THE BIBLE ADVENTURE!

An Inquisitive Christian Kid's Guide to Jesus and the Heroes of the Bible

TRACY M. SUMNER

ISBN 978-1-63609-987-3

Previously released as separate books: *Discover Jesus* and *Discover Bible Heroes*

Published by Barbour Publishing, Inc., 1810 Barbour Drive, Uhrichsville, Ohio 44683, www.barbourbooks.com

Our mission is to inspire the world with the life-changing message of the Bible.

Printed in China.

002415 0325 XY

HEY, KIDS. . .

SO YOU THINK YOU KNOW ALL ABOUT JESUS AND OTHER IMPORTANT BIBLE CHARACTERS? GREAT. . .BUT YOU'LL LEARN EVEN MORE HERE!

Jesus Christ, the Son of God, is the main character of the whole Bible. But God used many men, women, and children to fulfill His plan to bring salvation to the world.

The Bible Adventure! is written just for 8-to-12-year-olds, to help you get to know the 30 most important people in the Bible. Find out:

- who these people were and why they're important
- the things they did and said
- what the Bible says about them
- what their stories can teach us

From the Garden of Eden through the story of the early church—with a special focus on Jesus Christ—here are some of the most important Bible characters that you should know. You'll love their stories. . .which could truly change your life!

THE BIBLE ADVENTURE!

CONTENTS

BEFORE YOU GET STARTED

If someone were to ask you what you know about Jesus, what would you say?

You probably know that Jesus was born a little over two thousand years ago in the land of Israel in a town called Bethlehem. And you probably know that He died on a cross so that people could be forgiven for their sins. Maybe you've heard some great stories about the miracles He performed, or even the important things He taught about loving God and other people.

That's a good start. But with this book, you have the opportunity to learn a lot more.

Walking on the water, Jesus rescues Peter—who'd been walking on water too until he took his eyes off the Lord.

Jesus was the greatest man who ever lived. He changed how people came to God for forgiveness for their sins. He taught incredible lessons about how to live—and He set the perfect example of living a good life. He performed miracles so that people could know that He was telling the truth when He said that God had sent Him.

Some people believe that Jesus was just an unusually good man who left behind some guidelines on how people should treat each other. Yes, Jesus was a great teacher, and yes, He set a great example. But He was so much more than that.

The Bible calls Jesus "Immanuel," which means "God with us" (Matthew 1:23). That means that God Himself had come to earth! He was the only human being ever to follow every one of the Old Testament rules for living—what many call "the Law." He was the Savior who would take the punishment for people's sins by dying on a cross—and then be raised back to life. He is the one and only way people can come to God and live forever with Him.

Throughout history, lots of people have started religions. But Jesus was different from any other religious figure. For one thing, centuries before He came to the world, prophets predicted many things about Jesus—and they all came true! Also, Jesus didn't just claim to be sent from God. . .He claimed to be *God in a human body*. And He is the only religious figure to defeat death. God the Father brought Jesus back to life after His terrible death on a cross.

Jesus "has bought men for God from every family and from every language and from every kind of people and from every nation" (Revelation 5:9).

All the things you've just read about Jesus are recorded in the pages of the Bible. In this book, you'll learn about these things and many, many more, such as:

- The reason Jesus came to earth in the first place.
- "Prophecies"—things men who loved God and listened to Him said about Jesus long before He was born.
- The land of Israel when Jesus came to earth.
- Jesus' miraculous birth in Bethlehem.
- Jesus' life as a boy in the land of Israel.
- The incredible things Jesus did and said when He was on earth.
- Jesus' arrest, trial, and death on the cross. . . and how God raised Him from the dead.
- The start of "the church"—meaning all the people who believe in Jesus and follow Him.
- The amazing things Jesus' followers did after He had returned to heaven.

Each of the chapters in this book includes important stories and facts about Jesus. Each chapter also includes some interesting features having to do with that chapter's main topic:

- **"It's in the Bible!":** Verses related to the subject you're reading about.
- **"Who said that?":** Things people said or wrote in the Bible, and a quick profile of that person.
- **"What does that mean?":** Words and phrases describing truths from the Bible and what they really mean.
- **"What does that mean to me?":** Important verses and how they apply to your faith in Jesus.

This book doesn't include everything Jesus did and said while He was on earth, or everything that other people wrote about Him in scripture. To learn everything about Jesus, you'll need to crack open your Bible and start reading for yourself—and I hope you will.

By the time you finish reading this book, though, you'll probably know some things about Jesus you didn't know before. And you may find it easier to answer your friends and family members when they ask you about Jesus!

Tracy M. Sumner

Friends lower a paralyzed man down through the ceiling, seeking a healing from Jesus. You can read the whole story in Mark 2:1–12.

“The Trinity” is shown in art from an Austrian church. Though the Bible says no one has ever seen God the Father (John 6:46), many artists show Him as a bearded old man. Jesus, “the second person of the Trinity,” is identified by the Greek letters alpha [A] and omega [Ω] (Revelation 22:13). The Holy Spirit is represented by a dove (Matthew 3:16).

PART I

JESUS' STORY: HOW IT ALL STARTED

Every year around Christmastime, you hear people discussing the story of Jesus' arrival here on earth. The story includes a couple named Mary and Joseph, a stable in a little town called Bethlehem, angels announcing the birth, shepherds coming to worship the baby, and some really smart guys from the east bringing gifts.

It's a great story that we celebrate every year.

Did you know, though, that the story of Jesus didn't begin when Mary and Joseph traveled to Bethlehem for His birth? It's true! The Bible teaches that Jesus' story started *way* before that first Christmas more than two thousand years ago—before the beginning of time as we know it.

This is what the New Testament book of John says about Jesus:

The Word (Christ) was in the beginning. The Word was with God. The Word was God. He was with God in the beginning. He made all things. Nothing was made without Him making it. Life began by Him. His Life was the Light for men. The Light shines in the darkness. The darkness has never been able to put out the Light.

JOHN 1:1–5

Wow! This means that Jesus ("the Word") has always existed. As the second person of what we now call the "Trinity"—God the Father, God the Son, and God the Holy Spirit—He lived in heaven for all of eternity past. Not only that, John tells us that Jesus is actually our God and creator! Jesus confirmed these things when He prayed, "Now, Father, honor Me with the honor I had with You before the world was made" (John 17:5).

But "the Word," Jesus Christ, hasn't spent all of eternity in heaven. For a period of about thirty-three years, Jesus lived as a human being on earth. And He did that because He wanted to. God didn't *have* to become a man, living among other humans before dying a terrible death on a cross of wood. But He did it out of His love for us. Jesus willingly came to earth because He knew we needed to be rescued from the terrible effects of sin.

In the next two chapters, you'll learn more about why Jesus did what He did—and how God established a nation called Israel to bring the Savior into the world. It's an amazing story that will help you to understand just how much God loves you.

CHAPTER 1

LONG BEFORE BETHLEHEM

IN THIS CHAPTER:

- The creation story
- Adam and Eve's sin
- God's plan for saving humans
- The start of the nation of Israel
- Israel's part in bringing Jesus into the world

Did you know that another name for the book of Genesis is "the Book of Beginnings"? Genesis is at the *beginning* of the Bible, and it tells us the story of the *beginning* of the universe, the *beginning* of planet Earth, the *beginning* of all life on our planet, and the *beginning* of the human race.

That's a lot of beginnings, isn't it?

But Genesis tells of another beginning—the most important beginning for a world that needs God's forgiveness. We learn of the beginning of God's plan of salvation, the forgiveness of the sin of everyone who trusts Jesus Christ.

Everybody has done wrong, breaking God's perfect rules in one way or another. But in His great love, God sent Jesus to the world to make a way for us to be forgiven. And, believe it or not, that started in the book of Genesis.

WHY JESUS HAD TO COME TO EARTH (GENESIS 1–2)

In Chapter 3 of this book, "The *Real* Christmas Story," you'll read all about *when* and *where* God arrived on earth in the person of Jesus. But first, let's look at *why* He came. It all starts with Adam and Eve, the first two people God created, and how they messed up so badly that they (and everyone born after them) would suffer the effects of their disobedience.

Genesis, the first book of the Bible, opens with God creating everything simply by speaking it into being. He made the smallest microbes and the biggest and most distant galaxies, solar systems, and planets. He created everything on this earth—the oceans and rivers, the mountains and valleys, the forests and grasslands. . .all of it.

When God created every natural thing you see—as well as many things you can't see—He showed that He was creative and powerful. But when He created human beings, He showed that He was also *loving*. The Bible says God spent six days creating everything, but He waited until the last day to make a living being who could relate to Him like a child relates to its loving parent.

In the late 1700s, an English painter imagined the creation of Adam as looking like this.

On that sixth day of creation, God used simple dirt to form Adam, the first man who ever lived. Then God created Eve, the first woman, from Adam's body. Here's how the Bible describes the importance of people to God:

God said, "Let Us make man like Us and let him be head over the fish of the sea, and over the birds of the air, and over the cattle, and over all the earth, and over every thing that moves on the ground." And God made man in His own likeness. In the likeness of God He made him. He made both male and female.
GENESIS 1:26–27

When the Bible says that God made humans in His own "likeness," it means that we resemble Him in many ways. We don't know absolutely everything like He does—but we do know many things and have the ability to reason. We aren't all-powerful like He is—but we were created to rule over the earth and all the other living things God put here.

The most personal and loving part of the creation of humans was the way God "breathed the breath of life into the man's nostrils, and the man became a living person" (Genesis 2:7 NLT). At that point, Adam became much more than just an animal. His spirit could actually communicate with God. Adam could have a personal, loving relationship with his Creator.

Adam and Eve had it made! God had carefully and lovingly created them, along with everything they would need to live happy and healthy lives. They had the run of a beautiful garden—a garden God Himself visited every day. They had beautiful scenery to enjoy and lots of good food to eat. And best of all, Adam and Eve would get to live like this *forever*.

> **IT'S IN THE BIBLE!**
>
> "All men will die as Adam died. But all those who belong to Christ will be raised to new life. This is the way it is: Christ was raised from the dead first. Then all those who belong to Christ will be raised from the dead when He comes again" (1 Corinthians 15:22–23).

There was just one rule Adam and Eve had to follow. God told Adam, "You are free to eat from any tree of the garden. But do not eat from the tree of learning of good and bad. For the day you eat from it you will die for sure" (Genesis 2:16–17).

In a perfect garden, Adam and Eve spent time in the presence of a perfect God. There was no sin or death—in fact, they didn't know what sin and death were. No one had ever sinned or died! Adam and Eve didn't even know about good and bad, because everything was so good. Since there was no sin in the world, it didn't embarrass them that they weren't wearing clothes.

They only thing Adam and Eve knew about sin and death was that God never wanted them to experience it. Sadly, though, they learned about sin and death—in a very hard way—when they disobeyed God's command and ate from the "tree of learning of good and bad." That choice would also affect every human after them.

Satan looks over the Garden of Eden, making plans to ruin Adam and Eve's perfect home—and their relationship with God.

THE SADDEST DAY EVER (GENESIS 3)

One day, Eve was walking through the garden by herself. There was nothing to fear, since she and Adam lived in perfect harmony with their environment. Even the animals that can scare us today—like bears and lions and tigers—wouldn't harm them.

Then, crawling out of the bushes, a snake appeared in front of Eve. And it started *talking*.

Imagine Eve's surprise!

This was actually the devil in snake's clothing—and he was up to no good.

About now, you might be wondering how we know that the snake was really the devil in disguise. Genesis 3 doesn't mention the word *devil* or the name *Satan*. But if you fast forward through the pages of the Bible, you'll find a verse in Ezekiel 28 that most experts believe describes the devil:

> *"You were in Eden, the garden of God. Every stone of great worth covered you: ruby, topaz, diamond, beryl, onyx, jasper, chrysolite, turquoise, and emerald. And you had beautiful objects of gold. They were made for you when you were made."*
> EZEKIEL 28:13

Satan whispers lies into Eve's ear. In what is bad news for every human to come, she listens.

The snake started shooting tricky questions at Eve. She knew that God had warned her and Adam that they would die if they ate from that one forbidden tree, but the snake said, "No, you for sure will not die! For God knows that when you eat from it, your eyes will be opened and you will be like God, knowing good and bad" (Genesis 3:4–5).

The idea of a talking snake sounds weird to us today. Sure, some cartoon snakes talk, but we know that *real* ones don't. Real snakes make hardly any noise at all. But this snake wasn't like the ones we might see in a garden or a zoo today. It wasn't even like the other reptiles that lived in the Garden of Eden with Adam and Eve.

Eve's mind began to question what God had really told her and Adam. She wondered if maybe God was just keeping them from something worthwhile. *Besides,* she thought, *what could possibly be wrong with knowing good from bad?* God knew about good and evil, so why shouldn't she? Just one taste couldn't hurt, could it?

WHAT DOES THAT MEAN?

ORIGINAL SIN

The phrase "original sin" means that because Adam disobeyed God in the Garden of Eden, everyone who lived after them would be sinful people too. The New Testament explains it this way: "Sin came into the world by one man, Adam. Sin brought death with it. Death spread to all men because all have sinned" (Romans 5:12).

The Bible never says what kind of fruit grew on the tree that God told Adam and Eve to avoid. But many people imagine it as an apple.

Eve reached up into the tree's lower branches, picking one of the fruits God had told her and Adam to leave alone. When she took a bite, it probably tasted really good, so she urged Adam to try it too. Adam knew better—he remembered what God had told him. But he took the fruit from Eve's hand and ate some anyway.

At that very moment, something changed inside Adam and Eve. They suddenly felt shame for walking around the garden with no clothes on. So they gathered up some fig leaves to try to make clothing to hide their bodies.

Worst of all, for the first time Adam and Eve were *afraid* of God. Before, they had heard God in the garden and never felt a need to hide from Him. They knew He had made them, and they never questioned His love. But now they felt such shame and fear that they ran away when they heard their Creator in the garden. Before, they had walked around wearing no clothes and felt no embarrassment. But when God asked Adam why he and his wife had hidden themselves in the bushes, the man answered, "I heard the sound of You in the garden. I was afraid because I was without clothes. So I hid myself" (Genesis 3:10).

IT'S IN THE BIBLE!

"The dragon was thrown down to earth from heaven. This animal is the old snake. He is also called the Devil or Satan. He is the one who has fooled the whole world. He was thrown down to earth and his angels were thrown down with him" (Revelation 12:9).

God knew what Adam and Eve had done. He knew that they shouldn't even have known what it meant to be naked. God recognized that Adam and Eve now understood the difference between good and bad. But He wanted them to admit what they'd done. Neither one of them would take responsibility though. They just started pointing fingers—Adam blaming his wife for his own disobedience, and Eve blaming the snake for tempting her. Both people knew they had disobeyed God, and they knew they would be punished. Not only that, their children and their children's children, and every human being down to this day would suffer because of what Adam and Eve had done.

Since Adam and Eve's sin, every human being dies physically. But Jesus came to earth to provide spiritual life that lasts forever.

Adam and Eve's disobedience got them kicked out of the beautiful Garden of Eden.

Though God had said that they would die for their disobedience, they didn't die right away—at least not physically. There was an immediate death in the sense that their relationship with God was ruined. They'd never again be able to just walk around in the garden with God, enjoying being with Him. And in time—after living long, difficult lives—Adam and Eve both died physically.

But God didn't leave people without hope. He had a plan to bring human beings back to Himself, and that meant sending a Savior into the world to rescue us from our sin. So right there, on the same day He made Adam and Eve leave the Garden of Eden, He made a promise:

The Lord God said to the snake, "Because you have done this, you will be hated and will suffer more than all cattle, and more than every animal of the field. You will go on your stomach and you will eat dust all the days of your life. And I will make you and the woman hate each other, and your seed and her seed will hate each other. He will crush your head, and you will crush his heel."
GENESIS 3:14–15

When you first read those verses, you might think, *Okay, now I know why snakes crawl on their bellies and why women hate them.* (At least, many women!) *But what does that have to do with God giving us salvation through Jesus?* You don't see the name "Jesus" or the word *Savior* there, do you? Nope! But these words, straight from the mouth of God, meant that He would send a Savior who would be born from one of Eve's descendants—meaning the Savior would be born of a woman, just like you were.

Adam and Eve had messed up in the worst way possible, and God would have to punish them for what they had done. But they were still His most loved creation, and He wasn't about to let the devil completely ruin them—or all the people who would be born after them. God promised Adam and Eve that one of their future relatives—a grandchild's grandchild's grandchild, perhaps—would one day crush the devil's head.

Genesis 3:15 is the very first promise of the coming Savior, sometimes called "Messiah," in other parts of the Bible. This verse means that God would defeat the devil and punish him for what he had done to us humans. The devil's head would be crushed, meaning he would be completely destroyed. But God's victory would come at a cost to Him. The devil would crush Jesus' heel, causing Him real pain but not completely destroying Him. Satan would work through people who didn't believe in Jesus to get Him killed on the cross. But that wouldn't be final because God would bring Jesus back from the dead!

In the meantime, though, Adam and Eve paid a terrible price for their disobedience. God told them to leave the garden and never return. They left paradise and went into a broken world where they would have to work hard just to make a living, where people would treat one another in mean ways, and where people would suffer many bad things. All because they had disobeyed the God who loved them.

Now it was time for God to do what needed to be done to bring the Savior into the world. And how He did it is a great story!

Jesus talks with a woman at the well of Sychar, explaining that "salvation comes through the Jews."

THE START OF SOMETHING GREAT

One day as Jesus and His followers were traveling through a place called Samaria, they stopped at a well in the town of Sychar. After Jesus sent the others to town to get some food, He started talking with a woman at the well. They discussed her life, God, and what it really means to worship God. She was amazed that this man she had never met knew so much about her—including some stuff she wished He didn't! As they talked, Jesus said, "You Samaritans know very little about the one you worship, while we Jews know all about him, for salvation comes through the Jews" (John 4:22 NLT).

What did Jesus mean when He said, "salvation comes through the Jews"? Well, He didn't mean that the only way to be saved—the way to live with God in heaven for all eternity—was to convert to the Jewish religion. He simply meant that God had used the Jewish people to bring *Him* into the world. Those who had lived in the land of Israel and worshiped God as He instructed in the Old Testament produced the one Man who would offer salvation to people of every race and nation.

Jesus knew that God the Father's plan from the very beginning was to bring the Savior into the world through the Jewish people—descendants of a man named Abraham. (In the Old Testament, the Jewish people are also called "the children of Israel," "Israelites," and "Hebrews.")

After telling the story of Adam and Eve's disobedience in Genesis 3, the first book of the Bible goes on to describe other amazing interactions between God and human beings. You've probably read or heard about Noah, and how he saved his family by building a huge boat when God destroyed the world with a flood. (See the whole story in Genesis, starting in chapter 5.) By Genesis 12, you begin to see how God would set up and grow the nation of Israel, the people He chose to bring the Savior into the world.

WHAT DOES THAT MEAN?

BC AND AD

As you read this book, you'll see two sets of initials with the dates mentioned: BC and AD. In case you're not familiar with them, here's what they mean.

- BC is short for "before Christ." Since Jesus Christ is the most important person in all human history, His birth became the point from which we measure modern history. Things that happened earlier count down to Jesus' birth—so we say Moses lived around 1400 BC; King David, who came later, lived around 1000 BC; and Malachi, the last author of the Old Testament, lived around 400 BC.
- AD comes from "Anno Domini," a phrase in the old Latin language that means "in the year of our Lord." After Jesus was born, dates count up—so Jesus' last apostle, John, died around AD 100; the United States declared independence from England in AD 1776; and the Chicago Cubs won a World Series in AD 2016!

At God's invitation, Abraham looks at the stars—an indication of how many descendants he would have some day.

Here's how that happened: There was a man named Abram who lived in a place called Haran; that was located in what is now the country of Iraq. One day, around 1900 BC, God told Abram to gather his family members, pack up his belongings, leave his home in Haran, and travel to a place he would be shown. God promised Abram that he and his family would be blessed and that they would become famous. God also promised Abram that everyone on earth, no matter where they lived, would benefit if he did what he was told:

Now the Lord said to Abram, "Leave your country, your family and your father's house, and go to the land that I will show you. And I will make you a great nation. I will bring good to you. I will make your name great, so you will be honored. I will bring good to those who are good to you. And I will curse those who curse you. Good will come to all the families of the earth because of you."
Genesis 12:1–3

The Bible doesn't say that Abram asked God any questions. He didn't ask where he was going or how long it would take to get there. Abram, his wife Sarai, his nephew Lot, and all their family members just packed up and hit the road. Eventually, they settled in a place called Canaan, the areas of modern-day Lebanon, Syria, Jordan, and Israel. It was a beautiful place with lots of land that produced crops for farmers who lived there. It would be a great place for Abram and his family to live!

One night, years after Abram had settled in Canaan, he was resting in his tent when God appeared. The Lord said He would protect Abram and reward him for his faithfulness. But Abram's first thought was of an heir—someone to give his money and things to when he died. In those days, men all wanted to have children so there would be someone to carry on the family name.

Abram and Sarai were older than this elderly Jewish couple—which would have made starting a family quite difficult. But nothing is too hard for God!

But Abram knew there was a problem attached to God's promise: he had no children! Even worse, Abram and Sarai were too old to start having kids. So Abram told God that he would make a servant named Eliezer the heir of all he owned. But God had another plan:

Then the word of the Lord came to him, saying, "This man will not be given what is yours. But he who will come from your own body will be given what is yours." He took him outside and said, "Now look up into the heavens and add up the stars, if you are able to number them." Then He said to him, "Your children and your children's children will be as many as the stars."
GENESIS 15:4–5

And God kept that promise.

WHAT DOES THAT MEAN TO ME?

Then Abram believed in the Lord, and that made him right with God (Genesis 15:6).

One of the most important parts of the message of salvation through Jesus is that we are saved through faith in Him. That means that God sees us as right with Him when we tell Him we believe what He has said—that Jesus came to live on earth and then die so our sins could be forgiven.

Jewish people—descendants of Abraham—crowd the Western Wall in Jerusalem. Abraham is also called the "father" of all people who follow God by faith in Jesus.

To remind Abram of this promise, God started calling him "Abraham," which means "father of many." And God changed Sarai's name to Sarah.

Though Abraham and Sarah were both very old by this time—and Sarah had never been able to become pregnant—God miraculously gave them a son. They named him Isaac.

After Isaac grew up, he married a woman named Rebekah. They were unable to have children for a long time also, but God again performed a miracle and gave them twin sons, one who was named Jacob.

Many years later, God gave Jacob this promise: "Your descendants will be as numerous as the dust of the earth! They will spread out in all directions—to the west and the east, to the north and the south. And all the families of the earth will be blessed through you and your descendants" (Genesis 28:14 NLT).

An old postage stamp highlights the "twelve tribes of Israel." Look up Genesis 49 and try to match each tribe with its image.

Does that promise sound familiar? If so, that's because it's basically the same thing God had promised Jacob's grandfather, Abraham. Even though Abraham and Sarah had just one son together, their grandson Jacob had *twelve* sons, and the families of each of those twelve sons grew in number to become a large group of people called a "tribe." Since God at one point changed Jacob's name to Israel (Genesis 32:28), these family groups came to be known as "the Twelve Tribes of Israel." Each of them was important for a different reason. For example, the nation of Israel's priests came from the tribe of Levi, Jacob's third son. The kings all came from the tribe of Judah, Jacob's fourth son.

The Bible says Jesus came from the tribe of Judah. You can read about that in Matthew 1:1–16 and Luke 3:23–38, which are Jesus' family records, also called His "genealogy." In Revelation, the last book of the New Testament, Jesus is called "the Lion of the Tribe of Judah" (5:5 NLT).

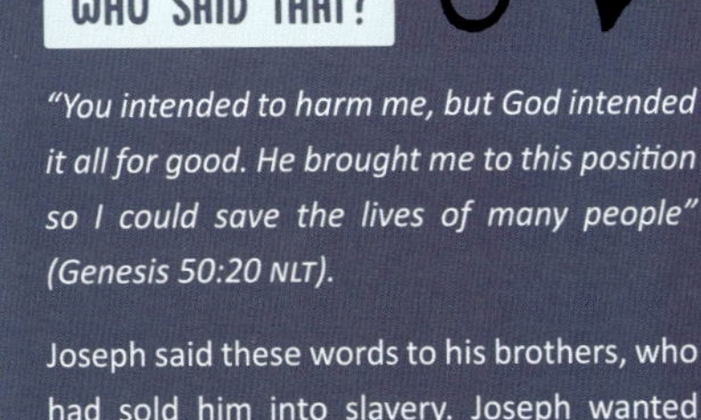

WHO SAID THAT?

"You intended to harm me, but God intended it all for good. He brought me to this position so I could save the lives of many people" (Genesis 50:20 NLT).

Joseph said these words to his brothers, who had sold him into slavery. Joseph wanted them to know that he would not seek to punish them because God had used the situation to ensure the survival of the people of Israel.

Jacob's second-youngest son, Joseph, played a huge role in the history of God's chosen nation, Israel. But for a long time, it didn't look like Joseph would be important at all.

Because he was Jacob's favorite, Joseph's brothers didn't like him very much. One day the brothers, in a fit of jealousy, sold Joseph to be a slave! He was carted off to Egypt, where he had to work for other people (and even spent time in jail for a crime he didn't commit). But eventually, miraculously, he became one of the most powerful men in the nation. As it turned out, God used the very thing Joseph's brothers had done to harm him to save the people of Israel from starvation. When God did that, He kept His plan on track for the salvation of people around the world.

Isn't it amazing? God used events long before Jesus came to earth to complete His plan of bringing the Savior into the world. When you read Genesis, you see how good God is, how much He loves you, and how He was working from the very beginning of time to make a way for you to spend eternity in heaven with Him.

Now that we've made our way through the book of Genesis, let's take a look at how God continued working out the plan of salvation through the rest of the Old Testament.

Joseph, great-grandson of Abraham, keeps his family—and God's plan for a Savior—alive during a famine.

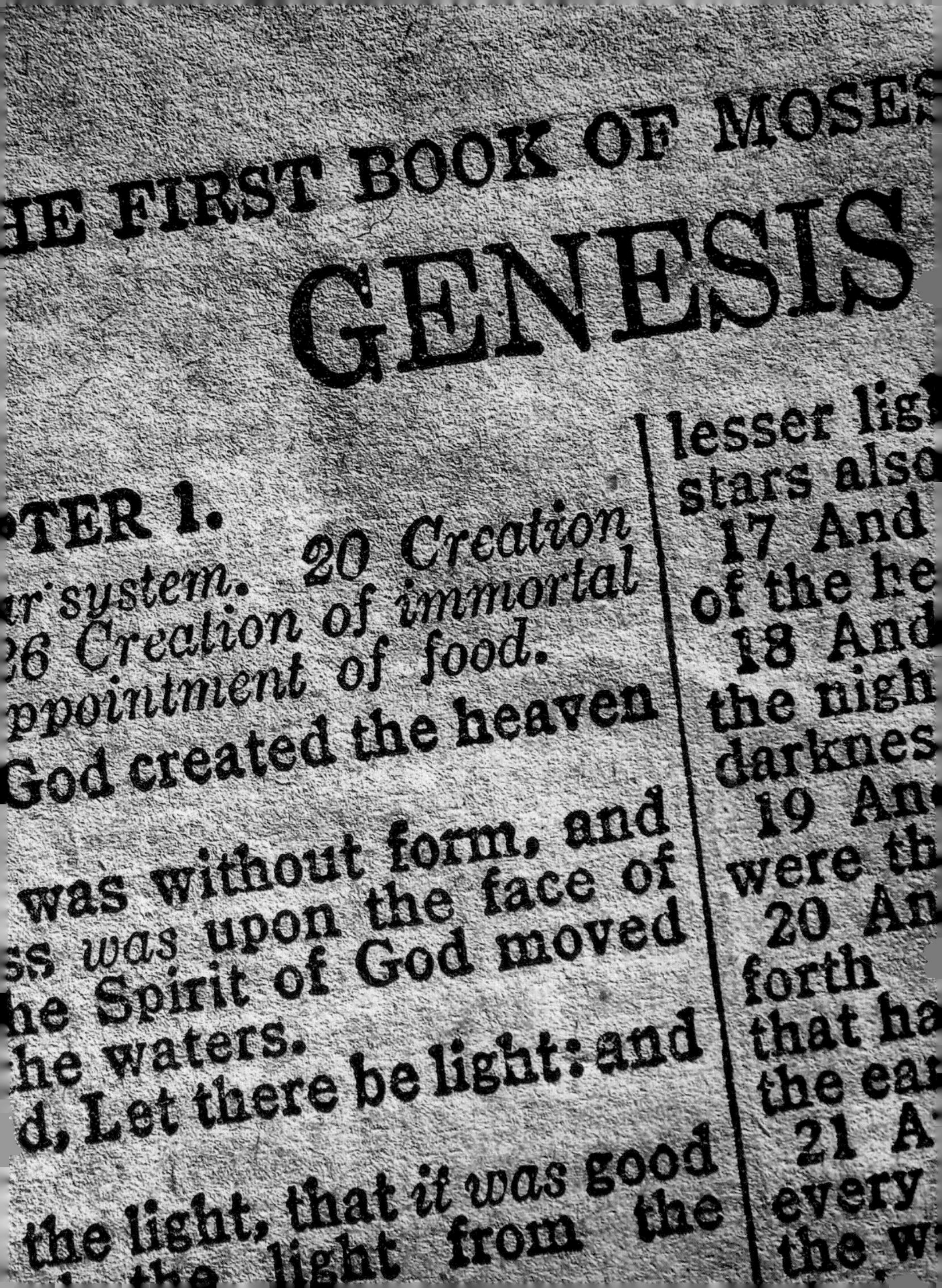

HE FIRST BOOK OF MOSES

GENESIS

TER 1.

r system. 20 *Creation*
26 *Creation of immortal*
ppointment of food.

God created the heaven

was without form, and
ss *was* upon the face of
he Spirit of God moved
he waters.
d, Let there be light: and

the light, that *it was* good
the light from the

lesser ligh
stars also
17 And
of the he
18 And
the nigh
darknes
19 An
were th
20 An
forth
that ha
the ea
21 A
every
the w

CHAPTER 2

THE OLD TESTAMENT: IT'S ALL ABOUT JESUS

IN THIS CHAPTER:

- How God protected His chosen people
- Old Testament sacrifices and what they had to do with Jesus
- When God had to discipline His people
- Old Testament prophecies about Jesus

When you think about which books of the Bible would tell you about Jesus, your thoughts probably go to the four Gospels—Matthew, Mark, Luke, and John—and the rest of the New Testament. But did you know that when you read the *Old* Testament, you're actually reading about Jesus? It's true! Even though Jesus' name isn't mentioned once in the Old Testament, those Bible books tell us a lot about Him.

You probably already know many of the cool stories from Old Testament. We've looked at the story of Adam and Eve and the account of Abraham, including God's promise to work through his descendants to bless many people throughout history.

After disobeying God, Adam and Eve are forced out of their home in the Garden of Eden. Their lives would be hard and they would ultimately die, but Adam and Eve could take courage in God's promise that one of their descendants would someday give birth to a Savior.

But these are more than just great stories. They're part of God's plan to bring Jesus into the world so He could teach and heal people, and then make forgiveness possible for everyone who has ever done wrong. That is, everyone!

In this chapter, we'll pick up where we left off in Chapter 1. Remember, God had called Abraham to leave his home in Haran and travel to a land he didn't even know about. That land, Canaan, was where God's people would live while He worked through one generation after another to prepare the world for Jesus' arrival.

But God didn't do this work in secret. He told many men about the coming of the Messiah, which is another name for Jesus Christ. These men are called "prophets," and they had a lot to say about Jesus, even though He would not arrive on earth for many centuries.

So keep reading. . .and prepare to be amazed. God did awesome things to make sure you could know Him and be a part of His plan for forgiveness and salvation.

A SAD LIFE IN EGYPT

Let's pick up the story of God's chosen people with Jacob's son Joseph, who became such an important person in Egypt.

Jacob and his family were living in Canaan when they suffered through a time of famine—that is, the people didn't have enough food for themselves or their animals. They were starving, so Jacob and seventy of his family members left Canaan and traveled to Egypt, where there was plenty of food to go around.

At first, the Egyptians welcomed the Israelites into their land. For many years after that, the people of Israel lived in peace with their new neighbors. But as more and more Israelites were being born (some people think as many as three million Israelites lived in Egypt at one time), the Egyptians began to worry that the Israelites might become too strong and take over the country.

To solve that "problem," Pharaoh (the ruler in Egypt) ordered that the Israelites work as slaves in Egypt. That was how it would be for the next four hundred years. Jacob's descendants built cities and roads for Pharaoh, who thought that if he worked the people hard enough, they would be too tired to have more children.

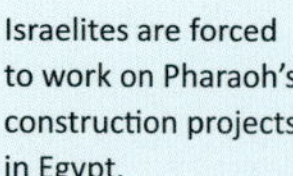

Israelites are forced to work on Pharaoh's construction projects in Egypt.

From a burning bush, God called Moses to lead the people of Israel into the promised land—where the plan of salvation from sin would continue to move forward.

HEADING HOME TO CANAAN

The people of Israel weren't happy living as slaves. They worked very hard every day for no pay, and the Egyptians treated them terribly. The people cried out to God about their treatment, and God heard them. He sent a leader to free them from Egyptian slavery and guide them in their travel back to their homeland—which was His plan all along.

Around 1450 BC, God called a man named Moses to lead the Israelites out of Egypt. Moses was a shepherd who lived with his wife and her family in a placed called Midian. The Bible says Moses had grown up in Egypt, but had to run away to Midian after he killed an Egyptian for beating one of his fellow Hebrews. When Pharaoh found out what Moses had done, he ordered him killed for his crime.

Since he was a wanted man in Egypt, Moses stayed in Midian for forty years, working for his father-in-law. But he never forgot the suffering of his people back in Egypt. He wanted them to be free like he was. And God would call Moses to do something about that suffering.

One day, Moses was just doing the things shepherds do when God spoke to him about leading the people out of Egypt. In the wilderness at Mount Sinai, which the Bible calls "the mountain of God," Moses saw something strange: a bush that was on fire but wasn't burned up!

At first, he probably rubbed his eyes and looked twice to make sure he wasn't just seeing things. But then a voice spoke from the bush—the voice of God! "Moses, Moses!" God called out. When Moses answered, God said, "Do not come near. Take your shoes off your feet. For the place where you are standing is holy ground" (Exodus 3:4–5).

Moses was afraid to look at the burning bush any longer, but God told him, "I have seen the suffering of My people in Egypt. I have heard their cry because of the men who make them work. I know how they suffer. So I have come down to save them from the power of the Egyptians. I will bring them out of that land to a good big land, to a land flowing with milk and honey" (Exodus 3:7–8).

But that wasn't all God had to say. He gave Moses the job of leading the people out of Egypt and back to Canaan, the land God had promised to give them.

At first, Moses didn't want to do what God had told him. He didn't think he was a good enough speaker. And he didn't see how a man as powerful as Pharaoh, the king of Egypt, would listen to anything Moses had to say. But God told Moses not to worry about those things because He would be with him. God promised to do amazing miracles to make sure Pharaoh would let the people of Israel leave.

So Moses did as God had told him. He went to Egypt and met with leaders of the people of Israel. Then he and the elders went to Pharaoh, telling him that God had commanded that the Israelites be allowed to leave Egypt and return to their homeland. At first, Pharaoh refused. But God sent a series of terrible disasters—called "plagues"—to Egypt, and Pharaoh finally agreed to let the Hebrew people go.

So the Israelites gathered together and headed out into the wilderness to start their journey back to their homeland.

IT'S IN THE BIBLE!

And God said to Moses, "I AM WHO I AM." And He said, "Say to the Israelites, 'I AM has sent me to you.'" Again He said, "Say this to the people of Israel, 'The Lord, the God of your fathers, the God of Abraham, the God of Isaac, and the God of Jacob, has sent me to you.' This is My name forever. By this name I am to be remembered by all people for all time" (Exodus 3:14–15).

The firstborn son of Pharaoh dies in the tenth and final "plague" on Egypt. God sent terrible tragedies on Egypt to convince Pharaoh to free the Israelites from their slavery.

Sheep, cows, and certain birds were among the animals Israelites could bring to God as sacrifices for sin. The sacrifices pointed to the time that Jesus would be the one perfect sacrifice for all time.

SACRIFICES FOR SIN

About three months after the Israelites left Egypt, they came to Mount Sinai. That is where God gave Moses laws for the Israelites. These laws, if followed, would keep the people happy and right with God. They included many laws about sacrifices for sin.

If you've read the first five books of the Old Testament, you'll see that the Israelites often disobeyed God. They worshiped fake gods and did many other things the one true God didn't want them to do. Not only that, they often complained on their journey through the wilderness on the way to Canaan. To deal with such sins, God required people to bring Him animal sacrifices.

The book of Leviticus tells how these animal sacrifices were done. But such sacrifices actually started way back in the Garden of Eden, after Adam and Eve disobeyed God. The first sacrifice happened when God killed some animals, then used their skins to make clothing for Adam and Eve (see Genesis 3:21). Later on, Adam and Eve's sons, Cain and Abel, brought sacrifices to God, but God only accepted Abel's—it was animals from his flock, while Cain brought fruits and vegetables. The Bible says that, after the flood, Noah sacrificed animals to God (Genesis 8:20–21). Abraham and others did too.

But why would God tell His people to make that kind of sacrifice? Why did they have to kill innocent animals so that people could be forgiven? Remember, back in the Garden, God said that if people did wrong, they would die. But God loved people so much that He made a way for another living thing to take their place when they did wrong. The New Testament book of Hebrews put it this way: "According to the law of Moses, nearly everything was purified with blood. For without the shedding of blood, there is no forgiveness" (Hebrews 9:22 NLT).

God looks "with favor" on Abel's animal sacrifice, but not on Cain's offering of "the fruits of the soil." Cain's jealous reaction led to the first murder in human history (see Genesis 4:1–16).

God had very strict rules when it came to sacrifices. The animals had to be perfect in every way, and they had to be offered in exactly the way God said. When the people did these things the way God told them to, they would have forgiveness of their sins.

Today, when you go to church, you don't see anyone sacrificing innocent animals so God will forgive them. That's because *Jesus* made the perfect sacrifice for our sins. The Bible says Jesus never sinned—He never did anything that made God unhappy with Him. It also says that Jesus took our sins on Himself, the same way those innocent animals did in the Old Testament. He sacrificed Himself on the cross so that God would forgive us for doing wrong.

Animal sacrifices in Old Testament times were kind of a preview of what Jesus did for us on the cross. In a very real way, Jesus was the sacrificial lamb dying in our place, allowing God to forgive us for every wrong thing we've ever done. That is what a man called John the Baptist meant when he said about Jesus, "See! The Lamb of God Who takes away the sin of the world!" (John 1:29)

WHO SAID THAT?

Christ never sinned but God put our sin on Him. Then we are made right with God because of what Christ has done for us (2 Corinthians 5:21).

A man named Paul (you'll read a lot about him in Chapter 8) wrote these words to Christians who lived in the city of Corinth in Greece. He wanted them to understand that Jesus was the ultimate sacrifice God had provided for their sins.

Mary holds the baby Jesus and a lamb in a painting called "Innocence." As a grown man, the innocent Jesus—called "the Lamb of God"—would die as a sacrifice for all people, of all times.

JOURNEY TO THE PROMISED LAND
Probable route of the Israelites' journey to Abel-shittim
King Sihon attacks the Israelites
Israelite battle missions
King Og attacks the Israelites
Land taken from Og and Sihon
0 10 20 30 mi
0 20 40 km
Mediterranean Sea
Hazor
BASHAN
Sea of Galilee
Ashtaroth
Yarmuk River
Edrei
Megiddo
Beth-shan
Jordan River
GILEAD
Ramoth-gilead
CANAAN
Shechem
Jabbok River
AMMON
PLAINS OF MOAB
Joppa
Jazer?
Rabbah
Jericho
Abel-shittim
Heshbon
Beth-jeshimoth
Mount Nebo
Jebus (Jerusalem)
Medeba
Moses dies
Dead Sea
Jahaz?
Dibon
Hebron
Gaza
Aroer
Kedemoth?
Gerar?
Arnon River
Ar?
Arad
Beersheba
MOAB
Besor Brook
Hormah?
Kir-hareseth
NEGEV
Zoar
Iye-abarim?
Zered Brook
Aaron dies
The King's Highway
Tamar?
Mount Hor?
Bozrah
Kadesh-barnea
WILDERNESS OF ZIN
Punon
EDOM
ARABAH
ARABIAN DESERT
WILDERNESS OF PARAN
Timna Mines
Elath
Jotbathah
Ezion-geber?
Red Sea
N
Copyright © 2007 by Barbour Publishing, Inc.

ISRAEL'S UPS AND DOWNS

The Israelites' trip to Canaan shouldn't have taken long, but the people didn't always listen to God. The people sinned, causing God to delay their entrance into the promised land. So instead of settling right away in Canaan, the journey took *forty years*.

Many of the Israelites who started the journey died along the way, and Moses himself wasn't allowed to enter the land because even he had disobeyed God. A man named Joshua took over as leader, and he led God's people to military victories over other people who had settled in Canaan while the Israelites were in Egypt.

The people knew that God had given them Canaan, but it took the next two hundred years to drive the other settlers out of the promised land. Eventually, around the year 1020 BC, the twelve tribes of Israel were united as a single nation under a king named Saul. Unfortunately, he failed to obey God, so he was replaced by a man named David. He ruled over Israel for the next forty years before his son Solomon took over as king and ruled for another forty years.

With Solomon as king, Israel grew to become the richest, most powerful nation in the world. But after he died, things went downhill fast. The ten tribes who had settled in the northern part of Israel split from the nation and kept the name "Israel." The remaining two tribes to the south took the name "Judah." The northern kingdom was led by a long series of rulers who didn't love or serve God. In Judah, there were a few kings who loved God, but most of them didn't serve Him or love Him either.

Israelites offer sacrifices to a false god—a golden calf—under their new king, Jeroboam. Ten of Israel's twelve tribes followed Jeroboam after King Solomon died, and the Jewish people would be divided for hundreds of years.

As the rulers and people of the two kingdoms continued to fall away from their faith in God, He sent a series of men who warned the people to return to Him. But the two nations didn't listen, and God judged both by allowing outside kingdoms to conquer them. In 722 BC, the army of Assyria invaded and defeated Israel. In 586 BC, the armies of Babylon (in modern-day Iraq) invaded and defeated Judah, taking many of its people back to Babylon with them.

In time, God kept His promise to allow His people to return to their home. But we'll focus on the way God spoke through prophets, at this specific time in Israel's history, to let people know that the Messiah was coming.

JESUS IN THE OLD TESTAMENT

When Jesus was on earth, He told a bunch of Jewish religious leaders, "You search the Scriptures because you think they give you eternal life. But the Scriptures point to me!" (John 5:39 NLT). When Jesus used the word *Scriptures*, He meant what we now call the Old Testament. The New Testament wasn't written until after Jesus had died, rose again, and ascended (or "went up") to heaven. So everything people could read about the Messiah was in the Old Testament.

And there was plenty to read!

God the Father had a plan—a plan to send Jesus into the world to be your Savior and the Savior of everyone who would believe in Him. Jesus knew about all the Old Testament prophecies of how He would be born, how He would teach, how He would treat people, and how He would die and then come back from the grave.

In Chapter 1 of this book, you read about God saying that a woman would one day give birth to someone who would destroy all the bad things the devil had done. You also read how God chose a man—Abraham—to be the father of the nation that would bring Jesus into the world.

From early in the book of Genesis until the end of Malachi, the Old Testament's last book, God was doing His work—preparing the world for the arrival of Jesus, so people could be saved through Him. Along the way, God told His

The resurrected Jesus walks with two disciples on the road to a town called Emmaus. The Gospel writer Luke says that, "beginning with Moses and all the Prophets, [Jesus] explained to them what was said in all the Scriptures concerning himself" (Luke 24:27 NIV).

prophets what He was doing, and they shared His message with the world. When the people of Jesus' day saw His life and teaching and death on the cross, God wanted them to know for sure that He was the one sent to bring salvation to the world.

Some experts say that there are more than 125 predictions of the coming Savior in the Old Testament. That includes more than three thousand Bible verses! The Old Testament foretold (that is, told ahead of time) everything from Jesus' birth to His resurrection from the dead.

Clearly, God used the Old Testament to say something about His plan for forgiving sins!

THE OLD TESTAMENT PROPHETS

The prophet Micah spoke to both Israel and Judah, the northern and southern Jewish nations. He predicted that the Messiah, Jesus, would be born in Bethlehem (Micah 5:2).

WHAT THE PROPHETS SAID

The Old Testament tells the stories of many people who spoke or wrote prophecies that God had given them. The word *prophecy* means a message straight from God, and the word *prophet* refers to the person God chose to speak His words to the people.

God called a lot of prophets during Old Testament times. Men such as Samuel, Elijah, Elisha, David, and many others *spoke* the messages God had given them. But there were other prophets God used to *write down* messages that became books of the Bible. The first of these books, as it appears in your Bible, is Isaiah. It's part of a group (Jeremiah, Lamentations, Ezekiel, and Daniel are the others) called the "major prophets." Daniel is followed by twelve books called "minor prophets"—in order, they are Hosea, Joel, Amos, Obadiah, Jonah, Micah, Nahum, Habakkuk, Zephaniah, Haggai, Zechariah, and Malachi. "Minor" doesn't mean these books are less important but simply that they are shorter than others.

So how did the Old Testament prophets get the messages God wanted them to share? Centuries after the last of these prophets

WHO SAID THAT?

"Brothers, I know you and your leaders did this without knowing what you were doing. In this way, God did what He said He would do through all the early preachers. He said that Christ must suffer many hard things" (Acts 3:17–18).

The apostle Peter spoke these words to the people of Jerusalem after Jesus had died, been raised from the dead, and returned to heaven. He wanted them to understand that Jesus' suffering and death were the fulfillment of God's Old Testament promises of the Messiah.

preached to God's people, Jesus' disciple Peter explained it this way: "No part of the Holy Writings came long ago because of what man wanted to write. But holy men who belonged to God spoke what the Holy Spirit told them" (2 Peter 1:21). That means that the Old Testament prophecies about Jesus came straight from the heart and mind of God!

The Old Testament prophets preached their messages mostly to Israel and Judah, but a few of them wrote to other countries. Most of the time, the people didn't like what the prophets said. They hated being told that they needed to turn to God or else face His punishment for their sins. They often treated the prophets badly, even though their preaching included a message of hope for the people if they turned back to God.

The prophets' most hopeful message was God's promise to one day send the nation of Israel a Messiah. The word *Messiah* means the same thing as "Christ"—it refers to God's Chosen One, the Savior. You can find the idea in Psalm 2:2, which says, "The kings of the earth stand in a line ready to fight, and all the leaders are against the Lord and against His Chosen One."

Many prophecies about the coming Messiah are very detailed and specific. That was so people could see those prophecies fulfilled in the things Jesus did and said. Then they could believe that He was the Savior God had sent to the world.

This book can't discuss every single prophecy about Jesus. But let's take a look at some things God's prophets wrote and said about the Chosen One's birth, life, death, and resurrection.

JESUS' BIRTH

You probably already know the basics about Jesus' birth—after all, you hear them every year around Christmastime! We'll get into the details of that amazing event in Chapter 4. But in the meantime, did you know that centuries before Jesus' birth, Old Testament prophets wrote some amazing predictions about *how* it would happen? Here are some examples:

- Jesus would be from the family tree of King David (Jeremiah 23:5–6).
- His mother would be a woman who had never been with a man (Isaiah 7:14).
- He would be born in a city called Bethlehem of Judah (Micah 5:2).
- He would be born as a baby like everyone else, and He would be called "Wonderful Counselor," "Mighty God," "Everlasting Father," and "Prince of Peace." He would also possess a kingdom that would last forever (Isaiah 9:6–7 NLT).
- Many babies would die around the time of Jesus' birth (Jeremiah 31:15). This happened when the evil King Herod, jealous after hearing about a newborn "King of the Jews," ordered all young male children killed in an attempt to make sure *he* remained king.

Jesus' mother was a young woman named Mary. His birth was a miracle, since she had never been with a man. God caused Jesus to grow inside her.

JESUS' WORK HERE ON EARTH

When Jesus was about thirty years old, He started traveling around Israel (called "Palestine" at the time), teaching, preaching, and caring for people by doing incredible miracles. God had shown Old Testament prophets many of the great things Jesus would do while He was alive on earth. Here are some things the prophets told about what is called Jesus' "earthly ministry":

- A man (John the Baptist) would appear before Jesus' ministry started, to prepare people for Him (Isaiah 40:3–4).
- He would start His work in a place called Galilee (Isaiah 9:1–2).
- He would perform miracles of healing (Isaiah 35:5–6).
- He would teach the people of Israel how to live in a way that pleases God (Psalm 40:9).
- He would teach by telling stories called parables (Psalm 78:1–2).
- People would not listen to His parables or understand them (Isaiah 6:9–10).
- He would be humbled so that He could serve people (Psalm 8:5–6).
- He would bring good news and set people free (Isaiah 61:1).

WHO SAID THAT?

But He was hurt for our wrong-doing. He was crushed for our sins. He was punished so we would have peace. He was beaten so we would be healed (Isaiah 53:5).

The prophet Isaiah wrote these words about the coming Messiah, Jesus, who would come to earth to die a painful death on the cross so that your sins could be forgiven.

Jesus heals a blind man by touching His eyes with spit on His fingers. You can read the whole story in Mark 8:22–26.

JESUS' DEATH AND RESURRECTION

All during His time on earth, Jesus knew that His most important mission was to die and then be raised from the dead, so that people could be forgiven for their sins. Old Testament prophets included an amazing number of details about Jesus' death on the cross—as well as His resurrection. Here are some great examples:

- Jesus would be a humble man who rode into Jerusalem on a donkey colt, bringing salvation to all the world. People would be happy when He arrived (Zechariah 9:9–10).
- He would be betrayed for thirty pieces of silver (Zechariah 11:12–13).
- His closest friends would abandon Him (Psalm 31:11).
- He would be ridiculed and mistreated (Isaiah 50:3–6).
- People would reject Him and He would suffer (Isaiah 53:3).
- He would be wounded for our rebellion against God and die for our sin. He would be beaten so that we could be healed (Isaiah 53:5).
- He would be forsaken (that is, left alone) by God (Psalm 22:1).
- He would die alongside sinners but be buried with rich people (Isaiah 53:9).
- His body would not rot in a tomb, but God the Father would raise Him from the dead (Psalm 16:10).
- He would come back to earth from heaven as the Son of Man (Daniel 7:13–14).
- The people of Israel would one day realize that Jesus, the one they rejected and crucified, was their Messiah (Zechariah 12:10).

So there you have it! The Old Testament is more than a collection of great stories and wise instructions for how to live. It's also the story of how God used people and events—some good, some bad—to prepare the world for the arrival of the Savior, Jesus Christ.

Jesus carries His own cross to the execution site. The crucifixion is a terribly sad story—but it's followed by the joy of Jesus' resurrection!

WHEN GOD STOPPED TALKING

Many centuries after the Old Testament prophets told people about Jesus, the apostle Paul wrote, "But at the right time, God sent His Son. A woman gave birth to Him under the Law" (Galatians 4:4). That means that God had chosen the specific time that Jesus would come to earth, fulfilling the prophecies made about Him.

The last Old Testament book, Malachi, was written about 430 years before Jesus was born. During those years, the prophecies about Jesus stopped.

In Malachi's time, the Jewish people had returned to the land of Israel after spending seventy years in captivity in Babylon. After Babylon, a world power called the Persian Empire ruled over Israel. The Persians allowed the temple in Jerusalem, which had been destroyed by the Babylonians, to be rebuilt. For a while, the Jewish people could follow God's laws in their homeland.

But then the land and people of Israel came under the control of other nations. In 332 BC, a Greek king named Alexander the Great conquered the Persian Empire. Greece made the land of Israel into a province for almost two centuries, and some rulers tried to force the Jews to live and worship like Greeks. That led to a period of war called the Maccabean revolt in 142 BC, which left the people of Israel more free from outside rule. But that changed again in 63 BC, when the Roman Empire took control of Israel.

In the years just before Jesus' birth, the Jewish people in the land longed for God to fulfill His promises for a Messiah. They wanted someone to free them from the rule of outside kings and armies. That wasn't exactly God's plan—His Messiah would free people from their sins. But the time was now right. God worked through several individuals who loved Him and listened to His instructions to finally bring Jesus to the world.

Caesar Augustus ruled the Roman empire—including the biblical land of Israel—when Jesus was born in Judea.

The apostle Paul said Jesus came to earth "at the right time" (Galatians 4:4). Many people believe the rule of Rome was part of that—there was peace in the world and a road system that made it easier to spread the message of the Gospel.

PART II

WHEN GOD CAME TO EARTH

The story of Jesus' life on earth is told in the first four books of the New Testament—Matthew, Mark, Luke, and John. These books are called the "Gospels," and *Gospel* means "good news." The Gospels tell us about Jesus' birth, His work here on earth (what many people call His "earthly ministry"), and His death and resurrection.

If you've ever read through the four Gospels (and if you haven't, you should!), it might seem like they sometimes tell different stories. Well, the four Gospel writers all tell the same story, but they tell it in different ways and from different perspectives. Some writers included details the others left out, and the stories about Jesus' life are not always in the same order. For example, only Matthew and Luke tell us the story of Jesus' birth, and the two books focus on different details of that important event.

One reason the four Gospels are so different is that the authors were writing to different audiences. Matthew, for example, was written to Jewish readers, so it highlights Jesus' family tree (His genealogy) and mentions many Old Testament references to the coming Messiah. That way, Matthew's readers could see that Jesus was the long-awaited Messiah they had read about in the Old Testament.

The writer of Mark was not one of Jesus' twelve closest followers (also known as "apostles"), but he had followed Jesus. Mark wrote his book to non-Jewish readers, so he left out the genealogy and the Old Testament references Matthew had included. The third Gospel was addressed to someone named Theophilus, and Luke included many details not found in the others. Luke was the only non-Jewish writer of New Testament books (he also wrote Acts), so his books helped Gentile readers understand who Jesus was and what He means.

John, who was one of Jesus' twelve original apostles, wrote the fourth Gospel. This one is very different from the other three because it focuses more on the fact that Jesus was God in the flesh and that He had existed with God in eternity past. John includes many of Jesus' statements about who He really was and what that meant to people who heard Him speak.

In the next five chapters, you'll read some of the "highlights" of Jesus' time on this earth—including His birth, His childhood, His work, and His death and resurrection—as they appear in the four Gospels.

CHAPTER 3

THE REAL CHRISTMAS STORY

IN THIS CHAPTER:

- Angels visit Mary and Elizabeth
- The birth of John the Baptist
- Mary and Joseph travel to Bethlehem
- The birth of the Savior
- Shepherds visit the baby Jesus

If you asked most people what they like about Christmas, *gifts* would probably be near the top of their lists. Giving Christmas presents to people you care about is a lot of fun, and of course receiving them is great too!

What do you think would be the perfect Christmas gift? Would it be something you really need? Or do you like receiving things that are just fun to have?

There was one *perfect* Christmas gift, and it was given on the very first Christmas more than two thousand years ago. That was when God sent His only Son, Jesus, to be born in a little town called Bethlehem. After Jesus had grown up and started preaching, teaching, and performing miracles, He put it like this: "For God so loved the world that He gave His only Son. Whoever puts his trust in God's Son will not be lost but will have life that lasts forever" (John 3:16).

The best gifts are the ones we give out of love. There's no greater love than the love God has for us people—and there's no greater gift than the One He gave in the form of the man Jesus.

You can read the story of Jesus' birth in Matthew 1:18–2:2 and Luke 1:5–2:20. As you read those Bible passages, you'll also learn about the birth of John the Baptist, who "prepared the way" for Jesus. The Christmas story includes some great promises, several amazing miracles, and angels sharing God's message that the time had come for the Savior's birth.

Christmas gifts are lots of fun—but God's gift of Jesus changes lives forever.

JOHN'S MIRACULOUS BIRTH

It may sound strange, but many people who study history think Jesus was born around the year 4 BC. Of course, you'd think Jesus would be born in the year zero, but apparently, a long time ago, someone made a mistake in figuring the date of Jesus' birth. But since everyone was already familiar with the wrong date, it was kept in place—and now we say Jesus was born "four years before Christ"!

He was born in a town called Bethlehem, which was part of the Roman province of Judea. Judea was located in the southern part of the land of Israel. The city of Jerusalem (another really important place in Jesus' story) was the capital of Judea, and Herod was the Roman king over the area.

Jesus arrived about three months after the birth of His relative John the Baptist. John would become a great preacher who helped get people ready for the Messiah to be revealed. The births of John and Jesus were miraculous events that could never have happened without God making them reality.

The Bible's story of these two births starts with a very special blessing for a Jewish priest named Zacharias and his wife, Elizabeth. This couple loved God and served Him with all their hearts. But even though they had prayed for years that God would allow them to become parents, Elizabeth could never have a baby. Both of them were now very old. Elizabeth was sad and felt ashamed that she had never become a mother.

In this five hundred-year-old painting, Mary holds Jesus, who looks at His relative John, who is just a few months older. John, who will become known as "the Baptist," prepared people to hear Jesus' message.

This model of the temple shows Zacharias's workplace—where he met an angel and heard that he would become the father of John the Baptist.

But one day, as Zacharias was working at the temple in Jerusalem, he saw an angel standing near the altar. Though Zacharias was a priest who had worked in God's temple for many years, he had never heard God's voice or seen an angel before. He was very frightened.

Gabriel, the angel, quickly told Zacharias not to be afraid and assured him that God had heard his and Elizabeth's prayers. They would become parents to a baby boy!

In those days, Jewish men usually named their first sons after themselves. But the angel told Zacharias that God wanted him to name his son John. Gabriel also told the priest that his son would grow to be a special man who would bless many people as he preached. He would urge the Jewish people back to their God and prepare them for the Messiah's arrival.

Even though an angel had just told Zacharias that God was going to perform a miracle by giving Elizabeth a baby, the priest had his doubts. "How can I be sure this will happen? I'm an old man now, and my wife is also well along in years," Zacharias said (Luke 1:18 NLT). So Gabriel replied that he had come from the very presence of God to tell Zacharias what was going to happen. As a sign that what the angel said was true, God kept Zacharias from being able to speak until his son was born.

WHAT DOES THIS MEAN TO ME?

"See, I am going to send one with news, and he will make the way ready before Me. Then all at once the Lord you are looking for will come to His house. The one with the news of the agreement, whom you desire, is coming," says the Lord of All (Malachi 3:1).

This verse is one of the many in the Old Testament that make predictions concerning the arrival of Jesus. It is about John the Baptist, who would later preach to people to prepare them for the arrival of the Messiah.

As Zacharias left the temple, he couldn't even tell people what the angel had just told him. He tried to communicate by using his hands, but no one understood what he was trying to say. He went home to be with his wife.

Everyone who knew Zacharias and Elizabeth was happy for them when John was born, and they praised God for blessing the couple with a son. When John was eight days old, his parents performed a religious act for new baby boys called "circumcision." They did that because they obeyed God's laws regarding their child. At the ceremony, Elizabeth shocked her family and friends by announcing that the baby would be named John. They all expected him to be named Zacharias, and they couldn't understand why he would be called John. Everyone turned to Zacharias and asked him the baby's name. Taking a writing tablet in his hands, Zacharias wrote, "His name is John."

WHO SAID THAT?

"This is what the Lord has done for me. He has looked on me and has taken away my shame from among men" (Luke 1:25).

Elizabeth, the wife of the priest Zacharias and mother of John the Baptist, spoke these words of praise to God when she realized that she was going to become a mother. Elizabeth was very old when this happened, so she knew God had blessed her by allowing her to have a baby.

God gave the angel Gabriel two very important jobs-telling the virgin Mary that she would give birth to God's Son, Jesus, and telling Zacharias the priest tha he and his wife, Elizabeth, would have a son called John the Baptist.

Having done everything God's angel had told him to do, Zacharias was immediately allowed to speak again.

Can you imagine how hard it would be to know something great was about to happen, but not be able to tell anyone about it? For nine long months, Zacharias could only smile when he thought about the birth of his son. But the first thing out of his mouth after he named his son John was praise to God. Zechariah then turned to the baby and said:

"And you, my little son, will be called the prophet of the Most High, because you will prepare the way for the Lord. You will tell his people how to find salvation through forgiveness of their sins. Because of God's tender mercy, the morning light from heaven is about to break upon us, to give light to those who sit in darkness and in the shadow of death, and to guide us to the path of peace."
LUKE 1:76–79 NLT

John would do all those things. He would come to be known as John the Baptist, because he told people that they needed to turn back to God and then be baptized so that their sins could be forgiven. John also told people that the Messiah they'd been waiting for would soon reveal Himself to them. (You'll read more about John in Chapter 5 of this book.)

Zacharias and Elizabeth's son, John, would live a lonely life in the desert until it was time to announce Jesus' ministry had begun. John the Baptist "had his raiment of camel's hair, and a leathern girdle about his loins; and his meat was locusts and wild honey" (Matthew 3:4 KJV).

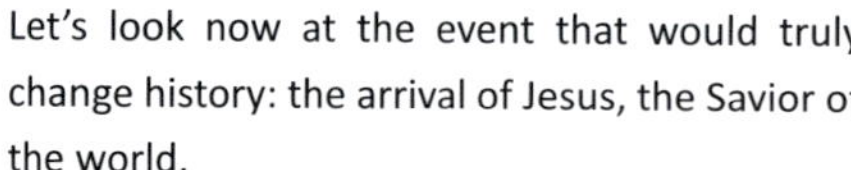

A WORLD-CHANGING ANNOUNCEMENT

Let's look now at the event that would truly change history: the arrival of Jesus, the Savior of the world.

Six months after Elizabeth learned that she would have a son, the angel Gabriel paid another woman a visit. This was a young lady named Mary, a relative of Elizabeth—probably her cousin. Mary was born and raised in a town called Nazareth, about sixty-five miles north of Jerusalem. Mary lived in the Roman province of Galilee in northern Israel, and she was engaged to be married to a carpenter named Joseph, who was also from Nazareth.

WHAT DOES THIS MEAN TO ME?

But at the right time, God sent His Son. A woman gave birth to Him under the Law. This all happened so He could buy with His blood and make free all those who were held by the Law. Then we might become the sons of God (Galatians 4:4–5).

These New Testament verses explain that God sent Jesus to earth at the time He had decided long, long before His Son arrived on earth. God's timing is always best.

Gabriel greeted Mary and told her, "You are honored very much. You are a favored woman. The Lord is with you. You are chosen from among many women" (Luke 1:28).

At first, Mary was confused by what the angel said. But then he told her, "Mary, do not be afraid. You have found favor with God. See! You are to become a mother and have a Son. You are to give Him the name Jesus. He will be great. He will be called the Son of the Most High. The Lord God will give Him the place where His early father David sat. He will be King over the family of Jacob forever and His nation will have no end" (Luke 1:30–33).

Many people believe that Mary was a young teenager when Gabriel told her that she would give birth to God's Son, Jesus.

Mary didn't know what to make of Gabriel'swords.Sheunderstoodthateverybabyhasa mom and a dad. She had a mom and a dad, just like you do! She also knew it wasn't possible for her to have a baby. She had never been with a man in that way. So Mary asked the angel how she could have a baby.

The angel explained that God would do an amazing miracle, causing her to become pregnant with Jesus. He also told Mary that her child would be holy, and called the Son of God. Finally, the angel told Mary that her relative Elizabeth would be having her miracle baby in another three months. Mary may have still wondered what God was doing, but she decided to trust Him. She told Gabriel, "I am the Lord's servant. May everything you have said about me come true" (Luke 1:38 NLT).

Relatives Elizabeth (left) and Mary (right) meet to discuss their miraculous pregnancies—Elizabeth was too old to have children and Mary was carrying God's own Son, Jesus.

WHAT DOES THIS MEAN TO ME?

INCARNATION

When you hear your pastor or someone else who knows fancy terms about the Bible use the word *incarnation*, they're talking about God becoming fully human in the person of Jesus Christ. He actually lived on earth among sinful and needy people! John 1:14 puts it this way: "Christ became human flesh and lived among us."

A few days after the angel's visit, Mary left Joseph, her friends, and family behind and traveled to Jerusalem to see Elizabeth. Elizabeth was very happy to see Mary, and the baby still growing inside her leapt. At that moment, the Holy Spirit revealed to Elizabeth who Mary's baby was—the Messiah! She was so excited that she cried out to Mary:

"You are honored among women! Your Child is honored! Why has this happened to me? Why has the mother of my Lord come to me? As soon as I heard your voice, the baby in my body moved for joy. You are happy because you believed. Everything will happen as the Lord told you it would happen."
LUKE 1:42–45

The Gospel of Luke says that Mary stayed with Elizabeth for three months before she returned home to Nazareth. Many believe Mary helped Elizabeth when John was born. Meanwhile, though, Mary's fiancé Joseph was worried—and maybe heartbroken—when he found out that Mary was expecting a baby too.

IT'S IN THE BIBLE!

MARY'S SONG OF PRAISE (LUKE 1:46–55 NLT)

After Elizabeth spoke a blessing to Mary, the mother of Jesus responded with a song of praise called "The Magnificat." Here's how it begins:

"Oh, how my soul praises the Lord. How my spirit rejoices in God my Savior! For he took notice of his lowly servant girl, and from now on all generations will call me blessed. For the Mighty One is holy, and he has done great things for me."

Mary's husband-to-be, Joseph, had a job as a carpenter. One time, when Jesus' neighbors doubted His authority to teach, they asked, "Is not this the carpenter's son?" (Matthew 13:55).

Joseph loved God and lived the way God wanted him to live. But he and Mary were not yet married, and he knew he was not the father of the child Mary was expecting. Joseph decided to break their engagement, but he wanted to deal with Mary kindly. He planned to end their relationship privately so she wouldn't be embarrassed in public.

But before Joseph could do this, an angel from God appeared to him in a dream. "Joseph, son of David," the angel said, "do not be afraid to take Mary as your wife. She is to become a mother by the Holy Spirit. A Son will be born to her. You will give Him the name Jesus because He will save His people from the punishment of their sins" (Matthew 1:20–21).

When Joseph woke up from his dream, he knew what God wanted him to do. What had happened was an amazing blessing to him as well as to Mary, so he did not break his engagement. Instead, Joseph married her and later raised Jesus as his own son.

TRAVELING TO BETHLEHEM (LUKE 2:1–20)

Before Jesus was born, Mary and Joseph lived in Nazareth in Galilee. That part of the world was controlled by the Roman Empire. Just before Jesus' birth, Emperor Augustus (who ruled from 27 BC until his death in AD 14), wanted a count of everyone in the empire so the Roman government could make sure they were paying their taxes. Augustus ordered everyone to return to the town where their families originated to register their names.

Joseph was a descendant of King David, so he and Mary traveled about seventy miles from Nazareth to Bethlehem (also known as the City of David) in Judea. Many other people had also journeyed to Bethlehem for the census, so Mary and Joseph couldn't find a place to stay the night. Every house was full and every bed taken, so they ended up in a stable—a place where people kept their animals! It wasn't a warm room with clean bedding, and it probably didn't smell very good. . .but it was better than sleeping outside.

That night, Mary's special baby was born. Back then, newborns were usually wrapped in a long, soft cloth called "swaddling clothes." Mary and Joseph wrapped the baby Jesus in the cloth to keep Him warm. Then they laid Him in a manger, a food box for cows.

WHO SAID THAT?

This happened as the Lord said it would happen through the early preacher. He said, "The young woman, who has never had a man, will give birth to a Son. They will give Him the name Immanuel. This means God with us" (Matthew 1:22–23).

These words were recorded by the Old Testament prophet Isaiah in his book of prophecy (Isaiah 7:14). The apostle Matthew, one of the twelve men who followed Jesus during His ministry here on earth, quoted Isaiah in his Gospel. Matthew wanted people to know that Mary's pregnancy with Jesus—even though she had never been with a man—was the fulfillment of Isaiah's prophecy.

This old Roman coin shows an image of Caesar Augustus—the ruler who demanded that everyone return to their family's hometowns to be counted—and taxed.

An angel "host"—meaning "a great number"—fills the sky above shepherds and sheep outside Bethlehem (Luke 2:8–14).

ANGELS, ANGELS EVERYWHERE! (LUKE 2:8–20)

Outside Bethlehem that night, some shepherds were watching over their sheep, keeping an eye out for thieves or wild animals that could drag their animals away. But the quiet of the night was broken by some amazing sounds and sights—suddenly, an angel of God appeared and the glory of God was shining all around the shepherds. They were terrified, and probably fell on their faces and trembled in fear.

But the angel quickly told the men, "Do not be afraid. See! I bring you good news of great joy which is for all people. Today, One Who saves from the punishment of sin has been born in the city of David. He is Christ the Lord. There will be something special for you to see. This is the way you will know Him. You will find the Baby with cloth around Him, lying in a place where cattle are fed" (Luke 2:10–12).

Just then, many more angels appeared on the scene, lighting up the nighttime sky, giving thanks to God, and singing, "Greatness and honor to our God in the highest heaven and peace on earth among men who please Him" (Luke 2:14).

What a scene that must have been!

After the angels returned to heaven, the shepherds looked at one another and said, "Let us go now to Bethlehem and see what has happened. The Lord has told us about this" (Luke 2:15). They hurried into town, where they found

Mary and Joseph, with the baby Jesus lying in a manger, just as the angel had said. Soon, the shepherds were telling people what they had seen and heard that night—and everyone who heard them was amazed and excited. The shepherds then returned to their flock of sheep, praising God all the way back for sending the Messiah they knew God had promised.

What an incredible night it was when Jesus was born! But that was just the beginning of the life of a man who would truly change the world.

Next, let's discuss something the Bible doesn't say very much about: Jesus growing up in Nazareth. You might be wondering why one famous part of the Christmas story didn't show up in this chapter. You'll find out as you read the next chapter!

Shepherds crowd the stable where Mary cares for the newborn Jesus.

CHAPTER 4

JESUS' CHILDHOOD: WHAT WE KNOW AND WHAT WE CAN GUESS

IN THIS CHAPTER:

- Jesus dedicated at the temple in Jerusalem
- Wise men seek—and find—Jesus in Bethlehem
- Jesus' family flees to Egypt, then moves to Nazareth
- Jesus amazes people at the Jerusalem temple
- Life for a Jewish boy in first-century Galilee

Most people know about Jesus' birth—after all, we celebrate it every year at Christmastime! Many people are familiar with things Jesus did during His ministry here on earth. And most know about His death on a wooden cross, and how God the Father raised Him from the dead. But what about the things that happened in Jesus' life in between His birth and the beginning of His ministry?

The Bible doesn't tell us a lot about Jesus' childhood years, and it says nothing about Him between the ages of twelve and about thirty. But a few passages give us a quick glimpse of Jesus' boyhood. We can also figure out some things about Jesus' early years by reading clues in the Bible and by looking at Jewish history—especially at the way Jewish children were raised and taught in Israel.

Why is knowing about Jesus' childhood important? Because it reminds us that while Jesus was "God in the flesh," He was also a human being who grew from childhood to adulthood—just like any other person.

So let's start this chapter by reviewing what we know for sure—in other words, the things the Bible says about Jesus as a baby and as a boy growing up in Nazareth.

Nazareth today is much larger then it was in Jesus' time. But He would have seen the same sky and hills when He looked out of His home.

DEDICATED AT THE TEMPLE (LUKE 2:21–40)

One reason Mary and Joseph were chosen to be Jesus' parents here on earth is that they both loved and obeyed God. Because they followed His instructions, they did everything required for their newborn son in the law that God had given Moses centuries before.

Jesus, Mary, and Joseph were Jewish people, and they obeyed the laws in what we now call the Old Testament. So when Jesus was eight days old, they "did the religious act of becoming a Jew on the Child" (Luke 2:21) and named Him "Jesus," just as the angel Gabriel had instructed them. That religious act is what the Bible calls "circumcision," and it was required of all Jewish males. (Remember, in Chapter 3 of this book, you read about the priest Zacharias and his wife, Elizabeth, holding the same ceremony for John.) This circumcision probably took place in Bethlehem, at a local Jewish place of worship called a synagogue.

But there was another step God wanted Mary and Joseph to take with their son.

Have you ever been to a church service where new parents bring their babies in front of the people and promise to teach them about how to live the way God wants them to? That's often called a "baby dedication service," and the Jewish people did something similar. At the time of Jesus' birth—and for thousands of years before that—God asked the Jewish people to bring their children to the temple in Jerusalem to "dedicate" them to His service.

Faithful old Simeon and Anna, who had waited many years for God's Messiah, finally get to see Him when Mary and Joseph bring baby Jesus to the temple.

When Jesus was forty days old, Mary and Joseph traveled from Bethlehem to Jerusalem for His dedication. (By the way, Jewish baby girls were also dedicated, but that was done when they were eighty days old, not forty.) The ceremony required parents to bring a lamb as a sacrifice to the Lord, but if the family didn't have enough money for a lamb, they could bring two pigeons or turtledoves. The Bible says that Mary and Joseph brought two turtledoves, which tells us they didn't have a lot of money.

In the temple to dedicate Jesus, Mary and Joseph met an amazing man named Simeon. He lived his life to please God. He had God's Spirit on him.

Simeon wanted more than anything to see the Messiah before he died, and God had promised Simeon that he would. We don't know how long Simeon waited, but it seems like he was an old man by the time Jesus was born. Simeon continued to believe God's promise, and one day it came true!

The Bible says that the Holy Spirit led Simeon to go to the temple on the same day Jesus was dedicated. He probably didn't know why God wanted him to go that day, but he did what he was told. When Simeon saw Mary and Joseph walking into the temple holding the baby Jesus, he instantly knew who he was seeing. God's Spirit told Simeon that the little one in Mary's arms was the Savior he had been waiting to see.

Simeon approached the young family with excitement and took Jesus into his arms. He probably had tears of joy streaming down his face when he said:

"Lord, now let me die in peace, as You have said. My eyes have seen the One Who will save men from the punishment of their sins. You have made Him ready in the sight of all nations. He will be a light to shine on the people who are not Jews. He will be the shining-greatness of Your people the Jews."
LUKE 2:29–32

God had already told Mary and Joseph who Jesus really was, but they were still amazed when they heard Simeon's praise to God. Simeon also talked to Mary and Joseph about Jesus' future and how people would respond to Him.

WHO SAID THAT?

"See! This Child will make many people fall and many people rise in the Jewish nation. He will be spoken against. A sword will cut through your soul. By this the thoughts of many hearts will be understood" (Luke 2:34–35).

Simeon, a man who loved God and lived for Him, spoke these words about Jesus when Mary and Joseph brought Him to the temple in Jerusalem for His dedication. Simeon's words meant that many people would believe in Jesus while many others would not. Some people would say wrong things about Him.

As Mary and Joseph listened to Simeon in the temple, an elderly woman approached them. Her name was Anna, and she was very, very old. Anna was a widow whose husband had died many years before. She actually stayed day and night in the temple, where she worshiped God every day. The Bible said she was a prophet (someone who tells people what God wanted them to hear), and it also says she knew who Jesus was right away. The moment she saw Jesus, she began thanking God for sending the long-awaited Savior.

Anna, a prophetess, thanked God for Mary's baby, then "told the people in Jerusalem about Jesus" (Luke 2:38).

Once Mary and Joseph dedicated Jesus as God required, they left Simeon and Anna in the temple and left Jerusalem. (Just imagine how happy those old believers must have been as they watched the younger couple leave with their baby. They had seen the Savior!)

Luke's Gospel says that Jesus' family traveled back to their home in Nazareth, but many people believe they first returned to Bethlehem and stayed there for a while. Why is that important? Keep reading. . .

The traditional image of the wise men—three kings, riding camels, following a star.

SOME WISE MEN VISIT JESUS (MATTHEW 2:1–12)

Nearly every Nativity scene on display at Christmastime includes the newborn Jesus, Mary and Joseph, shepherds, and three wise men from the east who came to worship Him. (And, every year, people sing the old Christmas song, "We Three Kings.")

But the Bible doesn't specifically say that the wise men (also called "magi") visited Jesus in Bethlehem at the same time as the shepherds. It also never says there were *three* of them!

Remember, the four Gospel writers included different details in their books. Some wrote down facts the others left out, and that can make it hard to put the story of Jesus' birth and childhood in perfect order. Even Bible experts don't agree on everything. But in the following paragraphs, we'll offer a good timeline for the wise men's arrival.

There's a lot we don't know about the wise men who visited Jesus. Even though some people believe their names were Gaspar, Melchior, and Balthasar, those names come from old Christian traditions. The Bible does not name them. And the Bible never says how many wise men there were. The only number mentioned in their story is three, and that is the number of gifts they brought with them: gold, frankincense, and myrrh. (Frankincense and myrrh are pleasant-smelling substances from trees in the wise men's homeland—both were very valuable at that time). It's possible there were three wise men, but there could have been two, or many more. In those days, people traveled long distances in large groups to be safer from robbers or wild animals, so it's likely the wise men traveled in a crowd.

They may not look like much to us, but the wise men's gifts—gold, frankincense, and myrrh—were valuable and useful to Mary, Joseph, and Jesus.

WHAT DOES THIS MEAN TO ME?

"The early preacher wrote, 'You, Bethlehem of Judah, are not the least of the leaders of Judah. Out of you will come a King Who will lead My people the Jews'" (Matthew 2:5–6).

The apostle Matthew wrote these words to help his Jewish readers understand that when Jesus was born in Bethlehem, He fulfilled an Old Testament prophecy about the Messiah. Matthew was quoting directly from Micah 5:2–4.

But here's what we know for sure: the wise men were from what the Bible calls eastern lands—probably a place called Persia, which is today the country of Iran. If they were from Persia, then they would have traveled more than *eight hundred miles* to see Jesus. They were very smart men who studied the stars and planets, and they had probably read old writings telling them that a new star would appear when a great king was born. Some believe that they had read some of the Old Testament prophecies about the coming Messiah.

The wise men found their way from their homeland to Judea—where Bethlehem and Jerusalem were located—by following what they called "his star." Many Christians now call it "the star of Bethlehem" or "the Christmas star." Some people believe this unusual light in the sky was a comet, and others think it was a supernova—a faraway exploding star—that appeared in the night sky around that time. Still others say it wasn't a natural object at all, but something God had miraculously placed in the sky so the wise men could follow it to find Jesus. Whatever it was, the wise men from the east knew it was a sign from God. The sign said that the King of the Jews had been born.

Now, about the timing of the wise men's visit to Jesus.

It's likely that the wise men first arrived in Jerusalem some time after Jesus' dedication at the temple. The Bible says that after Anna saw Jesus, she began telling people in Jerusalem

Even if the Christmas star was a "natural" comet, it was still a miracle—because it appeared just at the time and place to lead the wise men to young Jesus.

about Him. Word of Jesus' birth probably spread quickly throughout the city because the Jewish people there "were looking for the One to save them from the punishment of their sins and to set them free" (Luke 2:38).

When the wise men arrived in Jerusalem, they asked, "Where is the King of the Jews Who has been born? We have seen His star in the East. We have come to worship Him" (Matthew 2:2). That probably added to the excitement among the Jewish people, and it wasn't long before word got back to King Herod that the wise men had been asking about Jesus. This worried Herod because he didn't want another king competing for the people's loyalty.

"Herod the Great" was the Roman king of Judea, who became king around 37 BC and held that office until his death, which was between 4 and 1 BC. (As we noted earlier, most historians and Bible experts agree that Jesus wasn't born in the year zero, but instead was born between 6 and 4 BC.) Herod was a very bad man who treated many people in Judea cruelly. He didn't like anyone to challenge his authority in any way, and he killed many people who tried to stand up to him. Herod often did things to disrespect the Jewish religion. Even though he reconstructed their temple, he didn't do it to honor God—he just wanted Judea's capital to reflect well on himself.

When he heard about Jesus' birth, Herod hatched a plan—a *really evil* plan. He met with the Jewish religious leaders in Jerusalem and asked them where their Messiah was to be born. They told Herod that the scriptures said He would born in Bethlehem, a small town about six miles south of Jerusalem. Herod called the magi to meet with him and told them they could find the King of the Jews in Bethlehem. He also asked them to come back to him after they had visited the Messiah and tell him where He was—so that he could go and worship Him too. But Herod didn't plan on worshiping Jesus at all. He wanted to *kill* the new King before He had a chance to take Herod's place in Judea.

The wise men left Herod and continued to follow the light in the sky to Bethlehem. By the time the wise men arrived, Jesus and His parents had moved into a house, and the light stopped over the house where they were. The wise men's first response to seeing Jesus was to bow down and worship Him. Then they gave Him their gifts.

The Bible doesn't say how long the wise men stayed in Bethlehem, but it tells us that they never returned to speak to Herod about Jesus. They took another way home because God had warned them in a dream not to return to Jerusalem.

King Herod asks the wise men to tell him when they find Jesus, so "I can go and worship Him also" (Matthew 2:8). He really wanted to kill Jesus.

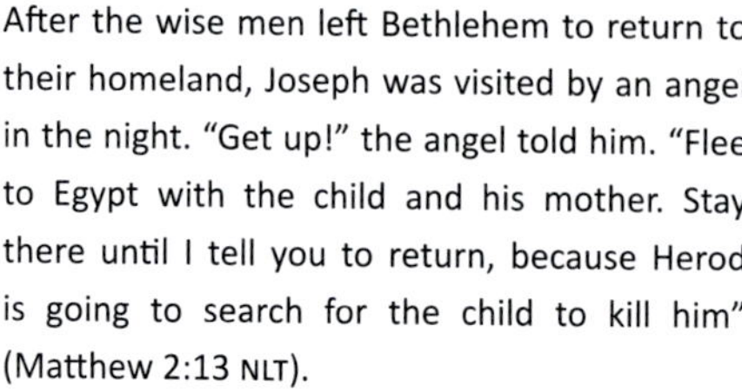

TO EGYPT AND BACK (MATTHEW 2:13–23)

After the wise men left Bethlehem to return to their homeland, Joseph was visited by an angel in the night. "Get up!" the angel told him. "Flee to Egypt with the child and his mother. Stay there until I tell you to return, because Herod is going to search for the child to kill him" (Matthew 2:13 NLT).

Joseph didn't even wait until morning to get his family moving toward Egypt. He got up out of bed that very night, got Jesus and Mary ready to travel, and headed for Egypt. God knew what Herod was planning to do, and He wasn't going to let an evil king stand in the way of His plans.

When Herod realized that the wise men had ignored his order for them to tell him where Jesus was, he became so angry that he commanded his soldiers to kill all boys two years old or younger in and around Bethlehem. Because of the wise men, Herod knew the place and time of Jesus' birth. By this point, though, Jesus, Mary, and Joseph had already left for Egypt.

Jesus stayed in Egypt with His parents until after Herod the Great died. Jesus may have been about two years old at the time. When it was safe for Jesus' family to return to Judea, an angel of God appeared to Joseph in another dream. "Get up," the angel said. "Take the young Child and His mother and go into the land of the Jews. Those who tried to kill the young Child are dead" (Matthew 2:20).

Joseph again did exactly as the angel told him. He took Jesus and Mary and headed back toward the land of Israel. But when Joseph heard that Herod's son Archelaus was the new ruler there, he was afraid to go to Judea. So instead, he and his young family traveled to Galilee and settled in Nazareth, Mary and Joseph's original hometown.

ONE AMAZING BOY! (LUKE 2:41–52)

After the journey to Egypt, there is only one other scene of Jesus' childhood in the Gospels.

IT'S IN THE BIBLE!

During the night he got up and left with the young Child and His mother for Egypt. He stayed there until Herod died. This happened as the Lord had said through an early preacher, "I called My Son out of Egypt." (Matthew 2:14–15).

Jesus lived in Nazareth until He started His "earthly ministry" when He was about thirty years old. He probably grew up like most Jewish boys in that part of the world. The Bible says Jesus was a healthy boy who grew up to become bigger and stronger every day. He probably helped Joseph in his work as a carpenter, and He probably studied the Bible in school, like the other Jewish boys living in Israel.

The famous pyramids of Egypt. Mary, Joseph, and young Jesus had to escape into Egypt to avoid King Herod's murderous plan.

Young Jesus was "filled with wisdom, and the loving-favor of God was on Him" (Luke 2:40). All Jewish boys at that time studied the Bible in school and learned about God's rules for life and His promises. So Jesus probably started attending school when He was around five years old. A collection of traditional Jewish writings called the Mishnah tells us how young boys were educated at that time. The schools were like the ones kids go to today in one way: students learned the simplest and most basic things first before moving on to more difficult and complicated topics.

Schools were connected with the local synagogues, and each community would hire its own teacher, called a "rabbi." The children started learning to read scripture (what we know as the Old Testament) at four or five years of age. At ten, they learned the Mishnah, and at twelve or thirteen, they were responsible for keeping God's commandments.

In addition to school, Jesus probably learned about the Bible at home too. Mary and Joseph built their life on what the Bible taught about God's love, His rules for life, and the promises He had made to them about Jesus. You can imagine that the family talked a lot about the scriptures and that they prayed to God together.

Most children who grow up in a home like Joseph and Mary's learn a lot about God's love and how He wants them to live. But Jesus understood the Bible and all rules and promises a lot better than other schoolchildren, even the ones who lived in good homes like His. There was something very special about this boy!

When Jesus was twelve years old, He put His learning and wisdom on display—and amazed some older, wiser men in the process.

As a boy, Jesus probably learned to read on a scroll of scripture something like this.

In those days, Jewish people from around the world would travel to Jerusalem once a year to take part in a Jewish celebration called "Passover." Mary and Joseph were no different, making the trip from Nazareth to remember God's love and protection of His people during their escape from slavery in Egypt. At twelve, Jesus was of the age when Jewish children celebrated Passover with the grown-ups. So the family packed everything they'd need for a seventy-mile trip and joined a large group of people to head to Jerusalem.

Mary and Joseph and Jesus stayed eight days in Jerusalem, and then it was time to head home to Nazareth. So Mary and Joseph packed up their belongings and joined the big caravan heading north.

Though Jesus' parents had left Jerusalem, He stayed behind. At first, Mary and Joseph didn't even realize He wasn't with the crowd heading back to Galilee. They probably assumed He was with friends or more distant family members. But when Mary and Joseph realized that Jesus wasn't in the larger group, they felt the panic any parent would in that situation. They started looking for Jesus and asking their friends and relatives if they knew where He was. But nobody knew!

Imagine how Mary and Joseph must have felt when they realized that the son God had so miraculously given them was missing. They left their traveling group and hurried back to Jerusalem to look for their missing son.

Finally, after three full days, Mary and Joseph found Jesus. He hadn't been playing with other kids in the area, and He hadn't gotten Himself lost when the people from Nazareth started for home. Instead, He was sitting near the temple, talking with some Jewish religious teachers, asking these learned men questions and answering their questions.

These teachers were well educated men. They knew and understood the Bible, and they knew how to teach others what they knew. But they had never seen a boy like Jesus. The men were amazed that a boy so young could understand the Word of God the way He did. The Bible doesn't say whether the teachers realized that Jesus was the Messiah, but one thing they did know: this was no ordinary kid!

Joseph and Mary must have been relieved to find Jesus safe. But at the same time, they didn't know quite what to make of what they were seeing. They might have expected their twelve-year-old son to go to the temple and ask someone to keep Him safe and give Him something to eat while He waited for His parents to come find Him. Yet there Jesus was, sitting with some of the smartest people in Jerusalem, calmly talking with them.

Mary was the first to speak. "Son," she said, probably with tears in her eyes, "why have you done this to us? Your father and I have been frantic, searching for you everywhere" (Luke 2:48 NLT).

But Jesus simply answered, "Why did you need to search? Didn't you know that I must be in my Father's house?" (Luke 2:49 NLT).

Mary didn't understand what Jesus meant when He said that, but from that day on, she remembered what had happened and Jesus' words to her. Jesus, though, understood everything about the situation. Even at age twelve—and probably well before that—He knew who He was. Jesus realized that He wasn't like the other kids at school. He knew that God had sent Him to earth, and He knew what His Father in heaven had sent Him to do. Jesus knew that He was the Son of God!

WHAT DOES THIS MEAN TO ME?

PASSOVER

Joseph and Mary went to Jerusalem every year to celebrate the Passover. The Passover started when the Israelites put lamb's blood around their doorposts and the Lord "passed over" their homes in the final plague on Egypt. All the firstborn in Egypt died because Pharaoh refused to let the Israelites return to their homeland of Canaan. God told the people to remember the Passover every year after they finally left Egypt (see Exodus 12:12–14).

Twelve-year-old Jesus discusses God's law with the religious teachers in Jerusalem. This story is the only information we have of Jesus' life from the time of the wise men's visit until He began preaching and teaching around age thirty.

Mary and Joseph find twelve-year-old Jesus in the temple at Jerusalem. ""Why were you looking for Me?" He asked. "Do you not know that I must be in My Father's house?" (Luke 2:49)

After the visit to the temple, Jesus and His parents returned to Nazareth. The Bible says that Jesus grew in wisdom, in physical maturity, and in the favor of God and all the people who knew Him.

Jesus spent the next eighteen years of His life growing and preparing Himself for the tremendous work His Father in heaven had called Him to do. He probably worked with his earthly father, Joseph, as a carpenter. People who knew Jesus as a young man in Nazareth called Him "just a carpenter" in Mark 6:3 (NLT).

As He was growing up in Nazareth, the Bible says Jesus obeyed His parents (Luke 2:51). That makes sense, because the Bible indicates Jesus perfectly kept the laws from the Old Testament—including God's commandment that children honor their mother and father. You can read that commandment in Exodus 20:12.

Many kids have brothers and sisters, and Jesus was no different. He shared His home with boys named James, Joseph, Judas, and Simon. He also had some sisters, but the Bible doesn't tell us how many or what their names were (Mark 6:3).

Everything Jesus learned as a child, everything He did, and everything He experienced as a son of Mary and Joseph and a brother to His siblings—all of that helped make Him ready for the life ahead of Him. When the time was right, Jesus began a traveling ministry that would change the world, starting with the land of Israel.

You can read about that ministry—and maybe learn a new thing or two about Jesus—in the next few chapters of this book!

WHAT DOES THIS MEAN?

You know how Jesus is often called "Jesus Christ"? The word *Christ* is not actually part of Jesus' name, but a title for who He is. It comes from the Greek word *Christos*, and it means "the anointed"—someone God had chosen. When used in the Bible, *Christ* is the Greek translation for the Hebrew word *Messiah*.

A man in Nazareth, Jesus' hometown, demonstrates carpentry as it probably looked in Jesus' time.

CHAPTER 5

FOLLOWING JESUS' FOOTSTEPS ON EARTH

IN THIS CHAPTER:

- Jesus' baptism in the Jordan River
- Jesus tempted in the wilderness
- Jesus calls twelve men to follow Him
- The travels of Jesus and His disciples
- What Jesus said about who He was
- Some amazing miracles

Think about the stories you've read or heard of Jesus' life on earth. Which ones come to mind first? The time He fed five thousand people with a few loaves of bread and some dried fish? Or the time He brought a dead man named Lazarus back to life? Or the time He walked on the water in front of His stunned followers?

Isn't it amazing to think that the Son of God—the man the Bible says was God in human form—actually lived here on earth and did all the incredible things the Bible describes?

The Gospel of Luke says that Jesus started His "earthly ministry" when He "was about thirty years old" (Luke 3:23). Between that time and the day Jesus died on a cross, He called twelve men to be His closest followers, and then walked countless miles with them, preaching the greatest sermons ever heard, healing huge numbers of really sick people, bringing some people back to life, and feeding thousands with just a little bit of food. He also turned water into wine, calmed storms with His voice, and walked on water. And while He was doing all that, Jesus set the greatest example ever of the life God wants all of us to live.

This story started when He met with a very special man God had sent to prepare people to meet Jesus.

John the Baptist pours water over Jesus in this painting from an Austrian church. Many artists show Jesus being baptized in this way, though some churches believe He was dunked into the water (or "immersed") because Matthew 3:16 says the heavens were opened and the Holy Spirit appeared like a dove "when Jesus came up out of the water."

JOHN BAPTIZES JESUS (MATTHEW 3:13–17)

Remember back in Chapter 3 of this book, when you read about the births of both Jesus and John the Baptist? Jesus and John were related through their mothers, and it's not hard to think that they got to know one another pretty well when they were kids—even though they did not grow up in the same town.

As Jesus was about to start His ministry on earth, John was busy telling others that they needed to ask God to forgive them for the wrong things they had done. John spoke about "repentance," and living lives that pleased God. John knew he wasn't the promised Messiah. He had been sent by God to prepare people to see Jesus.

Just as Jesus would fulfill many Old Testament promises of the coming Savior, John fulfilled God's promise of a messenger who would lead the way. The Gospel of Mark put it this like this:

This is the Good News about Jesus the Messiah, the Son of God. It began just as the prophet Isaiah had written: "Look, I am sending my messenger ahead of you, and he will prepare your way. He is a voice shouting in the wilderness, 'Prepare the way for the LORD's coming! Clear the road for him!' "
MARK 1:1–3 NLT

John the Baptist wasn't anything you might expect a preacher to be. He wore clothes made of scratchy camel hair, and he had a leather belt. He didn't have a house, but instead traveled all around looking for people to preach to. He probably slept outside most of the time, unless some nice people offered to let him spend the night in their home. Weirdest of all, John lived on a diet of honey and locusts (kind of like a grasshopper).

Does that look like lunch to you? It was for John the Baptist!

John probably didn't have much to call his own. He lived a simple life, not really caring about things. To John, it was much more important to do what God wanted him to do. He loved telling people about the good things God could do in their lives, and he wanted to get people ready to meet Jesus.

Some people thought John might be the Messiah they had been waiting for. But John told them that he wasn't—he was preaching to prepare the world for the real Messiah, the Savior. When religious leaders from Jerusalem learned many people were going out to hear John preach, they traveled to Bethany (about two miles away) to question him. They wanted to know who he was and why he thought he should be preaching to people and baptizing them.

John answered, "I baptize with water. But there is One standing among you Whom you do not know. He is the One Who is coming after me. I am not good enough to get down and help Him take off His shoes" (John 1:26–27). John also explained that while he baptized people with water, Jesus would baptize with the Holy Spirit (Matthew 3:11).

The very next day, Jesus approached John near the Jordan River, asking to be baptized. When Jesus waded into the water, John didn't want to baptize Him. John didn't feel worthy, and he told Jesus that it should be the other way around—Jesus should baptize John! But Jesus insisted, assuring John that it was God's will.

So John baptized his relative and Savior. When Jesus came up out of the water, the Holy Spirit came down on Him, and He heard God's voice saying, "This is my much-loved Son. I am very happy with Him" (Matthew 3:17).

After He was baptized, Jesus spent forty days in the wilderness, where He was tempted by the devil. The Bible writer Mark says, "He was with wild animals but angels took care of Him." (Mark 1:13).

WHEN JESUS SAID "NO!" TO THE DEVIL (MATTHEW 4:1–11, MARK 1:12–13, LUKE 4:1–13)

Can you remember the last time you were tempted to do something you knew was wrong? Everyone is tempted to do the wrong thing sometimes. Even Jesus was tempted here on earth! The Bible tells us that the devil appeared to Jesus personally, tempting Him to do things He knew weren't part of God's plan. But the temptation itself *was* part of His Father's plan.

After His baptism, Jesus went out to the desert to pray. He didn't just pray though, He also fasted, meaning He didn't eat anything at all—for forty days! In both the Old Testament and the New Testament alike, people who loved God often fasted when they prayed. When they did that, it showed their commitment to focus only on God. They were showing how serious they were about seeking Him and praying to Him. Jesus did the same thing. Since He was about to begin three years of traveling, teaching, performing miracles, and sacrificing Himself for our sins, He knew He needed to stay focused on His Father's plan.

The devil knew what God had in mind, and he tried his best to distract Jesus. During Jesus' forty days of fasting and praying, the devil thought he had the Lord right where he wanted Him. Knowing Jesus was hungry from not eating for so long, the devil approached Him and said, "If You are the Son of God, tell these stones to be made into bread" (Matthew 4:3).

Jesus could have done that easily—He had created the whole universe in the beginning. But Jesus knew that God the Father had taken Him into the desert so they could talk with one another. He wasn't about to let the devil keep Him from that important time with His Father in heaven, so He said, "No! The Scriptures say, 'People do not live by bread alone, but by every word that comes from the mouth of God' " (Matthew 4:4 NLT).

The devil then took Jesus to the highest part of the temple in Jerusalem and said to Him, "If you are the Son of God, jump off! For the Scriptures say, 'He will order his angels to protect you. And they will hold you up with their hands so you won't even hurt your foot on a stone' " (Matthew 4:6 NLT). But Jesus responded, "The Scriptures also say, 'You must not test the LORD your God' " (Matthew 4:7 NLT).

WHAT DOES THIS MEAN TO ME?

We have a great Religious Leader Who has made the way for man to go to God. He is Jesus, the Son of God, Who has gone to heaven to be with God. Let us keep our trust in Jesus Christ. Our Religious Leader understands how weak we are. Christ was tempted in every way we are tempted, but He did not sin (Hebrews 4:14–15).

Jesus was the Son of God, but He was also a human being who could be tempted to do the wrong things. These verses tell us that Jesus understands that we are weak when we are tempted to sin. But He also promises to give us strength to say "no" to temptation.

But the devil wasn't about to give up. He took Jesus to the top of a mountain and showed Him all the kingdoms of the world. Then Satan said, "I will give it all to you if you will kneel down and worship me" (Matthew 4:9 NLT). Now Jesus was finished with the devil for the day. "Get out of here, Satan," He said. "For the Scriptures say, 'You must worship the Lord your God and serve him only' " (Matthew 4:10 NLT).

When Jesus was tempted, all three times He answered the devil by quoting the Bible. When He did that, He showed two important things: (1) His commitment to do what His Father in heaven had sent Him to do, and (2) the power the words in the Bible have to help *us* fight off temptation.

Now it was time for Jesus to get busy! The Gospel of Matthew says that from the time of His baptism on, Jesus began preaching this message: "Be sorry for your sins and turn from them. The holy nation of heaven is near" (Matthew 4:17).

Satan tried—and failed—three times to get Jesus to do something wrong. To defeat the temptations, Jesus quoted God's Word, something we can do too.

The first four disciples Jesus chose were fishermen on the Sea of Galilee. They were also business partners and two sets of brothers: Peter and Andrew, and James and John.

TWELVE OF JESUS' CLOSEST FRIENDS (MATTHEW 4:18–22, MARK 1:16–34, LUKE 5:1–11)

Right after Jesus fought off the devil's temptations, He began calling a group of twelve men who would travel around with Him for the next three years. These men are sometimes called Jesus' disciples, but they are also called His "apostles."

These guys weren't the smartest or most talented people Jesus could have chosen. In fact, they all had flaws. But Jesus hand-picked them, and then He spent a lot of time teaching them how to live. He prepared them to spread the message of salvation around the world after He returned to heaven.

Here's a list of Jesus' disciples and some things we know about them:

- **Peter and Andrew:** These men were brothers, fishermen by trade, and they were the first disciples Jesus called. They lived in a place called Capernaum, a fishing village on the northern coast of the Sea of Galilee. The Gospel of Mark says, "Jesus said to them, 'Follow Me. I will make you fish for men!' At once they left their nets and followed Him" (Mark 1:17–18). If you want to read more about Jesus calling Peter and Andrew, look at Luke 5:1–11.

- **James and John:** They were the second pair of brothers Jesus invited to follow Him. Like Peter and Andrew, they were fishermen from Capernaum. Jesus called the pair "sons of thunder" (Mark 10:35–45), perhaps because they spoke without thinking. Jesus called James and John while they were in their boat working on their nets; they immediately left their father, Zebedee, to continue the work without them.
- **Philip:** A day after calling James and John, Jesus invited Philip to follow Him. Philip was from Bethsaida, another coastal village near the Sea of Galilee. After meeting Jesus, Philip brought the next disciple in this list to meet Him too.
- **Bartholomew:** The four Gospels don't tell us much about Bartholomew, other than that he was one of Jesus' twelve apostles. It's believed that he was also called Nathanael (see John 1:45–51). When Bartholomew/Nathanael first met Jesus, the Lord said, "Now here is a genuine son of Israel—a man of complete integrity" (John 1:47 NLT). That's high praise, coming from the Son of God!
- **Matthew:** He was an unlikely candidate to be one of Jesus' twelve disciples. Matthew, also called Levi, was a tax collector—and Jewish people didn't take kindly to his type. In fact, they *hated* tax-collectors. Matthew was working at his collection booth when Jesus called him (Mark 2:13–17). How important was Matthew? Well, if you've read the Gospel of Matthew, you've read something this disciple wrote!
- **Thomas:** Ever hear of someone called a "doubting Thomas"? That phrase started with this apostle, who needed proof that he was really seeing Jesus after the resurrection (see John 20:24–29). His nickname, Didymus, means "twin."
- **James:** Several men named James are listed in the New Testament, and two of them were disciples of Jesus. This one—not the brother of John—is identified as the son of a man named Alphaeus. He has been called "James the Less." Very little else is known about him.
- **Simon:** This disciple is mentioned only four times in the Bible—in the Gospels of Matthew, Mark, and Luke, and in the book of Acts (1:13).
- **Thaddeus:** The Bible doesn't tell us much about Thaddeus, but indicates he may also have been known by the name Jude or Judas. Some Bible experts believe he wrote the epistle of Jude, but most think the half-brother of Jesus did.
- **Judas Iscariot:** Judas is identified as the disciple who betrayed Jesus. When He chose His disciples, Jesus knew the future of each one—so why would He pick a man He knew would turn against Him? Because Judas's betrayal was part of God's plan to bring salvation to the world.

HITTING THE ROAD

The apostle John—not John the Baptist—wrote in his Gospel that Jesus "became human flesh and lived among us. We saw His shining-greatness. This greatness is given only to a much-loved Son from His Father. He was full of loving-favor and truth" (John 1:14).

John's words hint at Jesus' glory ("shining-greatness") as God. But most of the four Gospels describe Jesus' earthly ministry. These books show that during the last three years of His life on earth, Jesus traveled around Israel with His disciples. He stopped in many places to teach people how to love God, doing miracles that showed He really was the Son of God.

All of Jesus' earthly ministry took place in the land of Israel, which was under control of the Roman Empire. In the four Gospels, you can read about the places Jesus visited and things He did and said in each of them. Here are details on a few of those places:

- **Galilee**: Jesus spent a lot of His time in the region called Galilee, especially in the town of Capernaum, home of the apostles Peter and Andrew. Galilee is in the northern area of Israel, bordering on the Sea of Galilee, which plays a big part in Jesus' story. Jesus' boyhood hometown of Nazareth was in Galilee, and He visited other Galilean villages including Cana, Nain, Bethsaida, and Chorazin.
- **Jerusalem**: The Gospels include several stories of Jesus visiting the city of Jerusalem, which was in the Roman province of Judea. There are two examples of Jesus entering the temple in Jerusalem and angrily driving out merchants, people who were making money off the worshipers. Later in this book, you'll read about Jesus' final days on earth, which He spent mostly in Jerusalem.

Jesus surprises His disciples by speaking to a Samaritan woman at the well of Sychar.

- **Samaria**: During Jesus' time, Jewish people tried hard to avoid traveling through Samaria, an area between Judea to the south and Galilee to the north. Jews looked down on Samaritans, viewing them as impure since their family lines included other nationalities. But Jesus didn't see people that way, so He was happy to travel through Samaria. While there, He met and talked with a Samaritan woman, telling her many truths about Himself. (You can read the whole story in John 4:4–26.)

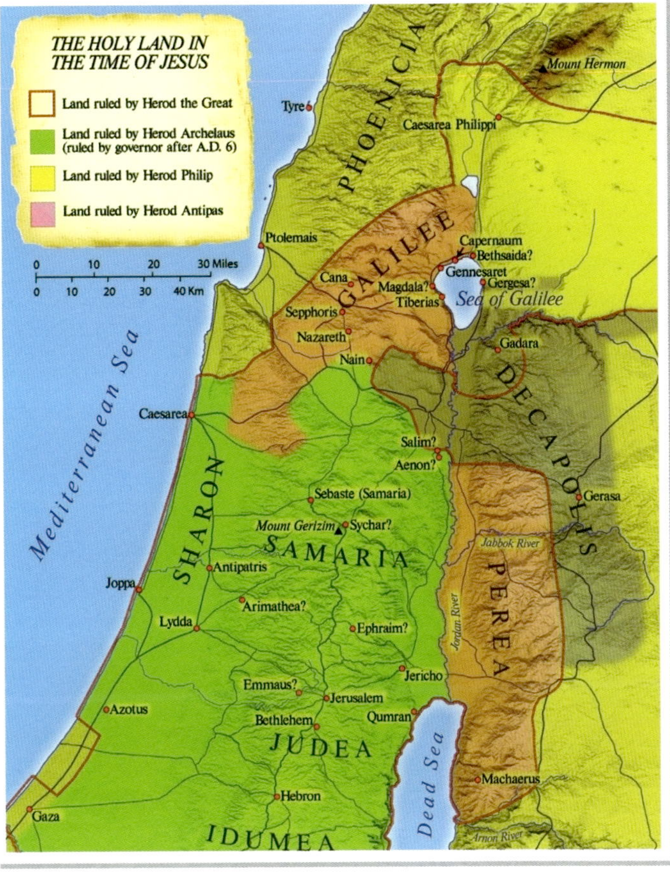

- **Bethany**: Three of Jesus' closest friends—sisters Mary and Martha and their brother Lazarus—lived in a small town called Bethany. It was located just a few miles east of Jerusalem.
  In Bethany, Jesus raised Lazarus from the dead.
  In the week leading up to His arrest, trial, and crucifixion, He spent His nights in Bethany. One evening that week, Jesus and the apostles had dinner in the house of a man named Simon. At dinner, Jesus' friend Mary washed His feet with perfume and dried them with her hair.
- **The Desert**: The Gospel of Luke says that Jesus "was led by the Holy Spirit to a desert" (4:1). He stayed there forty days to fast and pray. During that time, the devil tried unsuccessfully to get Jesus to sin. This desert was in Judea, probably an unpopulated area east of the Jordan River.
- **The Mount of Transfiguration**: People aren't exactly sure which mountain was the "Mount of Transfiguration." But we know that Jesus took three of His apostles—Peter, James, and John—to the top of a mountain, where they saw Moses and the prophet Elijah talking with Jesus. They also saw Jesus' "shining-greatness" and heard a voice from heaven saying, "This is My Son, the One I have chosen. Listen to Him!" (You can read this story in Luke 9:28–36.)

This book doesn't include every place Jesus traveled or everything He did and said. To get the full story, you'll need to read through Matthew, Mark, Luke, and John. For now, let's consider some very important things Jesus said about Himself.

WHO IS THIS GUY?

Jesus knew that God the Father had sent Him to earth to do some very specific things: teach, preach, perform miracles, and die on a cross so people could be forgiven for their sins. Some of the most important things Jesus said described who He really was and who had sent Him to earth.

Sometimes people believed Jesus when He spoke, and sometimes they believed when they saw the miracles He performed. But some people became very angry with Him. Many of the Jewish religious leaders thought He was speaking against God when Jesus said that God had sent Him—that He was the Messiah who had been promised long before. The leaders became even angrier when Jesus claimed to be equal to God—which He is! But the "important people" weren't the only ones who disliked Jesus' claim to be the Savior God had promised in the Old Testament.

Crowds often surrounded Jesus. Many people were interested in His miracles and message, and some—the religious leaders—were jealous of His popularity.

A view from "Mount Precipice," a spot near Nazareth. Some people today believe this is the place where Jesus' townspeople once tried to throw Him off a cliff.

A HOMETOWN ANNOUNCEMENT (LUKE 4:14–30)

Luke tells how Jesus went to the synagogue in His hometown of Nazareth. Synagogues were Jewish places of worship and teaching—kind of like churches for Christians today. Many of the people in the synagogue were probably friends or family members who knew Jesus when He was growing up. They had no doubt heard that He'd become a wonderful teacher.

Jesus stood in front of the congregation and read this passage from the book of Isaiah:

> *"The Spirit of the Lord is on Me. He has put His hand on Me to preach the Good News to poor people. He has sent Me to heal those with a sad heart. He has sent Me to tell those who are being held that they can go free. He has sent Me to make the blind to see and to free those who are held because of trouble. He sent Me to tell of the time when men can receive favor with the Lord."*
>
> LUKE 4:18–19

Jesus was reading from a scroll. When He finished, He handed the scroll to the attendant, sat down, and said, "The Scripture you've just heard has been fulfilled this very day!" (Luke 4:21 NLT). The people knew that Jesus had been reading an old promise of a coming Messiah—they probably liked what they were hearing. But that changed quickly when He seemed to scold them for just wanting miracles from Him.

The people were so angry that they surrounded Jesus and took Him to a nearby cliff to throw Him to His death. But Jesus miraculously left the scene before anyone could harm Him.

IT'S IN THE BIBLE!

Jesus' Seven "I am" Claims from the Book of John (all quotes from the New Living Translation)

- "I am the bread of life" (John 6:35).
- "I am the light of the world" (John 8:12).
- "I am the gate for the sheep" (John 10:7).
- "I am the good shepherd" (John 10:11).
- "I am the resurrection and the life" (John 11:25).
- "I am the way, the truth, and the life" (John 14:6).
- "I am the true grapevine" (John 15:1).

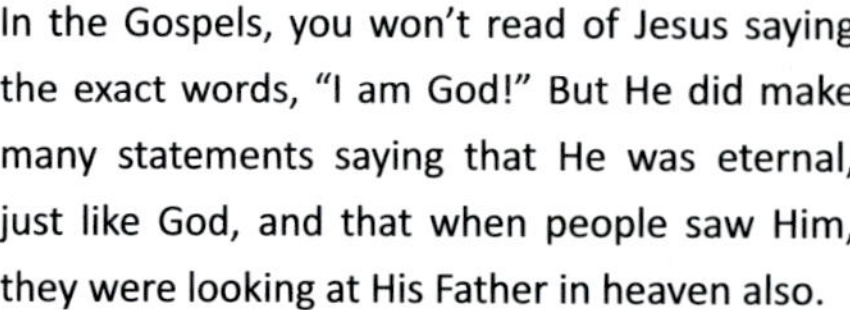

JESUS: "I AM!"

In the Gospels, you won't read of Jesus saying the exact words, "I am God!" But He did make many statements saying that He was eternal, just like God, and that when people saw Him, they were looking at His Father in heaven also.

One time when Jesus was at the temple in Jerusalem, He really shook up the religious leaders (who didn't like Him very much anyway) by saying that anyone who kept His word would live forever. And Jesus said that Abraham, who had lived hundreds of years earlier, had been glad to know that Jesus would someday come to earth.

Here's what happened next, straight from the Bible: "The people said, 'You aren't even fifty years old. How can you say you have seen Abraham?' Jesus answered, 'I tell you the truth, before Abraham was even born, I AM!'" (John 8:57–58 NLT)

These religious leaders knew exactly what Jesus was saying, and it made them very angry! He was claiming to be eternal and therefore equal with God. In fact, Jesus used the exact words that God had used to identify Himself to Moses, back in Exodus 3:14—"I AM." To the Jewish leaders, that was an insult to God that should be punished by death. They picked up rocks to stone Jesus, but He left before they could do anything to Him.

Jesus not only knew who He was, He wasn't shy about telling people about it. Here are some examples of the things He said about His own identity:

- "My Father and I are one!" (John 10:30).
- "Anyone who puts his trust in Me, puts his trust not only in Me, but in Him Who sent Me. Anyone who sees Me, sees Him Who sent Me" (John 12:44–45).
- "I am the Way and the Truth and the Life. No one can go to the Father except by Me. If you had known Me, you would know My Father also. From now on you know Him and have seen Him" (John 14:6–7).
- "Have I been with you all this time and you do not know Me yet? Whoever has seen Me, has seen the Father. How can you say, 'Show us the Father'?" (John 14:9).

Jesus said a lot about who He was, why He had come to earth, and who had sent Him. And He not only *said* those things, He *proved* them—by doing things only God could do.

WHAT DOES THIS MEAN TO ME?

In the Gospels, Jesus often called Himself "the Son of Man"—more than eighty times, in fact! What does that mean? In the Old Testament, there is a prophecy in which Daniel uses the phrase "like a Son of Man" in reference to the Savior (Daniel 7:13–14). When Jesus used this phrase, He was claiming to be the Messiah.

Jesus' very first miracle was turning water into wine, during a wedding in the small town of Cana.

SOME AMAZING MIRACLES

A big part of Jesus' ministry on earth was the miracles He performed in front of people. A miracle is something that that couldn't happen naturally, and in the Gospels we read about dozens of miracles Jesus performed. Not only that, but John's Gospel indicates that Jesus performed many more that aren't recorded in the Bible (see John 21:25). Have you ever wondered why Jesus performed so many miracles?

Jesus didn't do miracles just to show off, or because someone asked Him to do something cool. He performed miracles to show people—those who were really interested in who He was—that the things He claimed about Himself were true. After Jesus had died, risen from the dead, and returned to heaven, the apostle Peter told people in Jerusalem, "People of Israel, listen! God publicly endorsed Jesus the Nazarene by doing powerful miracles, wonders, and signs through him, as you well know" (Acts 2:22 NLT).

Not everyone who saw Jesus' miracles believed in Him, but many did. Here are some examples of miracles that met people's physical or spiritual needs—and how many people believed in Jesus because of what they had witnessed:

- **Turning water into wine (John 2:1–12):** Not long after His baptism—and after He'd sent the devil packing during His time of prayer and fasting in the desert—Jesus performed His very first miracle. He and some of His apostles, as well as His mother, Mary, were at a wedding in the village of Cana. It was about four miles north of His hometown of Nazareth.

After the ceremony, all the guests gathered for the reception, where they would eat and drink and offer their congratulations to the newly married couple. But shortly after the party started, something happened that was considered a big mistake in that culture: the host realized he had run out of wine.

Mary asked Jesus to help. Maybe she wanted Him to go buy some more wine in town, or maybe she believed He would do something miraculous. She simply told the servants working at the party, "Do whatever He says." Jesus asked the servants to fill some big stone jars with water, then dip some of the liquid out and take it to the wedding host. When they did as Jesus said, the wedding host was amazed—it was the best *wine* he had ever tasted!

John's Gospel says that when the disciples saw what happened at the wedding, they "put their trust in Him" (John 2:11).

- **Healing a Roman officer's servant (Matthew 8:5–13, Luke 7:1–10):** Jesus was in Capernaum when some men asked Him to help a Roman military officer called a centurion. The soldier's servant was in bed, unable to move, and in a lot of pain. Jesus agreed to go to the officer's home to heal his servant, but the centurion sent Jesus another message. He asked Jesus *not* to come to his home, because he didn't feel worthy to have the Lord under his roof.

  "Only speak the word, and my servant will be healed," he told Jesus. Jesus was impressed with the officer's faith, and said, "For sure, I tell you, I have not found so much faith in the Jewish nation. I say to you, many people will come from the east and from the west. They will sit down with Abraham and with Isaac and with Jacob in the holy nation of heaven" (Matthew 8:8–11). Jesus healed the centurion's servant without even seeing him!
- **Raising a widow's son from the dead (Luke 7:12–16):** Jesus was about to enter a village called Nain, which was in the north part of Galilee, when a funeral procession passed by. The people were mourning the death of a widow's only son. Feeling compassion for the woman, Jesus walked over to her and said, "Do not cry," and then touched the coffin and said, "Young man, I say to you, get up!" Immediately, the dead man sat up and started talking! The people were amazed at what they had seen and began praising God. "A great Man Who speaks for God has come among us!" they said. "God has cared for His people!"

A sad woman is thrilled when Jesus raises her only son from the dead. This 3-D picture, calle a "relief," is on the wall of a church in Italy.

Jesus, walking on the wild waves of the stormy Sea of Galilee, appears as a ghost to the disciples, working frantically to keep their boat afloat.

- **Feeding five thousand people (Matthew 14:13–21, Mark 6:35–44, Luke 9:12–17, John 6:5–14):** You can read about this miracle of Jesus in all four Gospels. Jesus had just learned that Herod Antipas, the ruler of Galilee at the time, had murdered His relative and friend John the Baptist. Jesus was near a village called Bethsaida, near the shore of the Sea of Galilee.

  Jesus went out on the sea in a boat to pray by Himself, but a huge crowd of people gathered to meet Him—five thousand men, plus many other women and children. Jesus felt compassion for the people, so He went back to shore and started healing the sick.

  It was late in the day, and Jesus knew the people would be getting hungry. So He told His disciples to gather up any food they could find, but all they got was a young boy's meal of five loaves of bread and two fish. But that was plenty for Jesus. He told the people to sit down on the grass, then prayed to thank God for the food. He started breaking the bread and fish and handing it to the disciples to give to everyone in the huge crowd. By the time they had finished, everyone had eaten until they were full—and there were twelve baskets of food left over. That was enough for each disciple to have a basketful! John wrote, "The people saw the powerful work Jesus had done. They said, 'It is true! This is the One Who speaks for God Who is to come into the world' " (6:14).

- **Walking on water (Matthew 14:22–33, Mark 6:45–52, John 6:16–21):** After Jesus had fed that giant crowd, He told the disciples to get into their boat and go to the other side of the sea of Galilee. Then He sent the crowd home, and went to a private place to pray.

  About three o'clock the next morning, the disciples were in deep trouble. A strong windstorm had whipped up some heavy waves that were battering their boat. As they struggled to keep the boat afloat—and probably prayed it wouldn't sink—Jesus approached them walking on the water! When the disciples saw Jesus, they thought He was a ghost. These twelve men—many of them experienced fishermen who had been in storms before—were terrified. But Jesus calmed their fears by saying, "Take hope. It is I. Do not be afraid!" (Matthew 14:27).

  Peter called out to Jesus, "If it is You, Lord, tell me to come to You on the water." Jesus invited Peter to come, and for a moment, he too walked on the water! But when the apostle took his eyes off Jesus and started focusing on the wind and waves, he sank like a rock. Peter cried out for help, and Jesus quickly pulled him to safety. "You have so little faith," Jesus said. "Why did you doubt?" As Jesus and Peter got back into the boat, the wind and waves stopped. After seeing what had happened, the disciples worshiped Jesus and said, "For sure, You are the Son of God!" (Matthew 14:28–33).
- **Healing a man who was born blind (John 9:1–41):** One day, Jesus and the disciples encountered a man who had been blind since the day he was born. The Twelve asked Jesus if the man had been born blind because he or his parents had done wrong things. But Jesus told them the man had been born blind "so the work of God would be seen in him" (John 9:3). Jesus then bent down and spit on the ground to make some mud. He rubbed the

Dead for four days, Lazarus walks out of his tomb at Jesus' command.

mud in the blind man's eyes and told Him to go wash his face in a nearby pool of water. When he did as Jesus said, he was able to see for the first time in his life.

- **Raising Lazarus from the dead (John 11:1–44):** In the town of Bethany, only a few miles from Jerusalem, Jesus had three close friends—Lazarus and his sisters, Mary and Martha. One day, Jesus received a message from Mary and Martha telling Him that their brother was very sick. Jesus loved Lazarus and his sisters very much, and He planned to heal His dear friend. He told the disciples, "This sickness will not end in death. It has happened so that it will bring honor to God. And the Son of God will be honored by it also" (John 11:4).

  But Jesus waited two days before He headed for Bethany. By the time He arrived, Lazarus had already been dead *four days*—and Mary and Martha were both in tears. Martha cried out to Jesus and said, "Lord, if You had been here, my brother would not have died" (John 11:21). Jesus went to Lazarus's grave, where He ordered people to roll the stone cover away from the opening of the tomb. Then Jesus prayed and shouted, "Lazarus, come out!" The people were amazed when Lazarus walked out of the tomb, still wrapped in the strips of fabric that Jewish people put around the dead. Jesus told them to take off Lazarus's grave clothes and let him go.

IT'S IN THE BIBLE!

"I am the One Who raises the dead and gives them life. Anyone who puts his trust in Me will live again, even if he dies. Anyone who lives and has put his trust in Me will never die" (John 11:25–26).

John, at the end of his Gospel, wrote, "There are many other things which Jesus did also. If they were all written down, I do not think the world itself could hold the books that would be written" (John 21:25).

Jesus indeed did many amazing things when He was here on earth—too many for even the Bible to include. But He also *said* some amazing things as He preached and taught people about living for God. In the next chapter, you'll read about some of those things.

CHAPTER 6

WHAT JESUS SAID—AND WHAT IT MEANS

IN THIS CHAPTER:

- Jesus' teaching in the Sermon on the Mount
- Jesus' teaching through stories called parables
- Jesus talks with a religious leader about being "born again"

Have you ever heard someone use phrases like "an eye for an eye, a tooth for a tooth" or "the blind leading the blind"? How about "wolves in sheep's clothing" or "he who lives by the sword, dies by the sword"?

These are just a few examples of things Jesus said that people still say today—even when they're not talking about Jesus or the Bible. But He had a lot more to say than just memorable phrases. A lot of what Jesus said truly changed the world.

Jesus spent a lot of time teaching. He shared very important stuff about who He was, who God the Father is, and how His followers should live, think, and treat other people. Sometimes Jesus taught just one person, and sometimes He taught small groups. On other occasions, He taught large crowds.

What were some of the important truths Jesus taught? For one thing, that people needed to turn away from doing wrong things and confess their sin to God (Matthew 4:17). And that people should "take up [their] cross and follow Me" (Matthew 16:24). He taught that people needed to have faith in God (Mark 11:22) and that they must be "like a little child" before they could enter the kingdom of God (Matthew 18:3).

Some people eagerly listened to Jesus. They knew God had sent Him to earth—even if they didn't fully understand why. Some people loved His teaching so much that they decided to follow Him. But other people heard what Jesus had to say and just went back to their daily lives. Still others didn't like what Jesus had to say at all. Some became so angry about Jesus' words that they wanted to kill Him!

In the coming pages, you'll see some of the things Jesus taught—just the highlights, we could say. But as you read, remember that you won't find everything Jesus said or taught—you'll need to go to your Bible for that.

Let's start with Jesus' teaching that Christians call "the Sermon on the Mount."

Many people believe Jesus' "Sermon on the Mo
took place here, overlooking the Sea of Galilee.

THE GREATEST SERMON EVER PREACHED (MATTHEW 5–7)

One time, a big crowd of people gathered on the shore of the Sea of Galilee (also known as Lake Gennesaret), near Capernaum, a small fishing town. Jesus went to the side of a hill and started teaching people in a way they'd never been taught before.

The crowd listened closely as Jesus delivered the greatest sermon anyone has ever preached. He talked about how people could live to please God, how they should treat others, and how they could think good thoughts.

HOW TO BE HAPPY

Jesus started His sermon by giving the people a list of blessings now called "Beatitudes." (That's a word from the old Latin language that means "happy," "blessed," or "fortunate.") There are nine Beatitudes listed in Matthew's Gospel. Most Bible experts believe the first eight were for the crowds gathered at the hillside that day, while the ninth was for those who had been following Jesus.

Here is how Jesus described blessed (or happy) people:

- "Those who know there is nothing good in themselves are happy, because the holy nation of heaven is theirs" (Matthew 5:3).
- "Those who have sorrow are happy, because they will be comforted." (Matthew 5:4).

- "Those who have no pride in their hearts are happy, because the earth will be given to them" (Matthew 5:5).
- "Those who are hungry and thirsty to be right with God are happy, because they will be filled" (Matthew 5:6).
- "Those who show loving-kindness are happy, because they will have loving-kindness shown to them" (Matthew 5:7).
- "Those who have a pure heart are happy, because they will see God" (Matthew 5:8).
- "Those who make peace are happy, because they will be called the sons of God" (Matthew 5:9).
- "Those who have it very hard for doing right are happy, because the holy nation of heaven is theirs" (Matthew 5:10).

Those are the first eight Beatitudes, that Jesus shared with the large crowd. The ninth, which was probably just for the disciples, was this: "You are happy when people act and talk in a bad way to you and make it very hard for you and tell bad things and lies about you because you trust in Me. Be glad and full of joy because your reward will be much in heaven. They made it very hard for the early preachers who lived a long time before you" (5:11–12).

MORE GREAT TEACHING FROM THE MOUNT

After Jesus spoke this list of things that make people happy and blessed, He shared some very simple teaching about how they should live. By living Jesus' way, people would be "salt" and "light" in the world around them (Matthew 5:13–16). Salt keeps food from spoiling, so Jesus was saying His followers would help to keep the world good. People need light to know where they're going, so Jesus was saying His followers would direct others to His truth. But Jesus went even further when He told the people that it's important to obey God from the heart—not just do the right thing because they think they have to. He taught the crowd some important truths about how the law of Moses really applied to them. Jesus said, in what we now know as Matthew 5:

- That refusing to forgive someone or talking bad about that person is as bad in God's eyes as killing that person (5:21–26).

Jesus called Himself "the light of the world" (John 8:12) and said His followers would be "the light of the world" as well (Matthew 5:14). What Jesus meant was that His teaching and Christians' example would show the world how to live.

- That looking at a woman with wrong thoughts was as bad as committing sin with her (5:27–30).
- That God expects people to honor their marriage vows, even though the culture allows them to get divorced (5:31–32).
- That you should always be honest with people and keep your word (5:33–37).

"Do not promise by heaven. It is the place where God is. Do not promise by earth. It is where He rests His feet. . . . Do not promise by your head. . . . Let your yes be YES. Let your no be NO. Anything more than this comes from the devil" (Matthew 5:34–37).

- That you shouldn't try to get even with people when they do things to hurt or anger you (5:38–42).
- That you should love everyone, even those who don't love you in return (5:43–48).

Matthew 6 tells us that Jesus told His listeners about devotion to God and what that should look like in the life of a Christian. He told them:

- We should give generously without expecting others to reward us or say good things about us (6:1–4).

WHAT DOES THAT MEAN TO ME?

"I tell you, do not use strong words when you make a promise. Do not promise by heaven. It is the place where God is. Do not promise by earth. It is where He rests His feet. . . . Let your yes be YES. Let your no be NO. Anything more than this comes from the devil" (Matthew 5:34–35, 37).

God wants you to be a person of your word, someone who follows through with what you've said. Then people will trust you, simply because you always do what you say you'll do.

- That we should not pray or fast so that others will see it and think better of us. Instead, we should get alone with God and pray in private. Not only that, we should forgive other people so that God can hear our prayers (6:5–18).
- That above everything else, we should seek what is best for God's eternal kingdom (6:19–34).

Jesus taught His followers to "knock" on God's door in prayer. "Everyone who asks receives what he asks for. Everyone who looks finds what he is looking for. Everyone who knocks has the door opened to him" (Matthew 7:8).

In Matthew 7, the final chapter that reports the Sermon on the Mount, Jesus discussed our relationships with other Christians and with God. (Yes, *God* wants us to have a personal relationship with Him!) Jesus told the crowd:

- That before we tell others that they've done wrong, we should make sure we're doing the things that please God (7:1–6).
- That we should ask God, our loving heavenly Father, for the things we need, knowing that He loves us and wants to do good things for for us (7:7–11).
- That we should treat others the way we want to be treated (7:12).
- That there is only one way to God—through Jesus Christ (7:13–14).
- That we should watch out for people who teach the wrong things (7:15–20).
- That our relationship with Jesus is based first on our faith in Him, not on the things we say or do (7:21–23).

INGREDIENTS FOR GOOD PRAYER (MATHEW 6:5–13)

Jesus knew that the people listening to Him had seen some bad examples of prayer. Sometimes the Jewish religious leaders would pray loudly, in public, to draw attention to themselves. So Jesus took time to teach the people how to pray in a way that really connected with God.

Jesus said people must be sincere when they speak to God. They should never pray just to look good to others. He urged His listeners to get alone with God, so they could pray without being distracted. And He told them that they should not just repeat the same things over and over when they prayed—they should pray from their hearts and speak to God like they would any other person. Finally, Jesus taught that people could believe that their prayers would be answered because their Father in heaven knows what they need before they even ask.

Even though Jesus was God in human flesh, He prayed often to His Father in heaven. And he taught us many important things about prayer.

Then Jesus gave the people a model for prayer, something we now call "the Lord's Prayer":

"Our Father in heaven, Your name is holy. May Your holy nation come. What You want done, may it be done on earth as it is in heaven. Give us the bread we need today. Forgive us our sins as we forgive those who sin against us. Do not let us be tempted, but keep us from sin. Your nation is holy. You have power and shining-greatness forever. Let it be so."
MATTHEW 6:9–13

A lot of people have memorized the Lord's Prayer and like to recite it word for word. There's nothing wrong with that, but Jesus didn't give this prayer just to be read back to God. It's an example of *how* people should pray. You could say it's a recipe for prayer, and here are the ingredients:

- When Jesus said, "Our Father in heaven," He meant that everyone should pray to the God who sent Him to earth, the God who identified Himself as our heavenly Father.
- When Jesus said, "Your name is holy," He meant that we are to praise God for what He really is—perfect and completely above human beings.
- When Jesus said, "May Your holy nation come. What You want done, may it be done on earth as it is in heaven," He meant that we should ask God to do what *He* wants to do, not what *we* want in our own lives and world.
- When Jesus said, "Give us the bread we need today," He meant that we should trust God to give us the things we need for life.
- When Jesus said, "Forgive us our sins as we forgive those who sin against us," He was reminding us that we should confess our sins to God—and that we should forgive others when they do things that upset us.
- And when Jesus said, "Do not let us be tempted, but keep us from sin," He wanted us to ask for God's help to overcome temptation, our desire to do and say the things that make Him unhappy.

HOW TO BE "GOLDEN"

Have you ever heard of "the Golden Rule"? Jesus didn't use that phrase, but the Golden Rule is one of His best-known teachings. It goes like this: "Do for other people whatever you would like to have them do for you. This is what the Jewish Law and the early preachers said" (Matthew 7:12).

Jesus knew He was talking to people who could be selfish and inconsiderate of others—just like all of us today! But He also knew that God had already told people how they should treat each other. The Golden Rule just simplified all of the earlier laws, so we could remember to treat other people with kindness, fairness, patience, forgiveness, and courtesy.

Think about how you want people to treat you. Do you like it when people are nice? Jesus says to be nice to them first. Do you like it when someone offers to help you? Jesus says to help others first. Do you like it when people forgive you after you've made a mistake? Jesus says to forgive others when they mess up. Do you like it when people include you in their circle of friends? Jesus says to include others, especially when you know they've been feeling left out.

When Jesus said, "Do for other people whatever you would like to have them do for you," He didn't mean we should only be kind to people who were kind to us first. He didn't mean we should only be kind to those who already like us. In fact, earlier in the Sermon on the Mount, Jesus said:

"But I tell you, love those who hate you. Respect and give thanks for those who say bad things to you. Do good to those who hate you. Pray for those who do bad things to you and who make it hard for you. Then you may be the sons of your Father Who is in heaven. His sun shines on bad people and on good people. He sends rain on those who are right with God and on those who are not right with God. If you love those who love you, what reward can you expect from that? Do not even the tax-gatherers do that? If you say hello only to the people you like, are you doing any more than others? The people who do not know God do that much."

MATTHEW 5:44–47

The Sermon on the Mount is well worth your time to read from beginning to end. But that's not Jesus' only great teaching. Let's look next at the way He taught using stories.

Every time you treat another person kindly, you're following Jesus' "golden rule."

Jesus' story of the "good Samaritan" was a parable—a story that teaches an important lesson.

JESUS' PARABLES: STORIES WITH REAL MEANING

Sometimes when Jesus taught, He just told people what He knew they needed to hear. For example, when He said, "love those who hate you," everyone knew exactly what He meant. Other times, though, Jesus taught by telling stories. These stories are called "parables," and Jesus told a lot of them.

Many times, people remember important lessons when they come in the form of interesting stories. Jesus also knew that the people who really loved Him and wanted to follow Him would listen closely so they could understand the important points of His stories.

Jesus used parables to teach on subjects such as the love and mercy of God, the importance of doing what God says, forgiving other people, God's eternal kingdom, and how God sees into our hearts.

During His time on earth, Jesus spoke more than forty parables. All of them are important, but here are five of the best-known:

- **Parable of the Good Samaritan (Luke 10:25–37)**—In Jesus' day, Jewish people and Samaritans didn't like each other very much. But in this story, a Samaritan man helped a Jewish man who had been beaten and robbed—and that was after two Jewish religious leaders had passed by the injured man. This story teaches that being a good neighbor means helping everyone who really needs it—even those we might think of as "enemies."

- **Parable of the Unmerciful Servant (Matthew 18:23–35)**—Forgiving other people is a huge deal to God. He wants us to forgive others the same way He's forgiven us. In this story, a king forgave his servant's huge debt, which the servant had no way of paying off. But that same servant soon found a man who owed him a little money and had him thrown in jail because he couldn't pay up. When the king learned what this unmerciful servant did, he demanded full payment of what he owed after all. There was no way the servant could do that.
- **Parable of the Pharisee and the Tax Collector (Luke 18:9–14)**—In Jesus' time, the Jewish people thought tax collectors were the worst people around. They worked for the Roman government, which had control over Israel. And they often collected more than what people owed and kept the extra money for themselves. In this parable, Jesus described a religious leader and a tax collector who went into the temple to pray. The tax collector cried out to God, asking for forgiveness because he knew he had done wrong to many people. But the religious leader was proud, thanking God that he wasn't as bad as the tax collector. Jesus said that the religious leader was *not* forgiven for his sins, while the tax collector was. That's because the tax collector knew he was sinful—he humbled himself and begged God for mercy. The religious leader didn't believe he needed God's forgiveness.

In a parable of Jesus, a Pharisee—a proud religious law-keeper—looks up and says to God, "I thank You that I am not like other men." But a humble tax collector bows before God, saying, "Have pity on me! I am a sinner!" (Luke 18:11, 13).

[Jesus said] "Whoever makes himself look more important than he is will find out how little he is worth. Whoever does not try to honor himself will be made important" (Luke 18:14).

- **Parable of the Wise and Foolish Builders (Matthew 7:24–27)**—With this parable, Jesus taught that it's important for people to build their lives on His teaching. He said people who listened to His words and did what He said were like a man who builds his home on a solid rock foundation, not on soft sand. When we build our lives on Jesus' teaching, He said, problems in life won't make us stop trusting in God or living for Him. But if we don't base our lives on Jesus' words, our problems will cause us to doubt God—we'll look for answers in something other than Him. It's always best to do what Jesus tells us to do.

- **Parable of the Prodigal Son (Luke 15:11–32)**—In this story, a young man asked his father to give him his inheritance early so he could move away from home. The boy went to the city, where he quickly wasted all his money on wild living with new friends. Before long, he didn't even have enough money to buy food, so he went to work for a pig farmer—and the slop he fed the hogs started to look good! The young man realized that even his father's servants were living better than he did, so he decided to go home and ask his father if he could become a servant himself. But as he got close to his father's home, he noticed his dad running to him! The older man welcomed the boy home—and as a son, not a servant. This story teaches many things about God, but perhaps the most important is that He is very happy to forgive us and welcome us back when we decide to return to Him.

In Jesus' parable of the lost son (also called the parable of the prodigal son), a loving father runs to welcome back the foolish young man who had left his home. The story was a picture of the way God the father welcomes sinful people into His own family.

THE WAY TO ETERNAL LIFE (JOHN 3:1–21)

One evening in Jerusalem, Jesus spoke what is probably the most important thing He ever said. A man named Nicodemus sat down with Jesus to discuss why He had come and what He planned to do. Nicodemus was a Pharisee, one of the Jewish religious leaders who specialized in Old Testament law—also known as the Law of Moses.

Many times, the Pharisees asked Jesus questions to try to trick Him, to trap Him into saying something they could use against Him. At best, they wanted to silence Jesus, but at worst they wanted to do away with Him completely. Nicodemus, though, was different. He asked Jesus questions because he sincerely wanted to know about Him.

Nicodemus didn't believe Jesus was the Messiah the Jews had been waiting for—at least not yet. They expected a powerful king or military leader who would lead the Jewish people in a revolt against the Roman government. But Jesus was not that kind of leader.

Nicodemus knew about the miracles Jesus had performed, and he might even have listened as Jesus spoke to the crowds of people who followed Him. The Pharisee knew there was something special about this man—he even told Jesus, "Teacher, we know You have come from God to teach us. No one can do these powerful works You do unless God is with Him" (John 3:2).

A Jewish religious leader named Nicodemus was the first person ever to hear what we now call John 3:16: "For God so loved the world that He gave His only Son. Whoever puts his trust in God's Son will not be lost but will have life that lasts forever."

Jesus didn't even acknowledge Nicodemus's statement. He really didn't need to. Both men knew Nicodemus had spoken the truth. Instead, Jesus talked about what gave people a right relationship with God. He told Nicodemus, "For sure, I tell you, unless a man is born again, he cannot see the holy nation of God" (John 3:3).

That didn't make sense to Nicodemus. The idea of being "born again" made him think of something that was not a physical possibility. How in the world could a fully grown man like him go back to his mother's womb? How could he be born all over again? And Nicodemus was probably thinking that he obeyed God's laws and insisted that others did too. That had to make him right with God and earn him a place in the eternal kingdom, didn't it?

Jesus patiently explained what He meant. He told Nicodemus, "For sure, I tell you, unless a man is born of water and of the Spirit of God, he cannot get into the holy nation of God" (John 3:5). Being born again means that the Holy Spirit gives a person a new spiritual life (3:6). Without the Holy Spirit, Jesus said, there is no way to be born again.

As a Pharisee, Nicodemus knew the Old Testament scriptures very well. So Jesus reminded him about a story from the book of Numbers. It was about Moses holding up a bronze snake on a pole so that Israelites who had been bitten by poisonous serpents could be healed. All they had to do was believe God and look at that metal snake.

Jesus then said that He was the Son of Man who had come down from heaven, telling Nicodemus, "As Moses lifted up the snake in the desert, so the Son of Man must be lifted up. Then whoever puts his trust in Him will have life that lasts forever" (John 3:14–15).

But Jesus also told Nicodemus something that each one of us needs to understand. Jesus had come to save people from their sins—it had nothing to do with anything good Nicodemus or any of us had done or ever would do. Salvation was all about what Jesus was going to do. He summed up the message of His Gospel like this:

Every human being is "born of water" (John 3:5), from the fluid inside the mother's womb. But Jesus said being "born again" comes through God's Spirit.

"For God so loved the world that He gave His only Son. Whoever puts his trust in God's Son will not be lost but will have life that lasts forever. For God did not send His Son into the world to say it is guilty. He sent His Son so the world might be saved from the punishment of sin by Him."
JOHN 3:16–17

Jesus knew He would one day be "lifted up" so that people could be saved through Him—He would be lifted up on a wooden cross. This was His most important mission: to take the punishment for our sins. By believing in Jesus' death and resurrection, we gain good standing with God. We become members of His family while we live here on earth, and we know we will always be with Him through eternity.

As you read Chapters 7 and 8 of this book, you'll learn more details of Jesus' death and the way God brought Him back to life.

WHO SAID THAT?

"How can a man be born when he is old? How can he get into his mother's body and be born the second time?" (John 3:4).

A man named Nicodemus asked Jesus this question one evening in Jerusalem. Nicodemus was a religious leader during Jesus' time on earth. He also played a part in Jesus' burial after He had died on the cross. (You can read about that in John 19:39–42.)

PART III

WHEN EVERYTHING CHANGED

In the past four chapters, you read about Jesus' birth and childhood, the things He did and the places He visited, and the lessons He taught. All of those things are important parts of Jesus' story. But every one of them was building up to His ultimate purpose for coming to earth.

From the time Jesus started His ministry, He knew it would end with His terrible death on a cross. But Jesus' crucifixion wouldn't really be the end—on the third day after His death, God would bring Him back to life! After that, Jesus would stay on earth for forty days. Many people would see Him, then go tell others that He was alive again—just as He had promised.

After those forty days, Jesus went back to His Father in heaven. But He left behind a group of followers who would continue preaching His message of salvation from sin. Jesus knew these men couldn't do this hard work all by themselves, so He promised to send a "Helper"—the Holy Spirit of God. And about a week after Jesus returned to heaven, He kept that promise. On the special day called Pentecost, the Holy Spirit filled everyone who followed Jesus—and the apostles became courageous preachers who would change the whole world.

In the next three chapters, you'll read about Jesus' final days on earth—His arrival in Jerusalem, His arrest and trial, and His death and resurrection. Not only that, you'll read about the amazing things His original apostles (as well as some other believers) did in the years after Jesus returned to heaven.

When you put all these things together, you have the incredible story of how much God loves us.

Jesus' death on the cross was sad but necessary. His resurrection—coming back to life—is the happy part of the story: This stained glass window shows Jesus, alive again and pointing out His wounds from the crucifixion!

CHAPTER 7

SOME FINAL PREPARATIONS

IN THIS CHAPTER:

- Jesus' final entry into Jerusalem
- Religious leaders oppose Jesus during "Holy Week"
- Jesus' farewell to the disciples at the "Last Supper"
- Jesus arrested in the Garden of Gethsemane

For about three years, Jesus traveled around Israel doing good for people. He taught them, encouraged them, healed them, and fed them. But He knew His ultimate mission was still ahead of Him.

Jesus had always known that He would go to Jerusalem to die on a cross, then be raised from the dead. He began to prepare His apostles for His death when they were visiting a place called Caesarea Philippi. But here's what the Bible says happened soon afterward:

From that time on Jesus began to tell His followers that He had to go to Jerusalem and suffer many things. These hard things would come from the leaders and from the head religious leaders of the Jews and from the teachers of the Law. He told them He would be killed and three days later He would be raised from the dead.
MATTHEW 16:21

Peter didn't like what Jesus was saying, and took the Lord aside to "correct" Him. "Never, Lord!" Peter said. "This must not happen to You!" (Matthew 16:22). But Jesus scolded Peter back, even more strongly: "Get behind Me, Satan! You are standing in My way. You are not thinking how God thinks. You are thinking how man thinks" (Matthew 16:23).

Peter thought he was doing good by scolding Jesus. After all, none of the apostles wanted Jesus to die on a cross! But at that time in Jesus' ministry, Peter and the others didn't fully understand why Jesus had come to earth. But Jesus did, and that's why He responded so strongly to Peter.

Then, not long before Jesus went to Jerusalem for the last time, He told His apostles:

"Listen! We are going up to Jerusalem. The Son of Man will be handed over to the religious leaders and to the teachers of the Law. They will say that He must be put to death. They will hand Him over to the people who do not know God. They will make fun of Him and will beat Him. They will nail Him to a cross. Three days later He will be raised to life."
MATTHEW 20:18–19

After hearing Jesus' words, the apostles probably wanted to go anywhere but Jerusalem. But they had faithfully followed Jesus for three years, so they followed Him now too.

A HUGE CELEBRATION (MATTHEW 21:1–11, MARK 11:1–11, LUKE 19:29–44, JOHN 12:12–19)

Around five hundred years before Jesus came to earth, God sent a message describing the way the Messiah would enter the city of Jerusalem for the last time. The Old Testament prophet Zechariah wrote, "Be full of joy, O people of Zion! Call out in a loud voice, O people of Jerusalem! See, your King is coming to you. He is fair and good and has the power to save. He is not proud and sits on a donkey, on the son of a female donkey" (Zechariah 9:9).

Every year, Christians from around the world gather in Jerusalem to remember the first Palm Sunday, when people laid their coats and palm branches on the road to make a path for Jesus.

There would be celebration in the streets of Jerusalem as the humble Jesus rode into the city. People had been waiting for many years for their Messiah—and though they didn't understand everything about the Savior's work, they knew Jesus was that Man.

Near the towns of Bethpage and Bethany, Jesus and His disciples prepared for His final entry into Jerusalem. Jesus told two of His followers to go to a village and get a young donkey for Him to ride. If anyone asked them why they were taking the animal, Jesus said to tell them, "The Lord needs it. He will send it back again soon" (Mark 11:3).

The two men walked to the village and found a mother donkey and her colt tied to a post on the street, just as Jesus had told them. They repeated what Jesus had instructed them to say to the people who asked what they were doing. Then they returned to Jesus and the other disciples. The disciples put their coats on the donkey's back, and Jesus sat on the young animal. It was time for what is called the "Triumphal Entry" into Jerusalem.

IT'S IN THE BIBLE!

When Jesus came into Jerusalem, all the people of the city were troubled. They said, "Who is this?" Many people said, "This is Jesus, the One Who speaks for God from the town of Nazareth in the country of Galilee" (Matthew 21:10-11).

It was the week before the Jews' Passover celebration. Thousands of visitors from all over the world were in Jerusalem to celebrate and worship God. As Jesus entered the city, people lined the roadway. Some spread their coats on the road ahead of Jesus, and others cut branches from palm trees to place on the road. (When Christians today remember the time Jesus entered Jerusalem, they call it "Palm Sunday.")

People crowded around Jesus as He made His way up the street. They were shouting, "Praise God for the Son of David! Blessings on the one who comes in the name of the LORD! Praise God in highest heaven!" (Matthew 21:9 NLT).

In many Bible versions, the words "Praise God" in Matthew 21:9 appear as *Hosanna*, a Hebrew word that means "oh, save!" in English. When the people cheered for Jesus on His way into the city, they thought they were welcoming a powerful king—one who would free them from Roman rule. Jesus did come to save them, but not from the Romans. He came to free them—and us—from sin.

JESUS' FINAL DAYS IN JERUSALEM

Many churches commemorate the days between Jesus' Triumphal Entry into Jerusalem and His resurrection as "Holy Week." It was a very dramatic time for Jesus.

He spent those days traveling back and forth between Bethany (where His friends Lazarus, Mary, and Martha lived) and Jerusalem, teaching, performing miracles, and preparing His disciples for what would happen to Him (and to them) as the week went on.

The Triumphal Entry took place on the first day of the week. While Monday is usually our first day of work or school each week, Sunday is actually the first day of the week. When Jesus entered Jerusalem, He went to the temple where He became very angry—people were buying and selling animals for the Passover sacrifices right in the place that they should have been worshiping God. Jesus chased the merchants out of the temple, turned over their tables, and shouted, "It is written, 'My house is to be called a house of prayer.' You have made it a place of robbers" (Matthew 21:13).

WHAT DOES THIS MEAN TO ME?

"For sure, I tell you this: If you have faith and do not doubt, you will not only be able to do what was done to the fig tree. You will also be able to say to this mountain, 'Move from here and be thrown into the sea,' and it will be done. All things you ask for in prayer, you will receive if you have faith" (Matthew 21:21–22).

Jesus wanted His followers to understand the importance of believing that God *wanted* to answer their prayers. What do you believe God wants to do for you today? When you ask for good things with faith, He'll do them for you!

Here is a side of Jesus that surprises many people—His anger over the misuse of God's temple, and the way He threw the greedy merchants out.

After this—what some people call "Jesus cleansing the temple"—He stayed for a while to heal the blind and lame people who came to Him for help. The religious leaders and teachers saw what He was doing, and they heard children looking toward the temple and calling out to Jesus, "Greatest One! Son of David!" (Matthew 21:15). These men had never liked Jesus, and they were very angry at what the kids were saying. So they complained to Jesus, "Do you hear what these children are saying?" The religious leaders wanted Jesus to stop the children, but instead He said, "Yes, have you not read the writings, 'Even little children and babies will honor Him'?" (Matthew 21:16).

After His visit to the temple, Jesus left Jerusalem and went to spend the night with His apostles in Bethany. But for the rest of the week, the Jewish religious leaders looked for reasons to arrest Jesus and have Him killed.

Sometimes the religious leaders tried to trick Jesus with difficult questions about the Old Testament law. But He always had an answer for them. One day, an expert in the law asked Jesus, "Teacher, which one is the greatest of the laws?" The religious leaders hoped they could accuse Jesus of disrespecting the rest of the Law by saying one rule was most important. But Jesus quickly answered:

" 'You must love the Lord your God with all your heart and with all your soul and with all your mind.' This is the first and greatest of the Laws. The second is like it, 'You must love your neighbor as you love yourself.' All the Laws and the writings of the early preachers depend on these two most important Laws."

Matthew 22:37–40

Jesus then asked the religious leaders a tough question that they couldn't answer (see Matthew 22:41–46). They stopped asking Him questions—but they kept trying to find ways to accuse and arrest Him.

THE PLOT TO KILL JESUS (MATTHEW 26:1–5, 14–16; MARK 14:1–2, 10–11; LUKE 22:1–6)

Even though Jesus was a good man who did many good things for others, some people in positions of authority wanted to kill Him. They didn't believe that God had a Son, so they hated it when Jesus claimed to be the Son of God. Jesus knew that the leaders were plotting against Him, but He also knew those things were part of God's plan.

A few days before Passover, Jesus reminded the disciples that He was going to die soon. He would be crucified, one of the worst possible ways to die. Meanwhile, the religious leaders in Jerusalem were meeting at the home of Caiaphas, the top Jewish leader in Jerusalem. There, they hatched a plot to have Jesus arrested and killed.

But it turned out that these men would have help from one of Jesus' own followers. Judas Iscariot slipped away from the disciples and approached the chief priests. He asked them what they would give him to hand over Jesus. The chief priests counted out thirty pieces of silver and sent Judas away. Then he waited for the opportunity to betray Jesus.

Jesus knew what Judas was doing. But He didn't stop the betrayal, because even Judas's terrible choice was part of God's plan to save people from their sin.

Judas Iscariot, at left, considers the Jewish priests' offer of thirty pieces of silver in exchange for leading them to Jesus.

IN THE "UPPER ROOM" (MATTHEW 26:17–35, MARK 14:12–31, LUKE 22:7–38, JOHN 13)

Jesus knew His time with the apostles was short, so He called them together for one final meal as a group. They met in an upstairs room of a house in Jerusalem. Many Bible experts believe this "upper room" belonged to the family of a young man named John Mark, who would later write the Gospel of Mark.

With all twelve apostles gathered around Him, Jesus began by showing them something very important. He knew that the Twelve had been arguing among themselves about which one of them was the most important (Luke 22:24). That was the wrong attitude for them to have, so Jesus showed His disciples what humbleness looked like.

Jesus got up from the table, then found a pan and filled it with water. Soon, He was washing and drying the apostles' feet, a job usually done by servants. Jesus wanted the men to understand that they should serve one another and think of others as more important than themselves. Then He told them:

"I am your Teacher and Lord. I have washed your feet. You should wash each other's feet also. I have done this to show you what should be done. You should do as I have done to you. For sure, I tell you, a workman who is owned by someone is not greater than his owner. One who is sent is not greater than the one who sent him. If you know these things, you will be happy if you do them."
JOHN 13:14–17

Later, as the apostles were eating, Jesus made a shocking announcement: "I tell you the truth, one of you will betray me" (Matthew 26:21 NLT). The apostles looked around at each other, wondering who would do something so terrible. But Jesus knew it would be Judas, a man whose feet He had just washed. Judas had already taken money to give Jesus up to the authorities, so he got up quickly and left the room.

Jesus washes His disciples' feet—a job usually done by a household servant—to set an example of humility that every Christian should follow.

IT'S IN THE BIBLE!

[Jesus said,] "I give you a new Law. You are to love each other. You must love each other as I have loved you. If you love each other, all men will know you are My followers" (John 13:34–35).

As part of the meal, Jesus took bread, gave thanks for it, and broke it. Then He gave each disciple a piece, telling them, "Take, eat, this is My body" (Matthew 26:26). He also took a cup of wine and told the men, "You must all drink from it. This is My blood of the New Way of Worship which is given for many. It is given so the sins of many can be forgiven" (Matthew 26:27–28).

SOME LAST-MINUTE INSTRUCTIONS (JOHN 14–16)

In a matter of hours, Jesus would die on a cross to provide a way for people to be forgiven of their sins. Now that He had gathered His apostles together for their last meal, Jesus gave them some final teaching. (You can read what He said in John 14–16. . .it's good stuff!)

Jesus started with comforting words: "Do not let your heart be troubled. You have put your trust in God, put your trust in Me also" (John 14:1). He assured the disciples that after He had returned to heaven, He would prepare a place where they could live with God forever.

Jesus also taught them some very important things. He said they should love God first and not love the world. He also told them, "Your hearts are full of sorrow because I am telling you these things. I tell you the truth. It is better for you that I go away. If I do not go, the Helper will not come to you. If I go, I will send Him to you" (John 16:6–7).

Jesus speaks to His twelve disciples during the Last Supper. Judas Iscariot (kneeling at front, holding a money bag) will soon leave to betray Jesus to the Jewish religious leaders.

IT'S IN THE BIBLE!

[Jesus said,] "For sure, I tell you, whoever puts his trust in Me can do the things I am doing. He will do even greater things than these because I am going to the Father. Whatever you ask in My name, I will do it so the shining-greatness of the Father may be seen in the Son" (John 14:12–13).

in His moment of greatest need. Peter didn't believe that, and told Jesus that he would never abandon his Lord. But Jesus told Peter that before the night was over—before the rooster crowed to signal the new day—he would deny three times that he even knew Jesus. Peter was very sad when he heard this, and he and the rest of the apostles promised they would never leave Jesus, even if it meant dying for Him that night.

The "Helper" Jesus mentioned was the Holy Spirit, who would come to the disciples weeks later. Jesus told the eleven remaining apostles (remember, Judas Iscariot had left the group) that the Holy Spirit would remind them of the things He had taught them. The Spirit would also show people that they needed God's forgiveness for their sins and lead them to Jesus. You'll learn more about the Holy Spirit's arrival in Chapter 9 of this book.

That night, the apostles would see Jesus arrested. But before they left to go to Jerusalem, Jesus prayed for Himself, for His apostles, and for every other Christian who would ever live. (If you want to see for yourself how much Jesus loves you, read that prayer in John 17.)

After dinner, Jesus and the apostles sang a song of praise to God. Then they left for a garden called Gethsemane. On the way there, Jesus told the disciples that they would all be ashamed of Him during His arrest. They would desert Him

The apostle Peter pledges his loyalty to Jesus, no matter what. Sadly, Peter couldn't keep his promise—but Jesus would forgive him. (Why is Peter holding a key? See Matthew 16:18–19.)

The garden of Gethsemane today. In this general spot, just before He was betrayed by Judas Iscariot, Jesus prayed. Then He was arrested and carried away to a trial.

ARRESTED LIKE A COMMON CRIMINAL (MATTHEW 26:36–56, MARK 14:32–52, LUKE 22:32–51, JOHN 18:1–13)

Jesus and the apostles walked through the Kidron Valley to the Mount of Olives, a place near the eastern side of Jerusalem. They went to an olive garden there called Gethsemane. Jesus told the apostles, "You sit here while I go over there to pray" (Matthew 26:36).

Then Jesus took His three closest friends—Peter, James, and John—and walked a short distance away from the other apostles. He told the three, "My soul is very sad. My soul is so full of sorrow I am ready to die. You stay here and watch with Me" (Matthew 26:38). He also told them, "Pray that you will not be tempted" (Luke 22:40). Jesus walked a short distance farther by Himself, fell to His face, and began to pray.

Jesus knew what was ahead for Him—terrible pain, sadness, and loneliness. His human side wanted more than anything to find another way. So He prayed, "Father, if it can be done, take away what must happen to Me." But He knew the hard things were part of God's plan, so He said, "Even so, not what I want, but what You want" (Luke 22:42).

Jesus had told Peter, James, and John to stay behind and pray, but they fell asleep. When Jesus had finished His own praying, He woke them up and told Peter, "Were you not able to watch with Me one hour? Watch and pray so that you will not be tempted. Man's spirit is willing, but the body does not have the power to do it" (Matthew 26:40–41).

Jesus went back to pray in private. Again He pleaded with God, asking if there wasn't another way to bring salvation to the people of the world. "My Father," He prayed, "if this must happen to Me, may whatever You want be done" (Matthew 26:42).

When Jesus returned to the apostles, they were asleep again! He went back to His private place a third time to pray. He was hurting so bad inside that sweat fell from His forehead like big drops of blood. The Bible says that God the Father sent an angel to encourage Jesus. When He returned to the apostles, He woke them up again and said, "Are you still sleeping and getting your rest? As I speak, the time has come when the Son of Man will be handed over to sinners. Get up and let us go. See! The man who will hand Me over is near" (Matthew 26:45–46).

Just then, Judas arrived, leading a crowd of Jewish religious leaders and Roman soldiers. Some of them carried clubs and swords and some carried torches. Judas walked up to Jesus and kissed Him on the cheek, a sign to let the mob know who to arrest. Jesus looked Judas in

Judas Iscariot leads Jewish religious leaders and a band of armed men to arrest Jesus. Notice Peter at lower right, drawing his sword on a man named Malchus.

the eye and asked him, "Judas, are you handing over the Son of Man with a kiss?" (Luke 22:48).

Jesus was prepared for what was about to happen. He asked the soldiers who they were looking for, and they answered, "Jesus of Nazareth." "I am Jesus," He told them. At the sound of His name, the crowd fell backwards for a moment. But they regrouped and surrounded Jesus again. He asked the mob to let His followers leave before they arrested Him (see John 18:4–9).

When Peter realized what was happening, he tried to defend Jesus. He pulled out his sword and started swinging it wildly at the men who had come to take Jesus away. Peter apparently wasn't a very skilled swordsman (remember, he'd always been a fisherman)—but he caught a man named Malchus, a servant of the Jewish high priest, on the side of the head and sliced off his ear. Jesus scolded Peter, and then touched the man's ear and healed his wound. Jesus then told Peter:

"Put your sword back where it belongs. Everyone who uses a sword will die with a sword. Do you not think that I can pray to My Father? At once He would send Me more than 70,000 angels. If I did, how could it happen as the Holy Writings said it would happen? It must be this way."
MATTHEW 26:52–54

Jesus knew and perfectly understood something that the apostles didn't. He had told them several times that He would die and then be raised from the dead, but they never really "got it." That's why Jesus told them right then that He was going to let these things happen. God could have stopped what occurred in the Garden of Gethsemane, but Jesus' arrest was a part of His plan—and He wasn't going to change that.

Jesus was tied up and led away. The apostles, terrified and heartbroken, ran away, just as Jesus had said they would. Only two—Peter and John—followed Him at a safe distance. For the next several hours, Jesus would be alone as He faced trial by the religious leaders and the Roman authorities. . .and after that, execution.

CHAPTER 8

JESUS' ULTIMATE MISSION

IN THIS CHAPTER:

- Jesus on trial
- Jesus condemned to die
- Jesus' death on a cross
- Jesus' resurrection
- The risen Jesus appears to His followers

We can only imagine the pain and disappointment Jesus' apostles—as well as the rest of His followers—must have felt after their Teacher and Lord had been arrested in the Garden of Gethsemane.

They had followed Him for three years, learning from Him and being amazed at the things He did for other people. He had told them that He was going to be arrested and then handed over to the Romans to be crucified. But somehow that message never sank in.

In their minds, it just wasn't supposed to end like this!

The story of Jesus' life on earth would have a wonderful, world-changing end. But before that happened, things would get worse—a *lot* worse—for the people who followed Him. Soon, however, their heartache and disappointment would be turned into the joy of knowing that Jesus had defeated death.

In this chapter, you'll read about Jesus' most important mission here on earth: to die a terrible death on a Roman cross before God the Father brought Him back from the dead. We'll start that part of Jesus' story with the trial—make that the *trials*—He would endure before He went to the cross.

A woman visits the "prison of Christ" in Jerusalem. Some believe Jesus stayed here before He went in front of the Roman governor, Pilate.

JESUS ON TRIAL (MATTHEW 26:57–27:10, MARK 14:53–15:20, LUKE 22:54–23:24, JOHN 18:13–19:3)

After Jesus' arrest in the garden, the mob of soldiers and Jewish religious leaders took Him to a man named Annas. He was the father-in-law of the top Jewish priest in Jerusalem at the time—in the Bible, this man is called the "high priest." Annas had been the Jewish high priest in the past, and he still had a lot of power and authority at the time He met with Jesus.

Annas asked Jesus about His followers and the things He had taught. But Jesus told him, "I have spoken very plain words to the world. I have always taught in the Jewish place of worship and in the house of God. It is where the Jews go all the time. My words have not been said in secret. Why do you ask Me? Ask those who have heard what I said to them. They know what I said" (John 18:20–21).

Then a soldier standing nearby slapped Jesus. He said, "Is that how You talk to the head religious leaders?" But Jesus told him, "If I said anything wrong, tell Me what was wrong. If I said what was right, why did you hit Me? (John 19:22–23).

Annas had heard enough to know that the religious leaders would want to put Jesus on trial. So he sent Jesus to Caiaphas, the current high priest. All the religious leaders and teachers gathered at Caiaphas's home to put Jesus on trial.

Caiaphas questioned Jesus, but He didn't answer. . .until the priest asked Him, "Are You the Christ, the Son of the Holy One?" (Mark 14:61). Jesus answered him, "I am! And you will see the Son of Man seated on the right side of the All-powerful God. You will see Him coming again in the clouds of the sky" (verse 62).

Jesus stands on trial before the Jewish religious leaders. They will call for His death.

That was all Caiaphas needed to hear. He tore his clothes, which was a Jewish way of showing extreme anger or sadness over something. "Do we need other people to speak against Him?" he asked the others in the room. "You have heard Him speak as if He were God! What do you think?" (Mark 14:63–64).

The religious leaders declared Jesus guilty of blasphemy—they said He was insulting God by claiming to *be* God. They spit on Jesus, covered His face and hit Him and then made fun of Him, saying "Tell us what is going to happen" (Mark 14:65). Even the soldiers hit Jesus as they led Him away and took Him to the palace of Pontius Pilate, the Roman governor of Judea.

At some point, while the religious leaders were questioning Jesus, Peter was in the courtyard of the high priest's home, watching what was happening. A young woman recognized Peter and said to him, "This man was with Jesus also." But Peter, fearing for his own life, told her, "Woman, I do not know Him" (Luke 22:57). Peter headed toward the gate, but someone else recognized Him as one of Jesus' followers and said, "You are one of them also," but Peter said, "No, sir, I am not" (verse 58). Not long after that, someone else in the crowd said to him, "For sure, this man was with Jesus also because he is from Galilee." But Peter said, "Sir, I do not know what you are saying" (verses 59–60). Immediately, Peter heard a rooster crowing. Just then, Jesus was passing by and looked directly at Peter. The apostle remembered that Jesus had predicted he would deny knowing the Lord three times. Peter went outside the courtyard gates and cried in shame.

A rooster, at upper left, gets ready to crow as Peter—warming himself by the fire—says he doesn't know Jesus.

Pilate, the Roman governor in Jerusalem, didn't believe Jesus had done anything wrong. But he gave in to the demands of the Jewish leaders and allowed Jesus to be crucified.

TRIED BY ROMAN AUTHORITIES

The Jewish religious leaders knew they could not execute anyone, even if they found a person guilty of blasphemy. Only the Roman government could kill a criminal. So they took Jesus to Pontius Pilate, the Roman governor of Judea.

When the religious leaders approached Pilate, he asked them what they were accusing Jesus of doing. They told the governor that Jesus claimed to be a king. They knew that claiming to be a king would be a serious challenge to the Roman government. When Pilate asked Jesus if He was the King of the Jews, Jesus answered, "My holy nation is not of this world" (John 18:36).

Pilate told the religious leaders that he didn't find Jesus guilty of anything. When they heard that, they became even more angry. So they said, "He makes trouble among the people. He has been teaching over all the country of Judea, starting in Galilee and now here" (Luke 23:5).

When Pilate heard the word *Galilee*, he decided to send Jesus to Herod Antipas, the son of Herod the Great, who was ruling the province of Galilee. Herod happened to be in Jerusalem at the time. He had heard of Jesus and the miracles He had done in Galilee, so Herod was glad to see Jesus in person. He hoped Jesus would even perform miracles for him, but when he asked Jesus questions, the Lord was silent.

Though Jesus didn't answer Herod's questions—and though the religious leaders kept saying false things about Him—Herod didn't find any reason to execute Jesus either. Herod and his soldiers said mean things to Jesus, and they put a robe on Him to make fun of His claim to be a king. But Herod sent Jesus back to Pilate.

WHO SAID THAT?

"I have sinned because I handed over a Man Who has done no wrong" (Matthew 27:4).

When Judas, one of Jesus' twelve apostles, learned that Jesus was on trial for His life, he felt very guilty. Judas went to the religious leaders who were plotting to have Jesus killed and tried to return the thirty pieces of silver he had received for betraying Jesus. When the religious leaders wouldn't hear him, Judas went out and killed himself.

The governor of Judea didn't want to crucify Jesus. Not only did he believe Jesus was innocent, he'd received a message from his wife that said, "Have nothing to do with that good Man. I have been troubled today in a dream about Him" (Matthew 27:19).

Pilate called the religious leaders and teachers and other people to meet with him outside his palace. He told the crowd that he hadn't found Jesus guilty of anything deserving death. Pilate was hoping to let Him go free.

The governor tried again to keep Jesus from crucifixion. He had Jesus stand in front of the Jewish religious leaders and again tried to persuade them to let Him to go free.

But the mob shouted back to Pilate, "If you let this Man go free, you are not a friend of Caesar! Whoever makes himself as a king is working against Caesar" (John 19:12). Pilate knew that the Jewish leaders could cause him big problems if they reported him to the Roman emperor, Tiberius Claudius Nero. But Pilate tried one last time to find a way to have Jesus set free.

Barabbas scuffles with his Roman guards, in a reenactment of the story of Jesus' trial and crucifixion. Barabbas was in prison for revolting against the government and for murder—but the Jewish religious leaders preferred him over Jesus.

It was tradition to release one prisoner during the Passover celebration. So Pilate brought out a known robber and murderer named Barabbas. Pilate believed the crowd would rather have Barabbas put to death than Jesus. But he was wrong.

"Which one of the two do you want me to let go free?" Pilate asked, and the crowd shouted out "Barabbas!" (Matthew 27:21). Pilate was out of ideas to free Jesus. When he asked the crowd one last time what He should do with Jesus, the people all said, "Nail Him to a cross!" (verse 23).

So Pilate gave in to the crowd's demands. But first, he brought out a basin filled with water and washed his hands in front of the people. He told the crowd, "I am not guilty of the blood of this good Man. This is your own doing" (Matthew 27:24). The crowd answered, "Let His blood be on us and on our children!" (verse 25).

Before He was crucified, Jesus was punished by flogging. At that time, criminals were often punished by being flogged or "scourged." This was a terrible beating with a whip made of leather straps, with metal balls or sharp pieces of bone braided into the leather.

In the Old Testament, God had commanded that no Israelite receive more than forty lashes. The Jews had cut off the punishment at thirty-nine lashes, to keep from accidentally breaking the law. But the Romans weren't limited to the Jewish law. The Bible doesn't say how many times they whipped Jesus, but these beatings were sometimes so bad that they caused a criminal to die before he could be crucified. Jesus was probably close to dying even before He went to the cross. But He was still alive, and that's because He hadn't yet finished the job God had for Him to do.

WHO SAID THAT?

"You brought this Man to me as one that leads the people in the wrong way. I have asked Him about these things in front of you. I do not find Him guilty of the things you say against Him" (Luke 23:14).

Pontius Pilate, the Roman governor of Judea in the land of Israel, said this to Jesus' accusers. When they wouldn't listen, Pilate gave in to their demands and ordered that Jesus be crucified.

Pontius Pilate washes his hands, a way of saying he didn't take responsibility for sending Jesus to the cross. He didn't want to crucify Jesus, but let the angry Jewish leaders have their way.

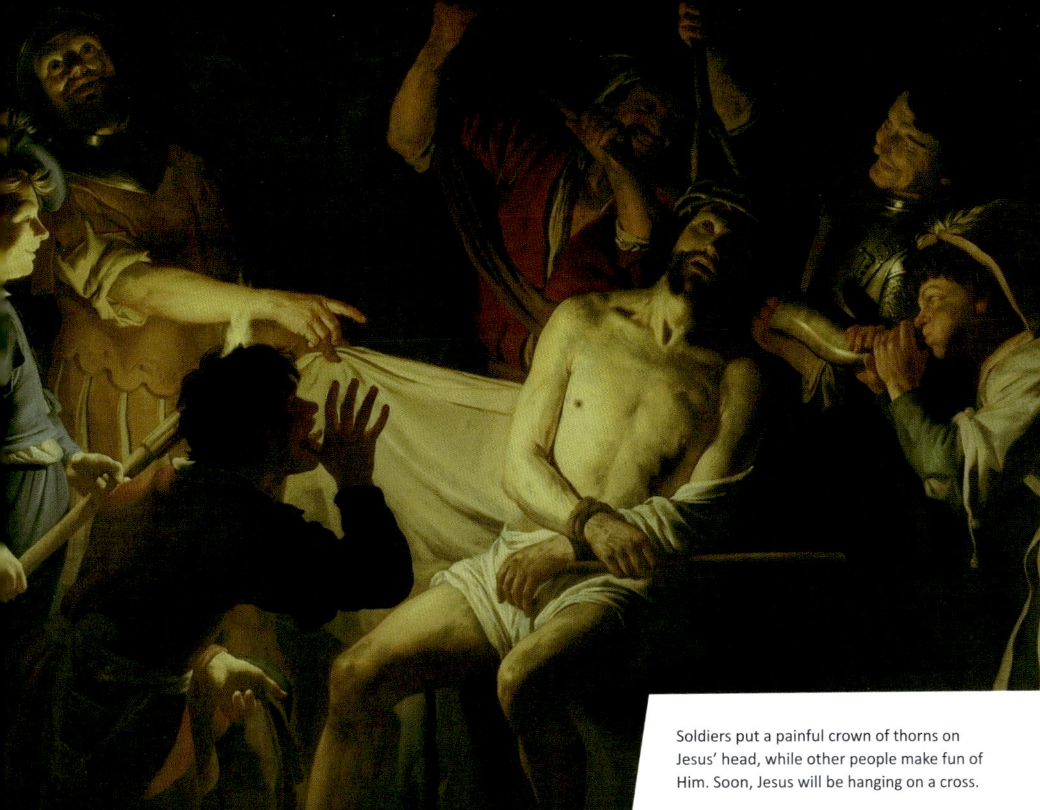

Soldiers put a painful crown of thorns on Jesus' head, while other people make fun of Him. Soon, Jesus will be hanging on a cross.

JESUS' DEATH ON A CROSS (MATTHEW 27:27–54, MARK 15:15–39, LUKE 23:26–49, JOHN 19:17–37)

After Pilate reluctantly sent Jesus off to be crucified, Roman soldiers took Him to their headquarters and put a purple robe on Him. They made a crown of thorns and put it on His head and then put a stick in His hand like a king's scepter. They were just making fun of Him, and saying things like, "Hail! King of the Jews!" (Matthew 27:29 NLT). They spit on Jesus and then hit Him on the head with a stick.

When the soldiers got tired of mocking Jesus, they took Him out to crucify Him. They made Him carry His own cross toward a place just outside the city of Jerusalem called "the Place of the Skull." It was also known as Golgotha, or Calvary.

Along the way, the soldiers forced a man named Simon to carry Jesus' cross. Simon was from a place in northern Africa called Cyrene, and he was probably in Jerusalem for Passover. Some believe that the soldiers forced Simon to help because Jesus was too weak—He had been beaten so badly that He didn't have the strength to carry the cross all the way by Himself.

The religious leaders and Roman soldiers led the way, but a crowd of others followed. There were many women following, so sad about what was happening to Jesus that they couldn't stop crying.

When they reached the Place of the Skull, the Roman soldiers nailed Jesus' hands and feet to the cross. Then they raised the cross so that everyone could see Jesus (remember how He had told His disciples that He would be "lifted up"?). Pilate put a sign on the cross reading Jesus of Nazareth, the King of the Jews. It was written in three languages: Hebrew, Greek, and Latin. When the top religious leaders saw the sign, they told Pilate, "Do not write, 'The King of the Jews'! Write, 'He said, I am the King of the Jews.'" But Pilate told them, "What I have written is to stay just as it is!" (see John 19:19–22).

In fulfillment of an Old testament prophecy (Psalm 22:18), the soldiers who had crucified Jesus divided His clothes among themselves, all except for His robe. They drew names to see who would get it.

Many people stood near Jesus' cross. Some of them made fun of Jesus and others cried for Him. Someone in the crowd yelled, "If you are the King of the Jews, save yourself" (Luke 23:37).

Jesus had spoken to His followers many times about forgiving others who had hurt them. As He hung on the cross, in terrible pain and about to die, He set a perfect example of this. Jesus actually looked down at the people who were crucifying Him and prayed, "Father, forgive them. They do not

WHAT DOES THIS MEAN TO ME?

For sure He took on Himself our troubles and carried our sorrows. Yet we thought of Him as being punished and hurt by God, and made to suffer. But He was hurt for our wrong-doing. He was crushed for our sins. He was punished so we would have peace. He was beaten so we would be healed (Isaiah 53:4–5).

Seven hundred years before Jesus was born, a prophet named Isaiah wrote these words to tell people about the terrible things Jesus would suffer for every Christian. Jesus was arrested, tried, beaten, and killed on a wooden cross so that we could be forgiven—so we could have peace with God.

Even though wicked people had put Him on the cross, Jesus prayed, "Father, forgive them. They do not know what they are doing."

know what they are doing" (Luke 23:34).

The religious leaders of Jerusalem, the ones who wanted Jesus to be killed, kept on mocking Him. "He saved others but He cannot save Himself," they yelled. "If He is the King of the Jews, let Him come down from the cross. Then we will believe in Him" (Matthew 27:42).

Jesus was crucified between two other people, criminals who had also been condemned to die. The Bible doesn't tell us their names or exactly what they had done to deserve death, but different Bible translations use words like *thieves*, *robbers*, *rebels*, or *revolutionaries*. One of them mocked Jesus, telling Him, "If You are the Christ, save Yourself and us." But the other criminal eventually came to understand who Jesus really was. He turned to his fellow criminal and said, "Are you not afraid of God? You are also guilty and will be punished. We are suffering and we should, because of the wrong we have done. But this Man has done nothing wrong." He then turned his head toward Jesus and said, "Lord, remember me when You come into Your holy nation" (see Luke 23:39–42).

Jesus offered compassion and love, even as He was dying a terrible death, by telling the criminal, "For sure, I tell you, today you will be with Me in Paradise" (Luke 23:43).

From the cross, Jesus made sure His mother, Mary, would be cared for after His death. Jesus told His favorite disciple, John, that he should consider Mary his own mother now, and Mary should see John as her son.

Jesus' mother, Mary, several other women, and the apostle John all stood near the cross. Looking down at them, Jesus said to Mary, "Woman, look at your son" and to John, "Look at your mother." The Bible doesn't say what had happened to Mary's husband, Joseph, but many people guess that he had died years before. After this day, John took Mary into his home and

IT'S IN THE BIBLE!

JESUS' SEVEN STATEMENTS FROM THE CROSS

- "Father, forgive them. They do not know what they are doing" (Luke 23:34).
- "For sure, I tell you, today you will be with Me in Paradise" (Luke 23:43).
- "[Mary,] look at your son". . . "[John,] look at your mother" (John 19:26–27).
- "My God, My God, why have You left Me alone?" (Matthew 27:46, Mark 15:34).
- "I am thirsty" (John 19:28).
- "It is finished" (John 19:30).
- "Father, into Your hands I give My spirit" (Luke 23:46).

cared for her as if she was his own mother (see John 19:26–27).

Jesus was crucified at nine in the morning. At noon, the sky went dark and stayed that way until three in the afternoon. Imagine that—even though it was the middle of the day, in Jerusalem for three hours it was like nighttime! Then, Jesus cried out, "My God, My God, why have You left Me alone?" (Matthew 27:46).

Jesus knew the time for His death had come. He had done what He came to do and now the time was very short. Jesus looked down from the cross and said, "I am thirsty." Someone soaked a sponge with vinegar and raised it up to Him on a stick. After He tasted it, Jesus loudly prayed to God, "Father, into Your hands I give My spirit" (Luke 23:46). Then He cried out, "It is finished," bowed His head, and died (John 19:30).

At that very moment, the huge curtain in the temple in Jerusalem split from top to bottom. A powerful earthquake struck the area, tearing rocks apart. Even more amazingly, tombs opened, and the bodies of people who loved God were raised from the dead! The Roman officer in charge of the crucifixion scene said, "For sure, this Man was the Son of God!" (Matthew 27:54).

Jesus' crucifixion took place on the day before the Sabbath. The Sabbath was a day of rest that God commanded, and the Jewish religious leaders had created many rules that went far beyond God's law. They didn't want the bodies of those who had been executed left on their crosses during the Sabbath. So the Roman soldiers broke the legs of the two criminals—this would make it harder for them to breathe and speed up their deaths. But when the soldiers came to Jesus, they realized He had already died, so they did not break His legs. John's Gospel tells us that this was a fulfillment of an Old Testament prophecy saying, "Not one of His bones will be broken" (John 19:36; see Psalm 34:20).

The Bible doesn't name the soldier who stuck his spear into Jesus' side. But some traditions call him Longinus, and say he became a believer.

A Roman soldier pierced Jesus' side with a spear to make sure that He was dead. The Bible says that "blood and water ran out" of the opening (John 19:34). John wrote that this also fulfilled an Old Testament prophecy, one that said, "They will look on the one they pierced" (John 19:37 NLT; see Zechariah 12:10).

JESUS BURIED

Pontius Pilate gave two men permission to take Jesus' body and prepare it for burial. The two men were Joseph of Arimathea and Nicodemus—yes, the same Nicodemus Jesus spoke to in John 3. Joseph of Arimathea was a member of the group of Jewish religious leaders who had called for Jesus' crucifixion. But Luke 23:51 tells us he had opposed the crowd's decision because he was a secret follower of Jesus.

Joseph and Nicodemus took Jesus' body down from the cross and then wrapped it in strips of linen fabric. Jesus had died the day before the Jewish Sabbath, so Joseph and Nicodemus had little time to do this work. They placed the body in a tomb belonging to Joseph; it was located in a garden not far from where Jesus had been crucified. They rolled a large stone into place to cover the entrance of the tomb. Then the Romans placed a guard at the tomb so that no one could steal Jesus' body.

WHAT DOES THAT MEAN TO ME?

He had done no wrong and had never deceived anyone. But he was buried like a criminal; he was put in a rich man's grave (Isaiah 53:9 NLT).

The Old Testament prophet Isaiah wrote these words several centuries before Jesus was born. This was a prophecy about Jesus' burial, and it was fulfilled when Jesus died like a common criminal, but was buried in the tomb of a rich and influential man named Joseph of Arimathea.

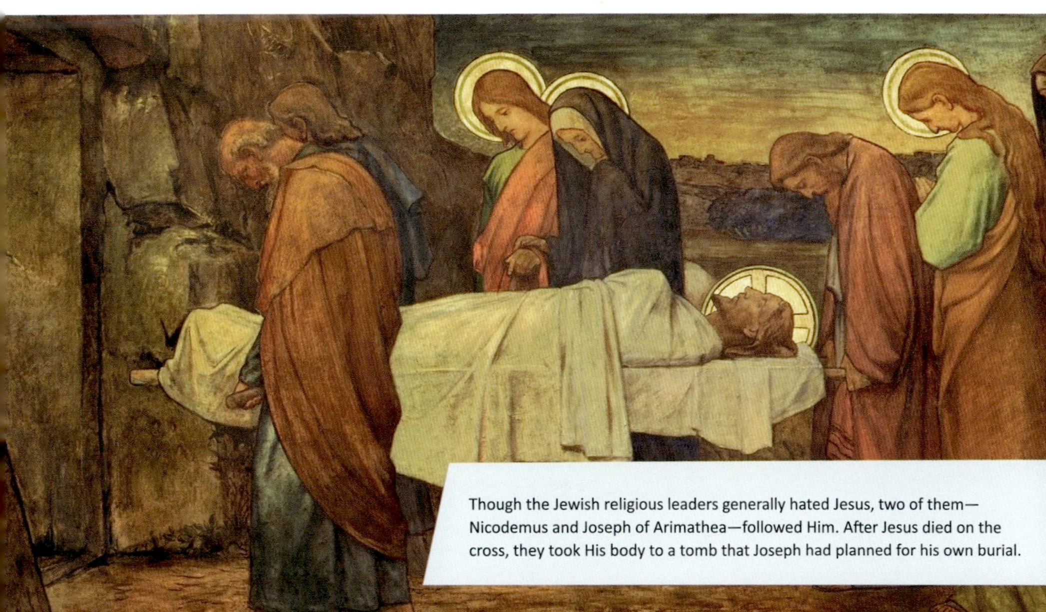

Though the Jewish religious leaders generally hated Jesus, two of them—Nicodemus and Joseph of Arimathea—followed Him. After Jesus died on the cross, they took His body to a tomb that Joseph had planned for his own burial.

Mary Magdalene is the first to see the resurrected Jesus, but she didn't immediately recognize Him. Mary thought the man was the keeper of the garden around the tomb, which is why the artist has shown Jesus holding a shovel.

DEATH COULDN'T KEEP HIM DOWN! (MATTHEW 28, MARK 16, LUKE 24, JOHN 20–21)

A man named Paul (you'll read more about him in Chapter 9) once wrote, "If Christ was not raised from the dead, your faith is worth nothing and you are still living in your sins. Then the Christians who have already died are lost in sin" (1 Corinthians 15:17–18).

That means that without Jesus' resurrection, the Christian faith is meaningless. If He hadn't come back from the dead, we'd still be separated from God for all eternity. But what Jesus had predicted about Himself was true: He died on a cross and was buried, and then God the Father raised Him from the dead! And literally hundreds of people saw Him alive after His resurrection.

The Bible records several appearances of Jesus between His resurrection and the time He went back to heaven. He appeared first to a woman named Mary Magdalene (see John 20:1–18). Mary had gone to Jesus' tomb very early on the Sunday morning following Jesus' death. But when she got there, she saw that the stone covering the entrance to the tomb was gone. So she ran to find Peter and John and told them that someone had taken Jesus' body. Peter and John then ran to the tomb. When they went inside, all they could find was the burial cloth the body had been wrapped in.

Later that morning, Mary was outside the tomb crying. The Gospels of Matthew and Luke tell us that other women were at the tomb that morning too. When Mary looked inside, she saw two angels, both dressed in white, sitting where Jesus' body had been laid. The angels asked her why she was crying, and she answered, "Because they have taken away my Lord. I do not know where they have put Him" (John 20:13). Suddenly, she heard a sound behind her and turned to see who was there. It was Jesus!

She threw her arms around Him, but He told her to go take the good news to the disciples. So Mary ran back to tell everyone what had happened.

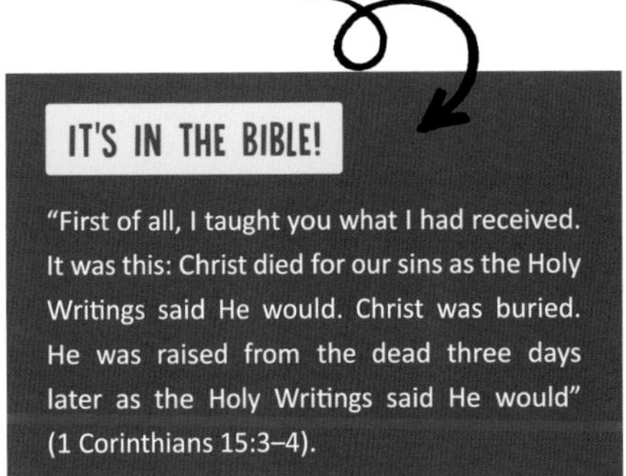

IT'S IN THE BIBLE!

"First of all, I taught you what I had received. It was this: Christ died for our sins as the Holy Writings said He would. Christ was buried. He was raised from the dead three days later as the Holy Writings said He would" (1 Corinthians 15:3–4).

Later that same day, two people who followed Jesus (but who were not among His apostles) talked to Him on the road to a place called Emmaus (Luke 24:13–32, Mark 16:12–13). They didn't recognize Him at first, but when they realized it was Jesus they had met, they rushed back to Jerusalem to tell the apostles that they had seen Him. Of the remaining eleven apostles, only Thomas wasn't in the room. Jesus miraculously appeared inside the room with them and showed everyone that He really was alive (Luke 24:36–43, John 20:19–23).

Eight days later, Jesus visited the apostles again, but this time Thomas *was* with them. The others had told Thomas that Jesus was alive, but he said he wouldn't believe it unless he could touch Jesus' wounds from the crucifixion. When Jesus appeared, Thomas believed.

On another occasion, Jesus visited with seven of His apostles on the shore of the Sea of Galilee. That day, He met with Peter, who had denied knowing Him. Jesus forgave Peter and told him that he would play a big role in building the church—that is, all the people who would believe the good news of salvation through Jesus. Jesus also hinted that Peter would one day die for Him. You can read this amazing story in John 21:1–24.

All eleven of the remaining apostles saw Jesus on a mountain in Galilee, where He told them, "All power has been given to Me in heaven and on earth. Go and make followers of all the nations. Baptize them in the name of the Father and of the Son and of the Holy Spirit. Teach them to do all the things I have told you. And I am with you always, even to the end of the world" (Matthew 28:18–20).

Jesus appeared to five hundred of His followers at one time and later to His half-brother James (1 Corinthians 15:6–7). And He visited with His apostles one more time before He went back to heaven, walking with them along the road to Bethany. On the way, Jesus told them to tell other people what they had seen and heard when they were with Him. But first, they were to go back to Jerusalem and wait for the power of the Holy Spirit to fill them. After that, Jesus left the disciples and went back to His Father in heaven (Luke 24:50–53).

"Doubting Thomas" sees the spear wound in Jesus' side and finally believes that the Lord has come back to life.

Now, Jesus' story would continue through His eleven remaining apostles—plus a few other really important people. You'll read about them and some of the incredible things they did in Chapter 9.

WHO SAID THAT?

"My Lord and my God!" (John 20:28).

The apostle Thomas spoke these words when He saw Jesus alive. The other apostles had told Thomas that Jesus had risen from the dead, but he wouldn't believe it until He had proof. Jesus told Thomas, "Thomas, because you have seen Me, you believe. Those are happy who have never seen Me and yet believe!" (John 20:29).

Why is the apostle Bartholomew often shown holding a knife? It's a hint at the terrible way he died, martyred for serving Jesus.

CHAPTER 9

SOME FOLKS GOD USED TO CHANGE THE WORLD

IN THIS CHAPTER:

- God sends the Holy Spirit
- Peter's sermon in Jerusalem
- Peter and John preach the Gospel
- The church in Jerusalem grows
- The apostle Paul and his travels

After Jesus' death and resurrection, He told His apostles, "Go and make followers of all the nations. Baptize them in the name of the Father and of the Son and of the Holy Spirit. Teach them to do all the things I have told you" (Matthew 28:19–20).

The first four books of the New Testament (Matthew, Mark, Luke, and John, also known as the Gospels) tell the story of Jesus' life, death, and resurrection. The fifth New Testament book, Acts—sometimes called the Acts of the Apostles—tells the story of how Jesus' followers did as He had instructed them. They took His message of salvation to other parts of the world, starting a movement that changed history.

In Acts 1, you can read about Jesus' final instructions to His apostles. Most Bible experts believe Jesus gave these instructions at the same time He told them to go into the world and make new followers. Jesus told His disciples, "Do not leave Jerusalem. Wait for what the Father has promised. You heard Me speak of this. For John the Baptist baptized with water but in a few days you will be baptized with the Holy Spirit" (Acts 1:4–5).

The apostles obeyed. They hung out in Jerusalem and waited for God to send His Holy Spirit to them. While they waited, they prayed and chose a man named Matthias to take Judas Iscariot's place as an apostle.

Then God sent the Holy Spirit. It was an amazing scene in Jerusalem!

Jesus' return to heaven—the "Ascension"—meant the Holy Spirit would soon come to live in believers' hearts. . .and help them change the world.

AN AMAZING DAY IN JERUSALEM (ACTS 2)

Before His death on the cross, Jesus told His followers, "Get your life from Me. Then I will live in you and you will give much fruit. You can do nothing without Me" (John 15:5). Jesus knew that His followers couldn't do what He wanted them to do just by their own power. On their own, they couldn't keep following Him and His teaching, and they wouldn't be bold enough to tell others about Him. Jesus had given them a tough assignment, and they needed His help if they were going to make it. That's why He promised to send the Holy Spirit. . .and why He fulfilled that promise not long after He went back to heaven.

On a Jewish holy day called Pentecost, 120 of Jesus' followers were gathered together in Jerusalem. Before He returned to heaven, Jesus had told them to stay there. In this place, and on this day, God would keep Jesus' promise by sending the Holy Spirit.

They probably never guessed it would be such a spectacular event!

The Holy Spirit, represented by the white dove, comes to earth to fill Jesus' followers on the special holiday called Pentecost. The little flames above each person are part of the miraculous event.

IT'S IN THE BIBLE!

[Jesus said,] "But you will receive power when the Holy Spirit comes into your life. You will tell about Me in the city of Jerusalem and over all the countries of Judea and Samaria and to the ends of the earth" (Acts 1:8).

As the people waited, they heard what sounded like a loud, powerful wind. It was so loud that people outside the house could hear it! Then what looked like flames of fire came down and touched each one of them. They were all filled with God's Holy Spirit, and now they were speaking in languages they didn't even know!

All the activity caught the attention of the people in Jerusalem—those who lived in the city, as well as those who were just visiting for the celebration of Pentecost. The visitors were from many other areas, and they spoke different languages—but then they heard these Spirit-filled Christians speaking in their own languages! Nobody knew what to make of it. Some people decided to make fun of these believers, saying they'd had too much wine to drink.

But the apostle Peter, filled with the Holy Spirit, told the crowds that these Christians hadn't been drinking. Peter said that the people in Jerusalem were eyewitnesses to the fulfillment of a promise God made through the Old Testament prophet Joel—that He would one day send His Holy Spirit to live inside people.

But that wasn't all Peter told the people in Jerusalem. Far from it!

Here is Peter, sculpted from rock. Jesus gave Him the name Cephas, which means "rock."

PETER: A CHANGED MAN

In Chapter 8 of this book, you read about the apostle Peter—one of Jesus' twelve closest followers—saying three times that he didn't even know the Lord. That fearful reaction to Jesus' arrest was just one of Peter's failings. When you read the four Gospels, you see that Peter often said and did the wrong things during the three years he followed Jesus' earthly ministry. Peter may have meant well, but that didn't always show in his words or actions.

That was Peter *before* God sent him (and all the other believers) the Holy Spirit. But *after* the Holy Spirit came, Peter was almost a completely different person. You can see how much he had changed in his very first sermon, which is recorded in Acts 2:25–41.

What a sermon it was!

Peter knew that some things he said in that sermon could get him into a lot of trouble with the religious leaders in Jerusalem. After all, those same things had gotten Jesus executed. But the Holy Spirit had given Peter amazing courage—plus the ability to remember exactly what Jesus had said to him and the other apostles.

Peter told a big crowd of people in Jerusalem that Jesus proved He was the Messiah through the things He said and did on earth—and by the fact that God raised Him from the dead. He also said that everyone could see how God had kept Jesus' promise to send the Holy Spirit to live in believers. The evidence was all around them, on that very day.

IT'S IN THE BIBLE!

[The Jews] said to Peter and to the other missionaries, "Brothers, what should we do?" Peter said to them, "Be sorry for your sins and turn from them and be baptized in the name of Jesus Christ, and your sins will be forgiven. You will receive the gift of the Holy Spirit" (Acts 2:37–38).

In an old Italian painting, Peter preaches to a small crowd. It would have been tough to paint the crowd he preached to on the day of Pentecost—enough for three thousand of them to believe in Jesus!

Peter's preaching was so powerful that it touched the hearts of many Jewish people in Jerusalem. That day, *three thousand* of them believed in Jesus and were baptized!

Amazing results, don't you think, for a former fisherman who didn't know when to talk and when to keep his mouth closed?

But that wasn't all Peter did. He remembered that Jesus had told him and the other apostles, "For sure, I tell you, whoever puts his trust in Me can do the things I am doing. He will do even greater things than these because I am going to the Father" (John 14:12). Well, Jesus did go to His Father in heaven, and Peter did do many of the great things he had seen Jesus do. He preached powerfully and he healed sick people, just as Jesus had.

As with Jesus, Peter made some enemies as he preached, taught, and healed people. A lot of people didn't like the things Peter and his friends were saying and doing, and they tried to stop him. They even threatened to put him in prison. But Peter wouldn't stop telling the good news of salvation through Jesus.

Acts 3 tells us that Peter and the apostle John went to the temple in Jerusalem and healed a man who had never been able to walk. This caught the attention of many people, so Peter preached another powerful sermon—this one at an area of the temple called Solomon's Porch. The sermon angered the religious leaders in Jerusalem, and they arrested Peter and John,

When a beggar asked Peter and John for money, Peter replied, "I have no money, but what I have I give you! In the name of Jesus Christ of Nazareth, get up and walk!" (Acts 3:6).

WHAT DOES THAT MEAN TO ME?

"There is no way to be saved from the punishment of sin through anyone else [but Jesus]. For there is no other name under heaven given to men by which we can be saved" (Acts 4:12).

You might hear people say that there are "many ways to God." But the Bible teaches there is only one way: through Jesus!

putting them in jail for the night. The two apostles didn't mind though, because many more people believed in Jesus because of Peter's preaching.

Peter did other great things to help the new church grow and become more powerful. Once, he traveled north to Samaria, where he taught Christians about the Holy Spirit (Acts 8:14–17). Not only that, he wrote two books that are in our Bibles today—1 and 2 Peter. In those books, he wrote about the things he had learned from Jesus.

THE CHURCH GROWS. . .AND EXPANDS (ACTS 3–8)

After God sent the Holy Spirit to Jesus' followers in Jerusalem, they performed miracles for people to see and preached the message of salvation through Christ. That first gathering of believers grew every day, and that got the attention of the religious leaders. They felt jealous because so many people were following Jesus, so they tried to stop Peter, John, and the rest of the church. When Peter and John refused to stop preaching, the religious leaders had them beaten and then sent them home.

One day, the religious leaders arrested a Christian man named Stephen, who had been accused of talking against God and the Old Testament Law. They brought Stephen in front of the whole assembly of religious leaders, but he wouldn't stop talking about Jesus. He reminded the angry religious leaders of Jewish history and the Old Testament prophets. Then he told them that they had murdered the promised Messiah, Jesus of Nazareth.

The godly Stephen, kneeling at left, is martyred—killed for his faith in Jesus—as an angry young Jew named Saul watches their coats (bottom right). Miraculously, Saul himself would soon become a follower of Jesus!

The crowd became furious with Stephen. They dragged him outside the city and threw rocks at him until he died. The Bible says that as Stephen was dying, he prayed, "Lord Jesus, receive my spirit" and "Lord, don't charge them with this sin!" (Acts 7:59, 60 NLT).

Stephen's death started a wave of opposition and violence against the Christians in Jerusalem. Because of this persecution, many Christians left the city and moved into different parts of Judea and Samaria. The Christians who stayed in Jerusalem, including the apostles, faced arrest and all sorts of bad treatment from the authorities.

One of the leaders of the persecution was a man named Saul, who was there when Stephen was killed and who "thought it was all right that Stephen was killed" (Acts 8:1). Saul spent a lot of time going to the houses of Christians in the city, arresting them and throwing them in jail because they followed Jesus.

But God had a plan even for Saul—who would later become known as Paul the apostle.

WHO SAID THAT?

See what great love the Father has for us that He would call us His children. And that is what we are. For this reason the people of the world do not know who we are because they did not know Him (1 John 3:1).

The apostle John, who was with Jesus for all of His earthly ministry, wrote these words many years after Jesus had returned to heaven. John also was with Peter during many of the events recorded in the book of Acts. John wrote the Gospel of John, plus 1, 2, and 3 John and Revelation.

AN UNLIKELY NEW FRIEND OF JESUS (ACTS 9)

The apostle Paul is a really important person in the Bible. He traveled thousands of miles over several years to tell people about Jesus and to start churches all over the known world. He wrote many letters to these churches and their leaders, thirteen of which are found in the Bible today. There is even evidence that he wrote other letters that aren't included as books of the Bible. Other than Jesus Himself, no one was more important in spreading the message of salvation throughout the world or in teaching people how to live as Christians.

But Paul didn't always love Jesus or His followers. Called Saul when he was born in a city called Tarsus, he grew up learning the Old Testament like most Jewish boys at that time. In Acts 23:6, Paul told the Jewish religious leaders that he was a Pharisee—that means he knew the Old Testament law and was very strict in following it.

As Saul's story begins in the book of Acts, he was doing everything he could to keep Christians from telling others about Jesus. When he found out that many of them had moved to a city called Damascus (in present-day Syria), he went to arrest them and bring them back to Jerusalem to be imprisoned. On his 175-mile journey to Damascus, though, another amazing miracle happened.

Right there on the road, a blinding light from heaven surrounded Saul. It was so bright that it caused him to fall to the ground, shielding his eyes. Then he heard a voice from heaven, asking him, "Saul, Saul, why are you working so hard against Me?" (Acts 9:3).

Saul hated Jesus, and tried to hurt Christians—until Jesus got Saul's attention on the road to Damascus. Suddenly, Saul himself was a Christian!

"Who are You, Lord?" the shaken and confused Saul asked.

"I am Jesus, the One Whom you are working against," the voice answered. "You hurt yourself by trying to hurt Me."

Saul knew he had no choice but to ask Jesus what He wanted. "Get up!" the Lord answered. "Go into the city and you will be told what to do."

Saul's traveling companions didn't see anyone, but they heard the voice speaking to Saul. When Saul got up from the ground, he couldn't see anything at all, so his friends led him into Damascus. Saul didn't regain his sight for three whole days.

Christians in Damascus had been worried about Saul's approach, because they knew how cruel he had been to their brothers and sisters in Christ. But one Christian man who lived in the city was prepared to *welcome* Saul into his home.

Ananias knew something about Saul the others didn't know, and he knew it because God had spoken to him in a vision. Ananias had heard all the terrible stories about Saul, and at first he didn't want to meet him. But God told Ananias that Saul had been chosen to take the message of Jesus to the non-Jewish world.

WHO SAID THAT?

"But Lord, many people have told me about this man. He is the reason many of Your followers in Jerusalem have had to suffer much. He came here with the right and the power from the head religious leaders to put everyone in chains who call on Your name" (Acts 9:13–14).

This was the response of a man named Ananias after God told him to welcome Saul into the church in Damascus. But God told Ananias, "Go! This man is the one I have chosen to carry My name among the people who are not Jews and to their kings and to Jews. I will show him how much he will have to suffer because of Me" (Acts 9:15–16).

Ananias prays for Saul—a new Christian soon to be known as Paul—to regain his sight.

God told Ananias that he would find Saul at the home of a man named Judas. (This was a common name at the time, and it is not the same Judas who had turned Jesus over to His enemies. By this time, Judas Iscariot had killed himself in sadness over his betrayal.) Ananias went, and while he was at Judas's home, he prayed for Saul to regain his sight. God answered Ananias's prayer.

Saul stayed for a while with the Christians of Damascus. They taught him more about Jesus, and before long, Saul began preaching and teaching others in the Jewish synagogue there. People were amazed that the same man who had beaten and killed people for being Christians was now preaching the message of salvation through Jesus.

Eventually, the man now known as Paul ended up in Antioch, a city in what is now the nation of Turkey. There was a big church there, and Paul helped the Christians in their faith. But then God called Paul to take a long journey to tell even more people about Jesus. God had enormous, world-changing plans for Paul—he was going to visit much of the known world, sharing the good news of Jesus and starting new churches in many cities.

PAUL'S FIRST MISSIONARY JOURNEY (ACTS 13–14)

Around AD 48, Paul and a Christian man named Barnabas set sail from Antioch. Paul's "first missionary journey" also included the young John Mark—Barnabas's nephew and the author of the Gospel of Mark. They landed first on a large island called Cyprus, where Barnabas was from. It's in the eastern Mediterranean Sea, south of modern Turkey and northwest of Israel.

The men docked at Salamis, then traveled from town to town preaching the good news of salvation through Jesus at Jewish places of worship. When they reached Paphos, a city on the western side of Cyprus, they stayed for a while. Paphos was the capital of Cyprus, and the home of the Roman governor of the island, Sergius Paulus. He was very happy to meet with Paul, and before he and his companions left Cyprus, the governor had become a Christian!

After Paul and Barnabas left Cyprus, they sailed to Asia Minor (modern-day Turkey) and landed in the area of Pamphylia. They then traveled about a hundred miles to a city called Antioch of Pisidia. By this time, John Mark had left the team and returned home to Jerusalem.

In Antioch, Paul went to the Jewish place of worship and told the people how God had brought Jesus to the world. But he also told non-Jewish people about Jesus, and many of them believed his message.

From Antioch of Pisidia, Paul and Barnabas departed for the city of Iconium, now called

SOME IMPORTANT MESSAGES FROM PAUL

The apostle Paul kept himself very busy traveling around the Mediterranean Sea, preaching the message of salvation through Jesus. But he somehow found time to write many of the books in the New Testament. Thirteen of Paul's letters (also called "epistles"), sent to churches and individual Christians, are in the Bible today. Those letters are Romans, 1 and 2 Corinthians, Galatians, Ephesians, Philippians, Colossians, 1 and 2 Thessalonians, 1 and 2 Timothy, Titus, and Philemon. Each of these letters contains instructions for living a good Christian life. They're all worth reading!

PAUL'S FIRST MISSIONARY JOURNEY
Paul and Barnabas's inbound journey
Paul and Barnabas's outbound journey
John Mark withdraws at Perga and returns to Jerusalem during inbound journey
0
100
200 mi
0
100
200
300 km
ASIA
GALATIA
CAPPADOCIA
Caesarea
Paul and Barnabas preach the gospel to the Gentiles after being rejected by the Jews.
Antioch (Pisidia)
After initially being mistaken for the Greek god Zeus, Paul is stoned and left for dead.
Iconium
PISIDIA
Lystra
LYCAONIA
Cilician Gates
Derbe
CILICIA
Paul and Barnabas begin their journey at Antioch.
Tarsus
LYCIA
PAMPHYLIA
Attalia
Perga
Seleucia
Antioch (Syria)
Myra
SYRIA
CYPRUS
Salamis
Paphos
Sergius Paulus, the governor of Cyprus, believes in the Lord after Paul rebukes Elymas the magician.
Sidon
Damascus
Tyre
Mediterranean Sea
Caesarea
PALESTINE
Jerusalem
Alexandria
EGYPT
N
Copyright © 2007 by Barbour Publishing, Inc.

Konya in Turkey. They stayed for a long time before moving on to Lycaonia, a large region in Asia Minor. In Lycaonia, they visited the cities of Lystra and Derbe. In Lystra, Paul healed a man who had never walked before.

Sadly, the people in Lystra thought Paul and Barnabas were mythical Roman gods come to earth. The people wanted to offer sacrifices to them, but Paul said that he and Barnabas were just men who had come to bring them the good news about Jesus. When Jewish people in Lystra found out what had happened, they turned the city's people against Paul and Barnabas. Before long, they were throwing rocks at Paul. Thinking he was dead, they dragged him out of the city.

Paul wasn't dead though—God still had work for him to do. So the very next day, he and Barnabas traveled to Derbe. After that, they returned to Lystra, Iconium, and Antioch. In every city, they taught and encouraged the Christians who lived there. After that, they started their trip back home.

By the time Paul and Barnabas completed their journey, they had been on the road for almost two years and traveled 1,250 miles. Along the way, they started many new churches and appointed leaders for those churches.

PAUL ON THE ROAD AGAIN (ACTS 16–18)

Around AD 50, before Paul started his second missionary journey, he and Barnabas traveled from Antioch to Jerusalem. They met with other Christians to discuss disagreements about what it took for non-Jewish people to become Christians. Some Jewish Christians believed the non-Jews needed to go through the Jewish religious ceremonies, but Paul disagreed.

At what is now called the "Council of Jerusalem," the men in attendance all agreed that non-Jewish Christians did not need to complete these ceremonies. After that, Paul and Barnabas traveled back to Antioch.

Paul wanted to take Barnabas on his second missionary journey, but they argued about whether John Mark should go with them. Remember, John had dropped out partway through the first trip. Barnabas wanted to give John Mark another chance, but Paul didn't. The issue was settled when Barnabas took John Mark to Cyprus and Paul recruited Silas, a church leader in Antioch, to travel with him in another direction.

Paul and Silas set out from Antioch, traveling through Syria and into Cilicia, which was a Roman province on the Mediterranean coast of what is now southern Turkey. Along the way, they made stops to encourage Christians in different towns. Then Paul went back to Derbe and Lystra. While there, he recruited a young Christian named Timothy to join him.

Paul's traveling party then made its way to Macedonia, another Roman province. Macedonia is now part of northern Greece, and it included cities such as Philippi, Thessalonica, and Corinth. Paul helped start churches in all three of those cities and later wrote letters ("epistles") that ended up being included in the New Testament: Philippians, 1 and 2 Thessalonians, and 1 and 2 Corinthians.

The Bible includes some great stories of Paul's visit to the city of Philippi. While he was there, a woman named Lydia became a Christian because of his preaching (Acts 16:14–15). Paul also cast out an evil spirit from a slave girl who had been making money for her master by telling people's fortunes (16:16–18). Paul and Silas ended up being beaten and thrown in jail in Philippi, but while they were there, they told the guard about Jesus. The guard and his whole family believed in Jesus and were baptized (Acts 16:19–34).

After Paul left Philippi, he visited several more cities, including Thessalonica, Berea, Athens, Corinth, and Ephesus. In Athens, Paul preached in the Areopagus, also known as "Mars' Hill."

WHO SAID THAT?

We took a ship from the city of Troas to the city of Samothracia. The next day we went to the city of Neapolis (Acts 16:11).

These words are from the pen of Luke, who wrote the third Gospel and the book of Acts. Luke was a physician and a historian. He was the only non-Jewish writer of a New Testament book. Acts 16:11 shows us that Luke actually traveled with Paul during his second missionary journey. This was the first time in telling the story that Luke used the word *we* to describe who was with Paul.

Paul and his missionary partner Silas were beaten and thrown in jail for their faithfulness in sharing the good news about Jesus. While they were being held in prison, they helped the jailer meet Jesus!

WHO SAID THAT?

"Sirs, what must I do to be saved?" (Acts 16:30).

A jailhouse guard in the city of Philippi asked Paul and Silas this important question. He was overseeing the two missionaries when an earthquake struck. The prison doors shook open, giving them an opportunity for an easy escape. The jailer figured they were gone. Knowing he would be in deep trouble with the Roman authorities if his prisoners got away, he pulled out his sword to kill himself. But Paul shouted, "Do not hurt yourself. We are all here!" The jailer had heard Paul and Silas singing and praying to God from their cell, so he asked the question above. Their answer? "Put your trust in the Lord Jesus Christ and you and your family will be saved" (Acts 16:31).

Several people believed Paul's message and became Christians (Acts 17:16–34). In Corinth, Paul met a married couple named Aquila and Priscilla, who would become important in the church in that city (Acts 18:18–21). After a short stay in Ephesus, Paul traveled back to Antioch.

Paul's second missionary trip took about three years, and it would change the world for good!

ONE LAST TRIP (ACTS 18:23–21:17)

Around AD 51, Paul started his third missionary journey. Before he went, he spent some time working with the church in Antioch. His first stop again was the regions of Galatia and Phrygia, which were located in modern-day Turkey. From there, he returned to Ephesus.

Paul had visited Ephesus during his second journey, but stayed only a short time. This visit, though, lasted almost two and a half years. He started out teaching in the Jewish places of worship, but some in the audience rejected his message and became abusive and rude. So Paul moved his teaching to a school run by a man named Tyrannus. He preached at the school every day for two years—to Jewish and Greek people alike.

God did amazing things through Paul in Ephesus. Miracles happened, people were healed, and evil spirits were cast out in Jesus' name. Paul's ministry grew so powerful that sick people would be healed of diseases and freed from evil spirits just by having cloth Paul had worn placed on their bodies!

Eventually, Paul's preaching in Ephesus got him into trouble. Many of the people who had come to faith in Jesus had been worshipers of a fake goddess called Artemis. An Ephesian silversmith named Demetrius had made a lot of money selling things related to the goddess, and he worried that if too many people switched from worshiping Artemis to Jesus, he would lose out. So he started a riot in the city, and Paul was nearly killed. After the violence died down, Paul and his traveling companions traveled to Macedonia and then to Greece. During this time, he avoided a plot by the Jews to kill him, and he raised a young man from the dead in a place called Troas.

PAUL'S FINAL YEARS (ACTS 21–28)

Paul eventually traveled back to Jerusalem. The Christians there were happy to see him, but after seven days, some of the Jews accused Paul of doing something in the temple that was against Jewish law. Paul was dragged out of the temple and beaten. He would have died, but Roman soldiers saw the trouble and stepped in. They put Paul in chains and took him away for questioning. The Romans later sent him to a place called Caesarea Maritima, the Roman capital of Judea, where he was held prisoner for two years.

From Caesarea, Paul and his traveling companions were sent to Rome so he could stand trial before the Emperor. Paul stayed in Rome for two years. He was allowed to go where he wanted, and he lived in a home he had rented. But Roman guards were always with him to keep him from escaping. While in Rome, Paul continued to tell people about Jesus.

The book of Acts ends with Paul in custody in Rome. But when we read his letters, it appears that he was eventually released and then made other visits as a missionary. Some believe that Paul was imprisoned in Rome a second time—this time in a very rough prison—and that he wrote many of his letters as he awaited a sentence of death.

Christian tradition holds that Paul was executed around AD 67 by order of the Roman emperor Nero, who was treating Christians very badly. Nero may have persecuted Christians because he blamed them for a huge fire that broke out in the city of Rome in AD 64. Four years later, Nero committed suicide.

During Paul's second imprisonment in

Paul tells the highly educated men of Athens about the "unknown God" they guessed was out there somewhere (see Acts 17:16–32).

Paul, who once approved of the death of Christians, was eventually killed for his own faith in Jesus Christ.

Rome, he wrote a farewell letter to a young pastor in Ephesus named Timothy. Paul knew that his time on this earth was short, and he said, "I have fought a good fight. I have finished the work I was to do. I have kept the faith" (2 Timothy 4:7).

Paul had done everything God had given him to do. He had preached the Gospel of salvation through Jesus in many places, and thousands of people came to faith in Christ because of it. He started many churches and also wrote to encourage and challenge them in their lives of faith.

Today, we know the message of salvation through Jesus, and we can thank Him for that. But we can also thank Paul, a man who changed the world because he loved God and did the things God had called him to do.

In the centuries after Paul and the other apostles died, the Christian faith would spread throughout the world. Millions of people came to believe in Jesus and embrace the life-changing message that He and His followers taught. That included one amazing promise Christians are still waiting to see fulfilled: Jesus, one day, will be coming back!

Boys read the Bible in Harare, Zimbabwe, Africa. More than two billion people around the world are identified as Christians, thanks in large part to the work that Jesus' apostles started two thousand years ago.

CHAPTER 10

HE'S COMING BACK!

In this book, you've read highlights of the Bible's teaching about Jesus. You've seen why He had to come to earth in the first place, as well as Old Testament prophecies about Him. You've learned about His birth, childhood, and earthly ministry. And you've read about Jesus' arrest, trial, death, and resurrection—plus the work of His followers after He returned to His Father.

It's an incredible story, isn't it? But there's still more to come. You see, Jesus' story didn't end when He ascended to heaven. And it didn't end with the work of Jesus' apostles either.

Jesus made some powerful promises when He was on earth, including this one: one day, He would return. That is the only promise Jesus hasn't fulfilled yet—but He will, and it could happen very soon.

Here is how Jesus described His return to earth: "Something special will be seen in the sky telling of the Son of Man. All nations of the earth will have sorrow. They will see the Son of Man coming in the clouds of the sky with power and shining-greatness. He will send His angels with the loud sound of a horn. They will gather God's people together from the four winds. They will come from one end of the heavens to the other" (Matthew 24:30–31).

Later on, just before Jesus was arrested, tried, and crucified, He promised His followers, "After I go and make a place for you, I will come back and take you with Me. Then you may be where I am" (John 14:3). That's a beautiful promise to everyone who has trusted Jesus for salvation.

When Jesus returns to earth, it will be with more attention than His birth in Bethlehem. Angels will announce Jesus' coming with trumpets!

Forty days after God raised Jesus from the dead, He returned to heaven. As Jesus rose up into the sky, His followers watched Him disappear from view. Just then, two angels appeared, saying, "You men of the country of Galilee, why do you stand looking up into heaven? This same Jesus Who was taken from you into heaven will return in the same way you saw Him go up into heaven" (Acts 1:11).

The New Testament includes many other promises about Jesus' return, which Christians call the "Second Coming." Here are some examples:

- "Do not be quick to say who is right or wrong. Wait until the Lord comes. He will bring into the light the things that are hidden in men's hearts. He will show why men have done these things. Every man will receive from God the thanks he should have" (1 Corinthians 4:5).
- "Christ is our life. When He comes again, you will also be with Him to share His shining-greatness" (Colossians 3:4).
- "Who is our hope or joy or crown of happiness? It is you, when you stand before our Lord Jesus Christ when He comes again. You are our pride and joy" (1 Thessalonians 2:19–20).
- "May the God of peace set you apart for Himself. May every part of you be set apart for God. May your Spirit and your soul and your body be kept complete. May you be without blame when our Lord Jesus Christ comes again" (1 Thessalonians 5:23).
- "It is the same with Christ. He gave Himself once to take away the sins of many. When He comes the second time, He will not need to give Himself again for sin. He will save all those who are waiting for Him" (Hebrews 9:28).
- "Christian brothers, be willing to wait for the Lord to come again. Learn from the farmer. He waits for the good fruit from the earth until the early and late rains come. You must be willing to wait also. Be strong in your hearts because the Lord is coming again soon. Do not complain about each other, Christian brothers. Then you will not be judged. See! The Judge is standing at the door" (James 5:7–9).
- "See! I am coming soon. I am bringing with Me the reward I will give to everyone for what he has done. I am the First and the Last. I am the beginning and the end" (Revelation 22:12–13).

IT'S IN THE BIBLE!

"But you must be sorry for your sins and turn from them. You must turn to God and have your sins taken away. Then many times your soul will receive new strength from the Lord. He will send Jesus back to the world. He is the Christ Who long ago was chosen for you. But for awhile He must stay in heaven until the time when all things are made right. God said these things would happen through His holy early preachers" (Acts 3:19–21).

In Chapter 2 of this book, you read about some Old Testament promises of Jesus' first arrival on earth. But other prophecies predict His return. For example, Psalms 2 and 110 describe God's chosen King—Jesus—who will rule on earth. And the prophet Isaiah wrote that in the end, "Every knee will bow down before Me. And every tongue will say that I am God" (Isaiah

The first time Jesus came to earth, it was as a helpless baby. In His second coming, He'll be the all-powerful King.

45:23). The apostle Paul used very similar words in Philippians 2:10–11: "So when the name of Jesus is spoken, everyone in heaven and on earth and under the earth will bow down before Him. And every tongue will say Jesus Christ is Lord."

Jesus' return to earth is a promise from the same God who sent Him in the first place. But the Bible tells us that only the Father knows exactly when it will happen. For centuries, Christians—even those who lived in the times of Jesus' apostles like Peter, John, and Paul—have looked forward to Jesus' return. Many Bible experts have read verses like the ones above and tried to guess when He will come back. Some people have even named specific dates, but all of them have been wrong.

Some believers in the first century—that is, the first one hundred years after Jesus' birth—believed He would return in their lifetime. And some of them worried that they might miss the big event. That's why the apostle Paul wrote, "Our Lord Jesus Christ is coming again. We will be gathered together to meet Him. But we ask you, Christian brothers, do not be troubled in mind or worried by the talk you hear. Some say that the Lord has already come. People may say that I wrote this in a letter or that a spirit told them" (2 Thessalonians 2:1–2).

Jesus told His followers that only His Father knew the exact schedule: "No one knows the day or the hour. No! Not even the angels in heaven know. The Son does not know. Only the Father knows" (Matthew 24:36). But now that Jesus is in heaven with His Father, we can imagine that He knows too. We still look forward to the day, because we know that God keeps all His promises!

A woman teaches about Jesus to children in India. Missionaries obey Jesus' "great commission"—to go and teach people around the world to follow Him. When the whole world has had the chance to hear about Jesus, He will return to earth as king.

Though we can't know the day or the hour of Jesus' return, the Bible gives clues about things that will happen before the Second Coming. First of all, Jesus said He wouldn't return until after the His Gospel message was preached to every nation in the world. Also, the apostle Paul wrote that Jesus' return would not happen until "the man of lawlessness" (who many call "the Antichrist") had been revealed. And Jesus taught that just before His return, there would be an increase in suffering and persecution against Christians throughout the world. To read about these signs, and others, look up these Bible passages: Matthew 24:4–29, 2 Thessalonians 2:1–12, and Revelation 6–18.

Jesus told His followers that His return would happen so suddenly that it would catch most people off guard: "The Son of Man will come as fast as lightning shines across the sky from east to west" (Matthew 24:27). The second coming will take place very quickly and that everyone on earth will know about it. The book of Revelation says, "See! He is coming in the clouds. Every eye will see Him. Even the men who killed Him will see Him. All the people on the earth will cry out in sorrow because of Him" (1:7).

Since many people are not ready to face God, Jesus' return will be a very bad and shocking surprise. To them, His return will mean judgment and eternal punishment for their sin. But for those who love and follow Jesus, it will be the day when every one of God's promises will be fulfilled. It will be the beginning of our eternity in heaven with Him!

IT'S IN THE BIBLE!

"For the Lord Himself will come down from heaven with a loud call. The head angel will speak with a loud voice. God's horn will give its sounds. First, those who belong to Christ will come out of their graves to meet the Lord. Then, those of us who are still living here on earth will be gathered together with them in the clouds. We will meet the Lord in the sky and be with Him forever" (1 Thessalonians 4:16–17).

This is how one artist imagines "the rapture"—as millions and millions of Christians are taken out of the world to be with Jesus.

Some people believe that part of Jesus' return is an event called "the Rapture." This is a moment when Jesus takes all living Christians, as well as the bodies of believers who had died before, off the earth to be with Him in heaven. Those who believe in the Rapture see this idea in 1 Thessalonians 4:13–18 and 1 Corinthians 15:50–54. After the Rapture, there will be terrible suffering in the world as God judges those left behind on earth. That time is called "the Tribulation."

Other Christians believe that Jesus' followers will not be removed from earth before the Tribulation. But when that terrible time is over, Jesus will come again to take believers away from all the suffering. Then He will completely destroy evil and the devil, beginning a reign of justice, peace, and righteousness on earth.

Jesus said His return to earth would come as a surprise to many people, so they should always try to be ready. "Be careful!" He said. "Watch and pray. You do not know when it will happen. . . . Watch!" (Mark 13:33, 37).

ARE YOU READY?

Jesus taught His followers how important it was for them always to be ready for His return. Since nobody knew the day or hour, Jesus told believers to keep watch at all times:

"Be ready and dressed. Have your lights burning. Be like men who are waiting for their owner to come home from a wedding supper. When he comes and knocks on the door, they will open it for him at once. Those servants are happy when their owner finds them watching when he comes. For sure, I tell you, he will be dressed and ready to care for them. He will have them seated at the table. The owner might come late at night or early in the morning. Those servants are happy if their owner finds them watching whenever he comes. But understand this, that if the owner of a house had known when the robber was coming, he would have been watching. He would not have allowed his house to be broken into. You must be ready also. The Son of Man is coming at a time when you do not think He will come."
LUKE 12:35–40

Jesus was saying we shouldn't try to figure out when He will return. Instead, we should always live our lives as if He could return at any moment—maybe even today!

People sometimes say things like, "You

know, two thousand years ago, Jesus said He would come back to earth. And ever since then, Christians have been thinking He would come back in their lifetimes. But He hasn't. Maybe the people who wrote the Bible misunderstood what Jesus meant. Or maybe He's not coming back at all!"

One of Jesus' closest friends on earth, the apostle Peter, wrote that there would always be people who said stuff like that. But he also wrote that we should be patient when it comes to Jesus' return, knowing that our timing is not the same as God's. Besides, Peter wrote, the longer Jesus waits to come back, the more people have a chance to come to Him for salvation! (see 2 Peter 3:3–9).

Yes, two thousand years is a long time for us humans. But to God, it's like the blink of an eye. God always keeps His promises, and one day He will keep His promise to send Jesus to earth for a second time. Until then, God wants us to live like Jesus is coming back today—not because we're afraid, but because we love Him. . .and love others enough to tell them about Him.

Jesus *is* coming back! When He does, it won't be an end but an incredible new beginning for everyone who trusts Him for salvation. The Bible says of that time, "See! God's home is with men. He will live with them. They will be His people. God Himself will be with them. He will be their God. God will take away all their tears. There will be no more death or sorrow or crying or pain. All the old things have passed away" (Revelation 21:3–4).

That's what your eternity with Jesus will look like. What an eternal life that will be!

Jesus loves children—like you! And He's eager for you to be part of His forever family!

ART CREDITS

Adam Jan Figel/Shutterstock 132
Adriana Mahdalova/Shutterstock 7 (right)
Alefbet/Shutterstock 92
Alena Sli/Shutterstock 102
Alex James Bramwell/Shutterstock 13
Anilah/Shutterstock 155
Anthony Rodriguez/Shutterstock 87
Arturo Escorza Pedraza/Shutterstock 49
Barbour Publishing, Inc. 34, 81, 144, 146, 148
Benjamin Haas/Shutterstock 157
Brian Maudsley/Shutterstock 46
Cecil Bo Dzwowa/Shutterstock 151
ColorMaker/Shutterstock 119
Comaniciu Dan/Shutterstock 72
Creatista/Shutterstock 21 (right)
Cris Foto/Shutterstock 137
CURAphotography/Shutterstock 39
Eduardo Estellez/Shutterstock 55
eFesenko/Shutterstock 59
Elena Schweitzer/Shutterstock 17
Everett Collection/Shutterstock 94 (left)
Everett Historical/Shutterstock 124
Everett—Art/Shutterstock 18 (left), 30, 48, 57, 75, 125
Fausto Renda/Shutterstock 6
Freedom Studio/Shutterstock 9, 78, 82, 90, 101
Gilmanshin/Shutterstock 42
Google Art Project/WikiMedia 35
Hamdan Yoshida/Shutterstock 43
Iosif Chezan/Shutterstock 52
JM71588/Shutterstock 18 (right)
Joachim Bago/Shutterstock 93
Johan Swanepoel/Shutterstock 12
John Theodor/Shutterstock 83
Jojojoe/WikiMedia 37 (Habakkuk)
Jorisvo/Shutterstock 16, 54, 126, 128, 138
Joyart/Shutterstock 33
Julia Raketic/Shutterstock 62
Jurand/Shutterstock 105
Kavram/Shutterstock 22
Kobby Dagan/Shutterstock 71
Lian_2011/Shutterstock 27
Lindasj22/Shutterstock 31
Maria Dryfhout/Shutterstock 159
Marilyn Barbone/Shutterstock 64 (left)
Mastapiece/Shutterstock 95
Monkey Business Images/Shutterstock 47
Morphart Creation/Shutterstock 149
Mountainpix/Shutterstock 153
Nancy Bauer/Shutterstock 58
Nicku/Shutterstock 38
Nyvlt-art/Shutterstock 74
Oleg Golovnev/Shutterstock 111
Oleg Ivanov IL/Shutterstock 68
Olga Plashko/Shutterstock 56
Olivier Le Queinec/Shutterstock 26
Piosi/Shutterstock 134
Rawpixel.com/Shutterstock 63
Renata Sedmakova/Shutterstock 10 (inset), 19, 32, 37 (Hosea, Joel, Amos, Jonah, Micah, Nahum, Zephaniah, Zechariah, Malachi) 40, 41, 50, 69, 70, 73, 77, 80, 86, 88, 98, 100, 106, 110, 116, 122, 127, 129, 130, 133, 135, 136, 140, 141, 142,
Roberta Canu/Shutterstock 51
Ruskpp/Shutterstock 24–25, 99, 139
Ryan Rodrick Beiler/Shutterstock 108
Sakkarin Sapu/Shutterstock 94 (right)
Salajean/Shutterstock 115
Sergey Kohl/Shutterstock 150
SpeedKingz/Shutterstock 97
Spiroview, Inc./Shutterstock 23
Stanislaw Tokarski/Shutterstock 123
Svitlana Bezuhlova/Shutterstock 158
The Yorck Project/WikiMedia 14
Triff/Shutterstock 64 (right)
Tung Cheung/Shutterstock 152
Vitaly Khodyrev/Shutterstock 156
Vlastas/Shutterstock 29
Vuk Kostic/Shutterstock 7 (left), 85
Welburnstuart/Shutterstock 104
WikiMedia 15, 21 (left), 28, 37 (Obadiah, Haggai)
WitR/Shutterstock 67
Zvonimir Atletic/Shutterstock 10 (main), 36, 37 (Isaiah, Jeremiah, Ezekiel, Daniel), 44, 53, 60, 65, 112, 113, 114, 120, 121, 147
Zwiebackesser/Shutterstock 118

THE BIBLE ADVENTURE!

CONTENTS

BEFORE YOU GET STARTED

Which person in the Bible do you find the most interesting? Maybe the first person you think of is Jesus—and that's a good thing, because He's the reason for the Bible in the first place. But consider some others you've read or heard about in church or Sunday school. You probably know some things about Adam and Eve, Moses, Joshua, David, the apostle Paul. . .maybe even Maher-Shalal-Hashbaz. (In case you didn't know, he was a son of the prophet Isaiah!)

Much of the Bible is the story of people—especially how they related to one another and to God. Some of those people were very important in God's plan to bring us salvation from our sins. Oftentimes, their lives serve as examples of things we should do as young Christians. Occasionally, their example is of things to avoid.

This book includes profiles of more than thirty important Bible characters—some you might already know, and a few who may be less familiar. Each section tells you who these people were, the things they did and said, and why they're important. And each profile will challenge you to think about the lessons you can learn from these Bible characters.

As you read, you'll learn things not only about biblical men and women, but also about God and His written Word. That's why God put these people in the Bible in the first place!

Each of the profiles in this book includes important stories and facts about these real people—starting with Adam and Eve and ending with Jesus, the most important person in all of human history. You'll also find some special features throughout this book:

- **"It's in the Bible!":** Key verses related to the person you're reading about.
- **"In Their Own Words":** Quotations directly from the mouths of these Bible characters.

And there are some other interesting and inspiring features that don't quite fit into the categories above. Don't forget to read and enjoy them too!

This book doesn't include *everything* the Bible says about these important people. But each entry includes a list of Bible references you can look up to find out more. And you should! Open up your Bible and start reading for yourself. We hope this book is interesting and helpful to you, but the Bible will truly change your life.

So, are you ready to get started? Let's go!

ADAM AND EVE

MEANING OF THEIR NAMES:
"Red" (Adam) and "Living" (Eve)

WHEN THEY LIVED:
Adam lived 930 years after the sixth day of creation; the Bible doesn't say how long Eve lived.

WHERE YOU CAN READ ABOUT THEM:
Genesis 1–5; Romans 5:12–21; 1 Corinthians 15:22, 45; 1 Timothy 2:13–14

WHY THEY'RE IMPORTANT:
Adam and Eve were the first humans God created, and that makes them the parents of every person who came after them. Adam and Eve are also important—in a not-so-good way—because their disobedience to God brought sin into the world.

The first two chapters of the book of Genesis, the very first book of the Bible, tell the story of God creating everything that exists by speaking it into being. He made the smallest microbes and the biggest and most distant galaxies. He created *everything* on our planet—the oceans and rivers, the mountains and valleys, the forests and grasslands, animals, birds, and fish—all of it.

This shows that God is very *creative*. But when He made humans, He showed that He is also *loving*. God spent six days creating everything you see around you now—but He truly saved the best for last. On the final day of creation, God made living beings who could relate to Him the way a child does to its loving parent.

On that special day, God used simple dirt to create the first man who ever lived. God named him Adam. Then God created the first woman, and Adam named her Eve. These first two humans were different from everything else God had made, because they shared the "likeness" of God Himself:

> *Then God said, "Let Us make man like Us and let him be head over the fish of the sea, and over the birds of the air, and over the cattle, and over all the earth, and over every thing that moves on the ground." And God made man in His own likeness. In the likeness of God He made him. He made both male and female.*
> GENESIS 1:26–27

When the Bible says that God made humans in His "likeness," it means we resemble Him in many ways. Though we don't know everything like God does, we have knowledge and the ability to think like He does. And while we aren't all-powerful like God is, we were created to rule over the earth and the other living things God put here.

The Bible says that when God created Adam, "He breathed into his nose the breath of life. Man became a living being" (Genesis 2:7). Adam, who was originally just a lump of dirt, was now alive, and he had a soul and spirit to communicate with God in a personal, loving way.

LIFE IN A PERFECT GARDEN

Genesis 2 tells us that before God created Eve, He made a beautiful garden for Adam to take care of. But God knew Adam was missing something very important. The animals in the garden all had a mate because God had made both males and females of each type. But Adam didn't have anyone to call his own mate. So God made Adam fall into a heavy sleep, then took a rib from his side to create Eve.

As the first man and wife, Adam and Eve had it made! God had carefully and lovingly created them, and He also made everything they would need to live happy and healthy lives with Him. They had the run of a beautiful garden—a garden God Himself visited every day. They had beautiful scenery to enjoy and lots of good food to eat. And best of all, Adam and Eve would get to live like this forever. Well, if they followed just one simple rule.

Nobody knows exactly what the Garden of Eden looked like. But many artists imagine it as full of friendly animals and lush green plants.

God told Adam, "You are free to eat from any tree of the garden. But do not eat from the tree of learning of good and bad. For the day you eat from it you will die for sure" (Genesis 2:16–17).

Adam and Eve were living in a perfect garden and spending time in the presence of the perfect God. There was no sin and no death. They didn't even know what sin or death were, because no one had ever sinned or died before! They didn't know the difference between good and bad, because everything in their lives was good. Adam and Eve were in the best place they could be to work and raise a family. Things were so good, they weren't even embarrassed that they weren't wearing clothes! (Imagine how embarrassed *you'd* feel if you found yourself standing in front of other people without a stitch of clothing on.)

Sadly, though, Adam and Eve would soon learn about sin and death. They broke the *one simple rule* God had given them. Adam and Eve suffered because of their foolish decision. Even worse, their choice affected every human being who would ever live after them.

"This is now bone of my bones, and flesh of my flesh. She will be called Woman, because she was taken out of Man."
GENESIS 2:23

THE SADDEST DAY EVER (GENESIS 3)

Adam and Eve lived in perfect harmony with the animals in the Garden of Eden. Even the animals we think are scary today—like bears and lions and tigers—were tame and friendly in the beginning. Humans had nothing to fear. Besides, because there was no sin or death, Adam and Eve didn't even know what fear was.

One day when Eve was alone, a snake crawled up to her. Eve wasn't afraid—but maybe she was surprised when it started *talking* to her.

We know that snakes can't talk to us. But this one wasn't like the snakes we see in our gardens today. It wasn't even like other reptiles living in the Garden of Eden. Eve didn't know it, but this was actually the devil in snake's clothing. And it quickly started shooting some tricky questions at her.

Eve knew God had warned her and Adam that they would die if they ate from one particular tree. But the snake said, "No, you for sure will not die! For God knows that when you eat from it, your

Eve disobeyed God by eating fruit from the one tree He said she should avoid. Then she offered a bite to Adam. . .and he disobeyed God too.

eyes will be opened and you will be like God, knowing good and bad" (Genesis 3:4–5).

Eve's mind began questioning what God had really told her and Adam. Had God really said "the tree of learning of good and bad" was off-limits? And what's wrong with knowing good from bad? Wouldn't it be nice to be like God? Just one taste couldn't hurt, could it?

So Eve reached up and picked a fruit that God had told her and Adam to leave alone. She took a bite, and then she took the fruit to Adam to try too. Adam knew better—he also remembered what God had told him. But he took the fruit from Eve's hand and ate some anyway.

At that moment, something changed in both Adam and Eve. For one thing, they felt guilty and embarrassed for walking naked around the garden. They quickly gathered some fig leaves and made coverings to hide their bodies.

Even worse, for the first time, Adam and Eve were *afraid of God*. They felt shame and fear, and they ran away when they heard the Creator in the garden. When God asked Adam why he and Eve had hidden themselves in the bushes, he told God, "I heard the sound of You in the garden. I was afraid because I was without clothes. So I hid myself" (Genesis 3:10).

Adam and Eve both knew they had disobeyed God—and they realized they were in big, big trouble. Sadly, their children and their children's children, and every human being down to this day, would suffer because of what they had done.

It was a sad, terrible day for all of humanity. Though God had said Adam and Eve would die if they ate from the tree of learning of good and bad, they didn't die right away—at least not physically. Adam would actually live 930 years (Genesis 5:5)!

Adam and Eve are kicked out of the Garden of Eden by an angel. It's just part of their punishment for disobeying God's one simple rule.

But Adam and Eve both died that day in the sense that their relationship with God was ruined. They would never again be able to just walk around with God in the garden and enjoy being with Him. Their lives would become very difficult, and at some point, their bodies would wear out and die.

That's the bad news. But God didn't leave Adam and Eve—or any of us—without hope. He had a plan to bring us back to Himself, and that meant sending a Savior to the world to rescue us from our sin. So on the same day He made Adam and Eve leave the Garden of Eden, God made this promise:

> *Then the Lord God said to the snake, "Because you have done this, you will be hated and will suffer more than all cattle, and more than every animal of the field. You will go on your stomach and you will eat dust all the days of your life. And I will make you and the woman hate each other, and your seed and her seed will hate each other. He will crush your head, and you will crush his heel."*
> GENESIS 3:14–15

When you read those verses, you don't see the name *Jesus* or the word *Savior* there, do you? But these words, straight from God's mouth, promised a Savior who would be born from one of Eve's descendants—meaning Jesus would be born of a mother just like you were.

IT'S IN THE BIBLE!

All men will die as Adam died. But all those who belong to Christ will be raised to new life. This is the way it is: Christ was raised from the dead first. Then all those who belong to Christ will be raised from the dead when He comes again.
1 CORINTHIANS 15:22–23

Adam and Eve had messed up in the worst way possible. But even though God had to punish them (remember, He had warned them they would die if they disobeyed), Adam and Eve were still His most loved creation. God wasn't going to let the devil keep them, or anyone who came after them, away from Him. He promised Adam and Eve that someone in their family line, many years down the road, would one day crush the devil's head.

What does that mean? That Jesus would one day come to earth as a baby, die to pay for people's sins, and rise again to life to defeat the devil forever.

WHAT WE CAN LEARN FROM ADAM AND EVE:

God wanted to bless Adam and Eve with the very best He had to give, but they lost everything when they broke one simple rule. They stand as a reminder for all of us to carefully listen to God when He speaks—and then obey Him.

NOAH

MEANING OF HIS NAME:
"Rest" or "Comfort"

WHEN HE LIVED:
Uncertain, approximately 2700–1750 BC

WHERE YOU CAN READ ABOUT HIM:
Genesis 5:32–10:32; Isaiah 54:9; Ezekiel 14:14, 20; Matthew 24:37–39; Luke 17:26; Hebrews 11:7; 1 Peter 3:20; 2 Peter 2:5

WHY HE'S IMPORTANT:
When God decided to destroy the entire world with a flood, He told Noah to build a giant boat to save his family. Then they would repopulate the earth after the flood was over.

WHAT BC IS ALL ABOUT

You probably noticed above that the date of Noah's life is followed by the initials BC. They stand for "before Christ." Anything that happened before Jesus was born in Bethlehem is counted backward, so the bigger the number, the earlier that event happened. So Noah was born around 2,700 years before Christ, King David around 1,000 years before Christ, and the prophet Daniel about 620 years before Christ.

After Jesus' birth, time counts upward. So the United States declared independence from England in 1776, and this book was published in 2025. These dates often have the initials AD, short for *Anno Domini*, "in the year of the Lord."

Adam and Eve's disobedience (also known as "the original sin") left the world in a terrible fix. Not only would Adam and Eve—and everyone who lived after them—die physically, they were also dead spiritually. That meant people did all sorts of terrible things, to each other and to God. As more and more people came into the world, things got worse and worse.

By the time of a man named Noah, people had become so wicked that God said He was sorry He had ever made them. Humanity had turned far away from God and gone their own evil way. God decided to destroy every living thing on earth with a huge flood and start over.

GOD'S PLAN FOR NOAH

People had become so bad in every way that God was planning to destroy the earth with a huge flood. But even then, He wasn't completely through with human beings. God had a plan to save one family and repopulate the earth. So Noah—a man the Bible says was "right with God. . .without blame in his time [and] walked with God" (Genesis 6:9)—was told to build a huge boat called an ark. It would protect Noah and his family and every kind of animal when the flood came.

Noah was the son of a man named Lamech. Sometime after he was five hundred years old (people lived a lot longer in those early days), Noah was told to begin building the ark. God gave him specific measurements for the boat—it would be about 510 feet long and 50 feet high. God even told Noah what kind of wood to use! God knew what He was doing. This boat had to be big enough to hold Noah, his family, and perhaps thousands of animals. And it had to be strong enough to stay afloat for months on what was probably some very rough water.

Can you imagine building a whole ship basically by yourself? That was the job that God gave to Noah.

IT'S IN THE BIBLE!

Because Noah had faith, he built a large boat for his family. God told him what was going to happen. His faith made him hear God speak and he obeyed. His family was saved from death because he built the boat. In this way, Noah showed the world how sinful it was. Noah became right with God because of his faith in God.

HEBREWS 11:7

Of course, building such a big boat would mean many years of hard work for Noah. The Bible says the flood came when Noah was six hundred years old, meaning it took him *decades* to finish the job. God's Word never says if Noah had any doubts about what God told him to do, nor does it describe what Noah's friends and neighbors thought of his project. The Bible only says, "Noah did just what God told him to do" (Genesis 6:22).

God was wiping the earth clean with this giant flood—people, animals, and birds would all die. But along with Noah and his family, God planned to save a pair of each kind of animal. After the flood, they would have babies and fill the earth again. So God told Noah to collect two of every creature living on the earth—one male and one female—and bring them into the ark.

Would you be surprised to learn that God also told Noah to bring *seven* pairs of some kinds of animals? Birds and "clean" animals—ones that people could later kill and eat—got onto the ark by fourteens.

Of course, there was more than just people and animals on the ark. Noah also had to store enough food in the boat to feed all the living creatures for what would be a ride of more than a year.

Animals gather, two by two, to enter Noah's ark. They, and Noah's family, will fill the earth after the flood.

STARTING OVER

A week before the flood began, Noah and his family started getting all of the animals into the ark. With that job done and all the people safely inside, God shut the ark's door. And then the water came!

Rain fell from the sky and "all the wells of water under the earth broke open" (Genesis 7:11). The incredible rain continued for forty days and forty nights, and before long, the entire earth was covered with water. Even the highest mountain peaks were swamped! Everything that breathed air—birds, bugs, animals, and human beings—died in the flood. Only the people and animals on the ark survived.

The water covered the earth for 150 days—about five months. About two months after that,

Noah and his family offer a sacrifice of thanksgiving to God, underneath the rainbow of God's promise.

as the water finally started to go down, the ark came to a rest on a mountaintop in a place called Ararat. By the time they were able to walk on dry land, Noah and his family had spent more than a full year in the ark! Imagine how happy they were when God told Noah, "Go out of the boat, you and your wife and your sons and your sons' wives with you. Bring out with you every living thing of all flesh that is with you, birds and animals and everything that moves on the earth. So they may give birth and become many upon the earth" (Genesis 8:16–17).

Noah was thankful to God, and he built an altar so he could offer a sacrifice—using some of those "clean" animals from the ark. God was happy with the sacrifice and said to Himself, "I will never again curse the ground because of man. For the desire of man's heart is sinful from when he is young. I will never again destroy every living thing as I have done. While the earth lasts, planting time and gathering time, cold and heat, summer and winter, and day and night will not end" (Genesis 8:21–22).

God told Noah and his sons—Shem, Ham, and Japheth—to have lots of children to fill up the earth again. He told them they could now eat both plants and animals. And God told Noah about His promise never to destroy the earth with a flood again. God even put a special sign in the sky as a reminder of His promise: a beautiful rainbow!

As God had commanded, Noah's sons and their wives had many children, and those children had many children, and on and on through the generations. Human beings once again had control over the earth. Noah probably saw many of his grandchildren, and great-grandchildren, and great-great-grandchildren, since he lived another 350 years after the flood. He died at age 950, as the third-oldest person in the whole Bible.

IT'S IN THE BIBLE!

"When the Son of Man comes, it will be the same as when Noah lived. In the days before the flood, people were eating and drinking. They were marrying and being given in marriage. This kept on until the day Noah went into the large boat. They did not know what was happening until the flood came and the water carried them all away. It will be like this when the Son of Man comes."
MATTHEW 24:37–39

WHAT WE CAN LEARN FROM NOAH:

God may sometimes ask us to do things that don't make sense—at least to us. But just as Noah obeyed God and built a huge boat when there wasn't a cloud in the sky, we should be willing to do what He tells *us* to do. Trust that the all-knowing God knows better than we do.

ABRAHAM

MEANING OF HIS NAMES:

"The father is exalted" (Abram) and "Father of a great multitude" (Abraham)

WHEN HE LIVED:

About 1996–1822 BC

WHERE YOU CAN READ ABOUT HIM:

Genesis 11–25; Matthew 1:1–17; Luke 16:19–31; John 8:31–47; Romans 4; Hebrews 11:8 –12

WHY HE'S IMPORTANT:

God chose Abraham to be the father of the Jewish nation—Israel—which also makes him the spiritual father of every Christian. Abraham had an unshakable faith in God, and he received every promise God had made to him.

Abraham is one of the most important people in the whole Bible. Why? Because he is considered the father of the Jews. Every Jewish person who has ever lived is descended from Abraham. And the Bible teaches that Christians are *spiritual* descendants of Abraham. If you take a few minutes to read Matthew 1 and Luke 3, you'll see that God used Abraham and his many, many descendants to bring Jesus into the world. That's what the apostle Paul meant when he wrote:

> *Be sure to remember that all men who put their trust in God are the sons of Abraham. The Holy Writings said long ago that God would save the people who are not Jews from the punishment of sin also. Before this time the Holy Writings gave the Good News to Abraham in these words, "All nations will be happy because of you."*
> GALATIANS 3:7–8

Abraham is the first of a line of Bible men who are called "patriarchs." The word *patriarch* means "father." In the Bible, a patriarch is the original father of a family or tribe. Abraham and his son Isaac, Isaac's son Jacob, and Jacob's twelve sons were the patriarchs of the Jewish people, also called Hebrews or Israelites.

IT'S IN THE BIBLE!

Because Abraham had faith, he obeyed God when God called him to leave his home. He was to go to another country that God promised to give him. He left his home without knowing where he was going. His faith in God kept him living as a stranger in the country God had promised to him.
HEBREWS 11:8–9

According to Genesis 11:27, Abraham was the son of a man named Terah. At birth, he was named *Abram*, which means "the father is exalted." But many years later, God changed his name to *Abraham*. We'll talk more about that in a bit.

ABRAM RECEIVES HIS CALL

Until he was seventy, Abram lived in a place called Ur in what is now the country of Iraq. Then he moved with his father and the rest of the family about six hundred miles northwest to the city of Haran. About five years later, Abram's father died, and not long after that, God spoke to Abraham with these instructions:

> *"Leave your country, your family and your father's house, and go to the land that I will show you. And I will make you a great nation. I will bring good to you. I will make your name great, so you will be honored. I will bring good to those who are good to you. And I will curse those who curse you. Good will come to all the families of the earth because of you."*
>
> GENESIS 12:1–3

Imagine God telling you to leave your home and everything you've ever known! Abram must have wondered what God had in mind. But he trusted God and obeyed. He didn't ask where he was going or how long it would take to get there. He just took his wife, his nephew Lot, and all their family members and hit the road.

Eventually, the family settled in a place called Canaan, an area that covers parts of modern-day Lebanon, Syria, Jordan, and Israel. It was a beautiful place that produced good crops for farmers. It would be a great place for Abram and his family to live.

One night, years after Abram had settled in Canaan, he was resting in his tent after a hard day's work. God appeared to Abram in a dream and made him a huge promise. The Bible says God took Abram outside his tent and said, "Look up into the heavens and add up the stars, if you are able to number them. Your children and your children's children will be as many as the stars" (Genesis 15:5).

Abram made God happy because he believed what God had told him (Genesis 15:6). Abram didn't know how God was going to keep His amazing promise. But he would see God perform a true miracle for him and his wife, Sarai.

ABRAM'S MIRACLE SON

Sometime later, God spoke to Abram again, telling him that he and his wife would get a name change. They wouldn't be Abram and Sarai anymore, but Abraham and Sarah. Then God made another promise to Abraham, one that he had a hard time believing—at least at first. God said Abraham would be the father of a son, and that Sarah would give birth to the child (Genesis 17:16).

Why was this such an amazing promise? Well, at the time Sarah was ninety years old—way past the age she should be having children—and Abraham was ninety-nine. But God told him, "Your wife Sarah will give birth to your son. And you will give him the name Isaac. I will make My agreement with him and for his children after him, an agreement that will last forever" (Genesis 17:19).

Abraham and Sarah went on with their lives, living in their tents in a place called Mamre. And then God stopped in for another visit. This time, He told Abraham that Sarah would have their son before another year had passed. Abraham believed what God said, but Sarah just laughed. *I'm much too old to have a baby*, she thought, *and Abraham is much too old to be a father*.

God knew what Sarah was thinking, and He said to Abraham, "Why did Sarah laugh and say, 'How can I give birth to a child when I am so old?' Is anything too hard for the Lord? I will return to you at this time next year, and Sarah will have a son" (Genesis 18:13–14).

And that's exactly what happened. When Abraham was a hundred years old and Sarah ninety-one, God miraculously gave them a son. They named him Isaac, which means "laughter." Through Isaac, God would continue His plan to bring salvation to the world. But before that could happen, Abraham would have to pass an incredible test of his faithfulness to God.

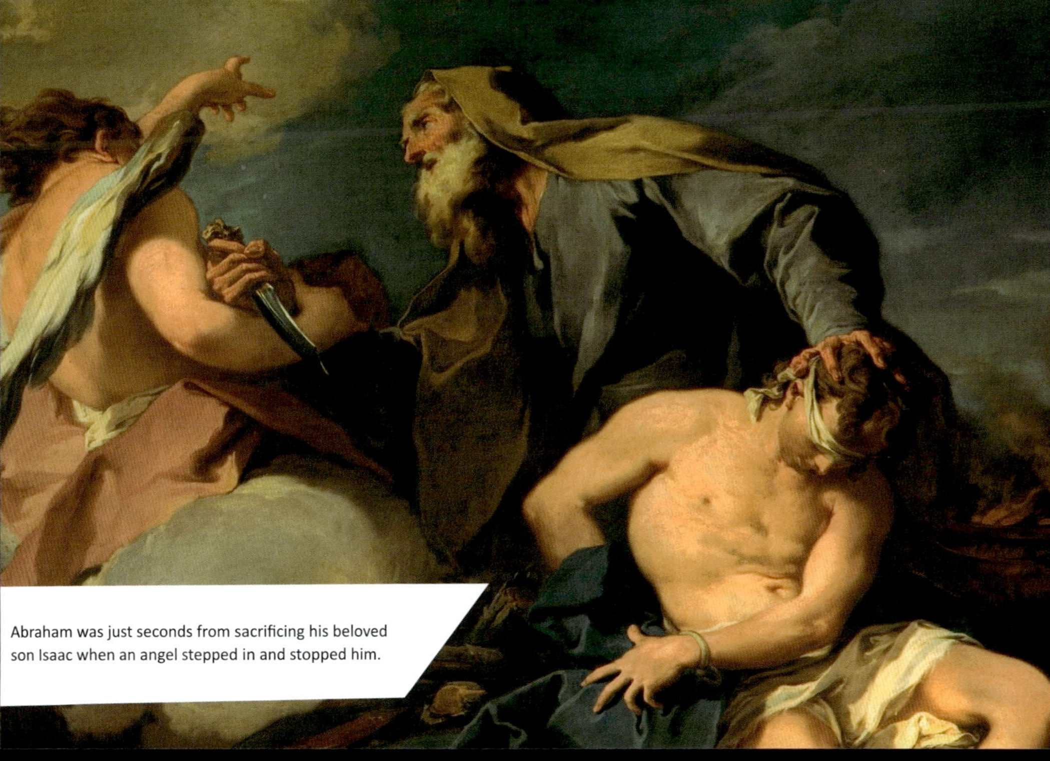

Abraham was just seconds from sacrificing his beloved son Isaac when an angel stepped in and stopped him.

GOD TESTS ABRAHAM'S FAITH

The story of Abraham includes several examples of God testing his faith. What that means is that God asked hard things of Abraham to see if he was willing to obey no matter what. The hard things started with the command for Abraham to leave his home and travel to a place he didn't even know. But Abraham's ultimate test is recorded in Genesis 22.

Isaac was probably a teenager when God told Abraham to do something that didn't make any sense at all. "Abraham!" God said. "Take now your son, your only son, Isaac, whom you love. And go to the land of Moriah. Give him as a burnt gift on the altar in worship, on one of the mountains I will show you" (Genesis 22:1–2).

Abraham traveled with his son to Mount Moriah, where he built an altar and prepared to sacrifice the son he loved so much. Isaac was just seconds from death when an angel of God stepped in and told Abraham, "Do not put out your hand against the boy. Do nothing to him. For now I know that you fear God. You have not kept from Me your son, your only son" (Genesis 22:12).

And then God reminded Abraham of His earlier promise:

> *"I will bring good to you. I will add many to the number of your children and all who come after them, like the stars of the heavens and the sand beside the sea. They will take over the cities of those who hate them. Good will come to all the nations of the earth by your children and their children's children. Because you have obeyed My voice."*
> GENESIS 22:17–18

When Isaac grew up, he married a woman named Rebekah. Like Abraham and Sarah, Isaac and Rebekah were unable to have children for a long time. But God did a miracle for them too and gave them a son named Jacob. You'll read about him in the next chapter of this book.

After Sarah died, Abraham married a woman named Keturah, who had at least six children with him. Abraham lived 175 years, and when he died he was buried with his wife in a cave near Mamre.

WHAT WE CAN LEARN FROM ABRAHAM:

Abraham was a great example of true trust in God. Even when he didn't understand God's ways, Abraham launched out and did what God told him to do. Real faith is like that. Do you love and trust God enough to do what He wants you to do, even when He hasn't given you all the details?

JACOB

MEANING OF HIS NAMES:
"Deceiver" (Jacob); "One who struggles with God" (Israel)

WHEN HE LIVED:
About 1837–1690 BC

WHERE YOU CAN READ ABOUT HIM:
Genesis 25–49; Matthew 1:1–2

WHY HE'S IMPORTANT:
Jacob, the son of Isaac and grandson of Abraham, became the father of sons who headed the "twelve tribes of Israel."

Earlier in this book, you read about Abraham, who is the first patriarch of the nation of Israel. Abraham was a good man who loved God and believed He would fulfill all His promises. One of those promises was that Abraham and Sarah would have a son. When God kept that promise, Abraham named his son Isaac. Later, Isaac and his wife, Rebekah, had twin sons—Jacob and Esau.

Jacob was very important in God's plan to bring salvation to the whole world. But as you read his story in the Bible, you see that he wasn't the nicest or most honest person. In fact, his name means "deceiver," and he often lived up to (or maybe we should say *down* to) the name. Fortunately, at one point in Jacob's life, God renamed him *Israel*, which means "one who struggles with God." Later, an entire nation—God's chosen people—was named after him. Perhaps you've heard of the "nation of Israel"?

As you read about Jacob, you'll see that he's not always a great example for Christians to follow. He had his strengths, but he also had some very big weaknesses—starting with a willingness to act and speak very dishonestly to get what he wanted.

Yet God still used Jacob to help establish the important nation of Israel—and play a big part in bringing salvation through Jesus Christ to the whole world.

JACOB'S BIG DECEPTION

Jacob and Esau were twins, but Esau came out first. In the culture of that time, he would get a bigger share of their father's wealth, as well as his father's blessing. This was an important prayer that asked God to make the oldest son successful.

Esau and Jacob were not identical twins, and

their personalities were very different. Esau was a hunter who liked being outside all the time. Jacob preferred to work around home. Esau had rough skin and a lot of hair on his body. Jacob was smooth.

Jacob knew that Esau was entitled to Isaac's wealth, but he wanted it for himself. So one day Jacob tricked his brother into selling his birthright. Esau had been out hunting, and when he came back to the family camp, he was starved. Jacob was cooking some stew, and Esau was so hungry that day he traded his birthright to Jacob. . .for a bowl of soup! (You can read the whole story in Genesis 25:27–34.)

Isaac was an older man when his twins were born, and now that they were young men, he was very old and almost unable to see. Isaac didn't know that Esau had sold his birthright to Jacob, and he still wanted to give his blessing to Esau. So he asked his older son to go hunting and then prepare some of his favorite food. Isaac had always favored Esau, but the boys' mother, Rebekah, preferred Jacob. So while Esau was out hunting, she came up with a plan for Jacob to take his father's blessing.

Rebekah told Jacob that she would prepare a meal that Isaac liked. While she was cooking, Jacob would put some scratchy, hairy goatskins on his hands and neck so he would feel like Esau. And he would put some of Esau's clothes over the goatskins so he could trick his old, blind father.

IN JACOB'S OWN WORDS

"If God will be with me and take care of me as I go, and if He will give me food to eat and clothes to wear, so that I return in peace to my father's house, then the Lord will be my God."
GENESIS 28:20–21

Sneaky Jacob tricks his father into giving him Esau's blessing. Jacob's name means "deceiver."

Jacob wasn't sure about his mother's plan. "But my brother Esau has much hair," he told her. "And my skin is smooth. If my father touches me, he will think of me as one trying to fool him. Then he will bring a curse upon me instead of good" (Genesis 27:11–12). Rebekah replied, "The curse will come upon me instead of you, my son. You do what I say" (verse 13).

Well, Rebekah's dishonest plan worked. Jacob lied to his father, making Isaac think that he was Esau, and he took the blessing Isaac intended for his older son. Because of that, Jacob, not Esau, would become the forefather of the Jewish people.

Later, Esau returned from his hunting trip. When he found out that Jacob had taken Isaac's blessing—the one that normally should have gone to Esau—he was furious. He even wanted to kill Jacob! When Rebekah learned that, she told Jacob to travel to a place called Haran and stay with his uncle Laban. Hopefully, Esau would cool down at some point.

One night, Jacob had a dream in which God promised to give his many, many descendants the land where he slept that night.

GOD'S PROMISE TO JACOB

One night on his way to Haran, Jacob had a dream. He saw a ladder reaching into the sky, with angels climbing up and down and God standing at the top. God spoke to Jacob and made these promises:

> *"I am the Lord, the God of your father Abraham, and the God of Isaac. I will give to you and your children after you the land where you are lying. They will be like the dust of the earth. You will spread out to the west and the east and the north and the south. Good will come to all the families of the earth because of you and your children. See, I am with you. I will care for you everywhere you go. And I will bring you again to this land. For I will not leave you until I have done all the things I promised you."*
>
> GENESIS 28:13–15

If that sounds familiar, it should! It's basically the same thing God had promised Jacob's grandfather Abraham, back in Genesis 15:5.

When Jacob woke up, he worshiped God. And he promised that if God would help him, he would give back one-tenth of everything the Lord gave him.

When Jacob arrived in Haran, he met Laban's youngest daughter, Rachel. Since Laban was his uncle, Rachel was Jacob's cousin. From the

The Bible says that Jacob wrestled with an angel and
refused to give up until the angel promised to bless him.

moment he saw her, Jacob knew he wanted Rachel as his wife.

Jacob offered to work seven years for Laban to earn the privilege of marrying Rachel. But Laban—who was quite sneaky himself—fooled Jacob. Laban tricked him into marrying Leah, Rachel's older sister! In those days, men sometimes had more than one wife, so Jacob worked seven more years for Laban so he could marry Rachel.

IT'S IN THE BIBLE!

Praise the Lord, for the Lord is good. Sing praises to His name, for it is sweet. For the Lord has chosen Jacob for Himself. Israel belongs to Him.
PSALM 135:3–4

Over time, with his two wives and their two servant girls, Jacob became the father of twelve sons and a daughter. God also changed Jacob's name to Israel (Genesis 32:28). The name *Israel* means "one who struggles with God." He received this new name after a mysterious "man" fought with him all night (Genesis 32:24). Jacob held on tight, demanding that the man "pray that good will come to me" (verse 26). That's when the man renamed Jacob "Israel" and said, "You have fought with God and with men, and have won" (verse 28). Jacob realized he had seen God face to face!

In time, Israel's twelve sons and the families of each of those twelve sons grew in number to become large groups of people called "tribes." These family groups came to be known as the "twelve tribes of Israel, and each one was important for different reasons. For example, Israel's priests came from the tribe of Levi, Jacob's third son. The great kings David and Solomon came from the tribe of Judah, Jacob's fourth son.

The Bible says that Jesus came from the tribe of Judah. You can read about that in Matthew 1:1–16 and Luke 3:23–38, which are Jesus' family records, also called His genealogy. The New Testament's final book, Revelation, calls Jesus "the Lion from the family group of Judah" (5:5).

Remember how God told Jacob that "good will come to all the families of the earth because of you and your children" (Genesis 28:14)? Jesus was the fulfillment of that promise!

WHAT WE CAN LEARN FROM JACOB:

Even though Jacob made some very bad decisions in his life, God still loved him and used him to help bring salvation to all people through Jesus. When you make bad decisions, remember that God still loves you too—and He can use you to do good for His kingdom as well.

JOSEPH

MEANING OF HIS NAME:

"He will increase"

WHEN HE LIVED:

About 1700 – 1600 BC

WHERE YOU CAN READ ABOUT HIM:

Genesis 37–50

WHY HE'S IMPORTANT:

Joseph played a role in the history of Israel and Egypt, saving many people in both countries from starvation during a famine. But he was also a part of God's plan to bring the Messiah—Jesus—into the world.

Joseph was the eleventh son of Jacob, whose story you just read. He was the first son of Jacob's favored wife, Rachel. Joseph is first mentioned in Genesis 30:24, where Rachel—who waited a long time to have a child—says, "May the Lord give me another son."

Seventeen years later, Joseph was shepherding his father's flocks in Canaan (Genesis 37:2). In this chapter of the Bible, we quickly learn that Joseph's brothers didn't like him very much. Why? It seems Joseph was a bit of a tattletale who told his father, Jacob, about some bad things his brothers were doing. Not only that, we read that Jacob (also called Israel) "loved Joseph more than all his sons, because Joseph was born when he was an old man. And Israel made him a long coat of many colors" (Genesis 37:3).

Joseph's brothers were so mad at him that they never said anything good to him. But Joseph made things even worse when he told his brothers about some dreams he'd had. In his dreams, Joseph's brothers were bowing down to him (Genesis 37:5–11)!

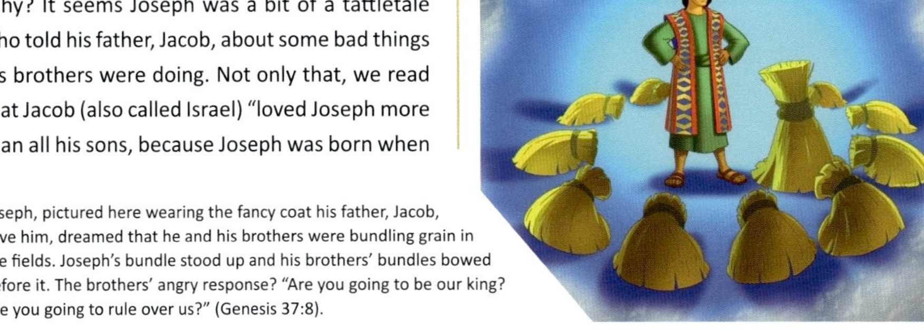

Joseph, pictured here wearing the fancy coat his father, Jacob, gave him, dreamed that he and his brothers were bundling grain in the fields. Joseph's bundle stood up and his brothers' bundles bowed before it. The brothers' angry response? "Are you going to be our king? Are you going to rule over us?" (Genesis 37:8).

Not long after Joseph told his brothers about his dreams, they made a plan to get rid of him—forever. One day, Joseph's father sent him out to the fields to check on his brothers. When they saw him coming, several of them wanted to *kill* him. Fortunately for Joseph, the oldest brother, Reuben, said, "Do not put him to death. Throw him into this hole here in the desert. But do not lay a hand on him" (Genesis 37:22). Reuben was planning to rescue Joseph and return him to Jacob after the other brothers moved on.

When Joseph arrived, his brothers grabbed him, stripped off his beautiful robe, and threw him into an empty well. Then—can you believe this?—they sat down to have lunch!

Later, a group of merchants came by, carrying items to sell in Egypt. One of Joseph's brothers had an idea: rather than *kill* Joseph, they should *sell* him. The merchants liked that idea, so Joseph was pulled out of the pit and taken to Egypt. There, he would become a slave.

IT'S IN THE BIBLE!

Because Joseph had faith, he spoke of the Jews leaving the country of Egypt. He was going to die soon, and he told them to bury his body in the country where they were going.

HEBREWS 11:22

If selling Joseph wasn't bad enough, the older brothers then tricked their father into believing that a wild animal had killed his favorite son. Jacob was heartbroken. But Joseph was still alive, and he was about to have an amazing life in the land of Egypt.

JOSEPH BLESSED IN EGYPT

When the merchants who had bought Joseph from his brothers arrived in Egypt, they sold him to a man named Potiphar. He was an important assistant to Pharaoh, the king of Egypt. Potiphar liked Joseph very much—he could see that Joseph was trustworthy and that God was with him in everything he did. So Potiphar put Joseph in charge of his home and everything he owned.

That's when Joseph's life took a very strange turn. Potiphar's wife accused Joseph of doing something very bad, but she was lying. Even though Joseph was innocent, Potiphar had Joseph thrown in jail. Even then, God was with Joseph, working behind the scenes for Joseph's good.

Like Potiphar, the jail warden trusted Joseph, so he put him in charge of all the other prisoners. God was with Joseph, making everything he did in jail go well for him.

At some point, two of Pharaoh's workers were sent to Joseph's jail. The king's baker and cupbearer—important people who handled Pharaoh's food and drink—had somehow made him mad. Joseph, still a prisoner himself, was told to watch over them.

One night, both of the men had strange dreams. Joseph could see that they were troubled, so he asked what was upsetting them. They described the dreams to Joseph, and God gave him understanding of what their dreams meant. Bad news for the baker: Pharaoh was still mad at him, and he was going to be killed. The news was better for the cupbearer, though—he would be released from jail and go back to serve the king again. "Remember me when it is well with you, and show me kindness," Joseph told him. "Say a good word about me to Pharaoh. Get me out of this prison" (Genesis 40:14).

The cupbearer was so happy to be set free that he forgot all about Joseph—so Joseph remained in jail for two more years. But then *Pharaoh* had a strange dream he couldn't understand. Nobody else could explain it to him either. At that point, the cupbearer remembered Joseph. He told Pharaoh that Joseph had explained his own dream, and Pharaoh sent for Joseph.

When the two men met, Pharaoh asked Joseph if it was true that he could tell what dreams meant. Joseph answered, "Not by myself. God will give Pharaoh a good answer" (Genesis 41:16). So Pharaoh described his dream, which included seven skinny, ugly cows eating seven nice, fat cows.

"God has shown Pharaoh what He is about to do," Joseph told the king (Genesis 41:25). He explained that the dream meant seven years were coming when the land of Egypt would produce huge crops—but that would be followed by seven years of famine, when there would be no new food.

After his brothers threw him into an empty well, Joseph's view might have been something like this.

A FAMILY REUNION

When those seven years of plenty in Egypt were over, the seven years of famine started—just as Joseph had said. And the famine affected countries all around Egypt too.

Because Egypt had prepared, it had lots of food. People from all over came to buy grain from Joseph. That included ten men who traveled from Canaan. . .Joseph's older brothers!

When the brothers came before Joseph, they didn't recognize him. Since Joseph was the most important person in Egypt after the pharaoh, they bowed—just like his dreams had predicted all those years ago. Joseph had the authority to punish or even kill his brothers, but God wouldn't want him to do that. Instead, when he showed them who he was, Joseph told his brothers not to be afraid of him or angry at themselves. God was using what they had done to save the lives of many people.

Joseph's brothers went back to Canaan and told their dad, Jacob, that Joseph was still alive. He could hardly believe it! Soon, Jacob and his sons and his sons' families moved from Canaan to Egypt, where there was plenty of food for everyone. Because they were Joseph's family, they had the best of everything, and their families grew bigger and bigger.

IN JOSEPH'S OWN WORDS

"Do not be afraid. Am I in the place of God? You planned to do a bad thing to me. But God planned it for good, to make it happen that many people should be kept alive, as they are today."
GENESIS 50:19–20

Joseph lived to be 110 years old. Before he died, he promised his brothers that God would one day rescue their descendants and take them back to Canaan. And, as with the dreams he explained, what he said was absolutely correct.

WHAT WE CAN LEARN FROM JOSEPH:

Joseph was blessed in a huge way because he was faithful to God no matter what. God wants to bless us today too, and He will do that when we stay close to Him and live in a way that pleases Him.

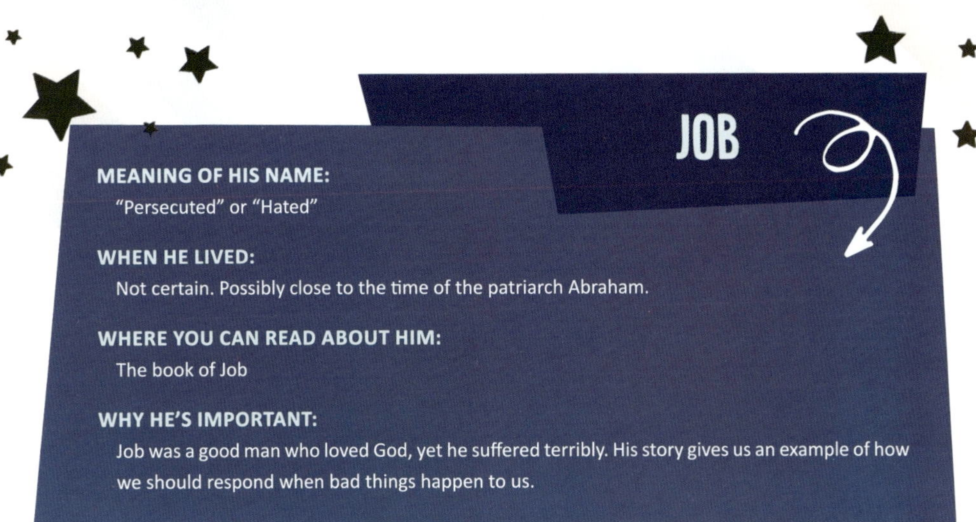

JOB

MEANING OF HIS NAME:
"Persecuted" or "Hated"

WHEN HE LIVED:
Not certain. Possibly close to the time of the patriarch Abraham.

WHERE YOU CAN READ ABOUT HIM:
The book of Job

WHY HE'S IMPORTANT:
Job was a good man who loved God, yet he suffered terribly. His story gives us an example of how we should respond when bad things happen to us.

Have you ever gone through a tough time and wondered if you'd done something to make God mad? Or have you ever gone through one of those tough times, but you *knew* you hadn't done anything to "deserve" it? If so, you might identify with a man named Job.

Job's story is told in the Old Testament. He has a whole book named after him, which you can find between the books of Esther and Psalms. No one knows for sure who wrote down Job's story, but some believe it was Moses. Some people think Job is the oldest book in the whole Bible—older even than Genesis.

Job lived in a place called Uz (Job 1:1). Nobody knows exactly where that was, but it might have been located east of the Jordan River. Job probably lived before or at the same time as Abraham, and he was about seventy years old when the events in the book of Job took place. He was a wealthy man with a wife, seven sons, and three daughters. He owned 7,000 sheep, 3,000 camels, 1,000 oxen, and 500 female donkeys. He also had many servants who worked for him (1:3).

Job was rich and well respected in Uz, but that isn't the first thing the Bible tells us about him. What set Job apart from others was his love for God. The Bible says that Job "was without blame. He was right and good, he feared God, and turned away from sin" (1:1).

But even though Job loved and obeyed God, he went through a time of suffering most people would find hard to imagine, let alone endure! Job's response to that suffering makes him an important example for all of us.

IT'S IN THE BIBLE!

We think of those who stayed true to [God] as happy even though they suffered. You have heard how long Job waited. You have seen what the Lord did for him in the end. The Lord is full of loving-kindness and pity.
JAMES 5:11

JOB'S TIME OF TESTING

The Bible tells us that the devil took notice of Job. Job appeared to love and obey God in every way, so Satan complained to God. The devil said that Job only loved God because God had given him so much. If Job lost his money and things, the devil argued, Job would curse God (Job 1:8–11).

God knew Job very well, so He told Satan, "See, all that he has is in your power. Only do not put your hand on him" (1:12). That meant that the devil could take everything Job had—except he couldn't attack Job's body.

In a time when wealth was counted in animals, Job had literally thousands of sheep, camels, cows, and donkeys!

From that day on, Job began losing everything. First, a man came to Job with the news that his oxen had been taken away and many of his servants killed (1:13–15). As Job heard this terrible news, another man came to him and told him that a fire from the sky wiped out his sheep and more of his servants (1:16). But that wasn't the last of the bad news that day. A third man then came to Job and told him that the Babylonians had come and taken Job's camels and killed still more of his servants (1:17).

IN JOB'S OWN WORDS

"Why should I take my flesh in my teeth, and put my life in my hands? Even though [God] would kill me, yet I will trust in Him. I will argue my ways to His face."
JOB 13:14–15

Then came the worst news of all. As the third man was describing Job's losses, a *fourth* man arrived to say that a strong desert wind had destroyed Job's oldest son's house. The collapse killed all ten of Job's children as they were eating (1:18–19).

We can only imagine how sad Job was when he learned this news. But he never questioned God or sinned in any way. He just said, "Without clothing I was born from my mother, and without clothing I will return. The Lord gave and the Lord has taken away. Praise the name of the Lord" (1:21). But things were going to get even worse for Job. God next gave the devil permission to take away Job's health—and ugly, painful sores broke out from the top of his head to the bottom of his feet. To make matters worse, Job's own wife lost heart. She said to him, "Do you still hold on to your faith? Curse God and die!" (2:9). But Job remained faithful to God. Not once did he say or do anything sinful because of his suffering.

A LONG HAUL, A HAPPY ENDING

Most of the book of Job (chapters 3–37) describes his talks with three friends—Eliphaz, Bildad, and Zophar. They had come to help Job make sense out of something that made little sense: Why should such a good man have to suffer so much?

Job had friends who came to comfort him in his trouble. . . but ended up accusing him of sin.

Job's friends were sure that God must be punishing him for some sin he had committed. Job told the three men that they were wrong—he was innocent. Job admitted that he wanted to die and told the men that he had asked God many questions about what was going on.

A fourth friend, a younger man named Elihu, arrived and tried to speak to Job's other friends on God's behalf. But then God Himself spoke to Job. God didn't answer all of Job's questions, but He proved that He knew so much more than Job did (Job 38–42). Even though Job never fully understood why God allowed him to suffer, he responded to God humbly. Job said he had been wrong in speaking of things he didn't fully understand.

Then God turned to Job's friends, saying He was angry with them. They had said things about God that were not true—unlike Job, who had spoken only the truth. God forgave Eliphaz, Bildad, and Zophar after they offered Him sacrifices—and after Job prayed for them.

In the end, God gave Job back two times as many animals as he'd had before, as well as ten more children. In fact, God "brought more good to Job in his later years than in his beginning" (42:12). Job lived 140 more years after his time of suffering.

WHAT WE CAN LEARN FROM JOB:

Christians sometimes think God won't allow bad things to happen to them—or that if bad things happen, it's because we are doing something to make God unhappy with us. But Job was a good and godly man who went through a time of terrible suffering. Bad things sometimes do happen to good people, but we can take heart in God's promise to do good through even the worst things that happen to us (see Romans 8:28).

MOSES

MEANING OF HIS NAME:
"Taken out" or "Drawn forth"

WHEN HE LIVED:
About 1393–1273 BC

WHERE YOU CAN READ ABOUT HIM:
The books of Exodus, Leviticus, Numbers, and Deuteronomy

BIBLE BOOKS HE WROTE:
Genesis, Exodus, Leviticus, Numbers, and Deuteronomy. He also wrote Psalm 90 and may have written the book of Job.

WHY HE'S IMPORTANT:
God chose Moses to lead the Israelites out of their slavery in the land of Egypt. Moses also wrote the first five books of the Bible—also known as the "Pentateuch."

Have you ever been asked to do something you didn't think you could do? If so, you might have an idea of how Moses felt when God sent him on a mission he thought was too big for him.

By the time Moses was born, the people of Israel had lived in Egypt for hundreds of years. (If you want a reminder of how and why they were there, reread the profile of Joseph earlier in this book.) For a long time, the Hebrews had it good in Egypt. They married and had many children. But as their numbers grew, a new pharaoh in Egypt got worried. He thought the people of Israel would become too powerful, so he turned them into Egypt's slaves.

It's terrible to be a slave, so the Israelites cried out to God to free them. God heard their prayers and chose Moses to deliver them. He was supposed to get them out of Egypt and lead them to their true homeland of Canaan.

IT'S IN THE BIBLE!

Moses was taught in all the wisdom of the Egyptians. He became a powerful man in words and in the things he did.
ACTS 7:22

Moses was born into an Israelite family. His mother was named Jochebed and his father Amram. Moses also had a sister named Miriam and a brother named Aaron.

Just before Moses was born, Pharaoh ordered the death of all the male babies of Israel. Moses'

God first spoke to Moses from a burning bush in a place called Horeb, the Mountain of God.

mother hid him for about three months, then placed him in a floating basket in the Nile River, hoping someone would find him alive. Pharaoh's own daughter found Moses, felt sorry for him, and adopted him as her own son! From there, Moses grew up in the pharaoh's family.

When Moses was about forty years old, he had to leave Egypt in a hurry. Why? He killed an Egyptian slave master who was beating an Israelite! Moses journeyed to a place called Midian, where he worked as a shepherd for a man named Jethro. They got along well, and Moses married Jethro's daughter.

Moses had spent about forty years working for Jethro when one day God used a miracle to get his attention. While out with his flock of sheep, Moses saw a bush that was burning but never burned out. Curious, he stepped up to look closer—and God spoke to Moses from the bush. He was being called to free the people of Israel from their slavery in Egypt.

"The cry of the people of Israel has come to Me," God told Moses. "I have seen what power the Egyptians use to make it hard for them. Now come, and I will send you to Pharaoh so that you may bring My people, the sons of Israel, out of Egypt" (Exodus 3:9–10).

Moses heard what God said—but he didn't think he was the right man for the job. Moses told God that he wasn't qualified, that he didn't have the right words to say, and that he wasn't a great speaker. God got angry with all of Moses' excuses, but He didn't let Moses off. God promised to be with him when he traveled back to Egypt to confront Pharaoh.

BACK TO EGYPT

After all his resistance, Moses finally obeyed God and began his journey back to Egypt. Along the way, he connected with his brother Aaron, who God said would speak for Moses. In today's world, we call that person a "spokesman."

Moses commanded Pharaoh to allow all the Israelites to leave Egypt, but Pharaoh refused—several times. Because the Egyptian leader was so stubborn, God sent ten terrible plagues on the country. After the final plague—the deaths of every Egyptian firstborn baby—Pharaoh finally set the Hebrews free. Now they could return to their "promised land" and serve God.

So Moses led the people of Israel out of Egypt. After they miraculously crossed the Red Sea (you can read that amazing story in Exodus 14), Moses met with God at Mount Sinai. On this rocky peak in the desert, God gave His laws for the Israelites to live by. Sadly, they didn't always obey God, or even trust Him to take care of them. Because of their sin, God punished the people by making them wander in the desert for a long, long time. A trip that should have taken a few weeks ended up lasting *forty years*!

Moses led the Israelites for almost all of those forty years. And during that time, he wrote the first five books of the Bible—Genesis, Exodus, Leviticus, Numbers, and Deuteronomy. These are also called the *Pentateuch*, a word which means "five books."

After his slow start, Moses accomplished amazing things for God and His people. Sadly, though, Moses didn't get to complete what he started.

THE TEN PLAGUES OF EGYPT

1. The waters of the Nile River turn to blood (Exodus 7:17–18)
2. Frogs cover the land (Exodus 8:1–4)
3. Lice cover people and animals (Exodus 8:16–17)
4. Flies swarm Egypt (Exodus 8:20–22)
5. Livestock die (Exodus 9:1–4)
6. Boils, a bad kind of sore, break out on people and animals (Exodus 9:8–9)
7. Hail pounds Egypt (Exodus 9:22–23)
8. Locusts swarm the land and eat every green plant (Exodus 10:4–5)
9. Total darkness covers Egypt for three days (Exodus 10:21–22)
10. Every firstborn of Egypt—people and animals—dies (Exodus 11:4–7)

One frog can be cute—but millions and millions of them covering the entire countryside? Probably not!

MISSING OUT ON GOD'S PROMISE

Out of all the people of Israel, God had chosen Moses to lead them into the promised land. But Moses missed out on that honor because even he didn't always obey God. And it was such a simple thing! The people were complaining about being thirsty, and God told Moses to speak to a large rock, which would miraculously send out water. But Moses was angry with the people, and he used his shepherd's staff—a long stick—to *hit* the rock instead. God still provided the water, but He told Moses, "Because you have not believed Me and honored Me as holy in the eyes of the people of Israel, you will not bring these people into the land I have given them" (Numbers 20:12).

IN MOSES' OWN WORDS

"So know this day, take it to your heart, that the Lord is God in the heavens above and on the earth below. There is no other."
DEUTERONOMY 4:39

A beautiful sunrise at Mount Sinai, where God gave Moses His laws and commandments for the Hebrew people.

Moses was a very good man, but even he made mistakes. His choice to disobey a plain command of God got Moses banned from the promised land.

The Israelites were just about to enter the promised land of Canaan. God took Moses to a nearby mountain where he could look into Canaan—but he wouldn't be allowed to set foot there. Moses must have felt very sad about that, but instead of complaining, he prayed and asked God to do good things for the Israelites in their new homeland. Then Moses died on that mountaintop, at age 120.

God already had Israel's next leader in mind. His name was Joshua, and you'll read about him in the next chapter.

WHAT WE CAN LEARN FROM MOSES:

Moses is truly one of the great heroes in the Bible, and he did many great things for God and for God's people. But Moses wasn't able to enjoy God's blessings in the promised land because he didn't obey God completely. God wants to give each of us His very best. Our part of the bargain is that we do everything He tells us.

JOSHUA

MEANING OF HIS NAME:

"Jehovah is his help" or "Jehovah is salvation"

WHEN HE LIVED:

1355–1245 BC

WHERE YOU CAN READ ABOUT HIM:

Exodus 17:7–14; Numbers 13:16–14:38, 27:13–22; Deuteronomy 31:1–23; the book of Joshua

WHY HE'S IMPORTANT:

After Moses' death, Joshua took over as leader of the Israelites who had been wandering in the wilderness, and he led them into the promised land. Joshua's faith in God helped him gain military victories over the people already in Canaan.

As we saw earlier, Moses' story didn't end as happily as it should have. Because he disobeyed God, he wasn't allowed to finish the Israelites' journey to the promised land. As it turned out, the final part of the forty-year trip would be led (with God's help!) by a man named Joshua.

The Bible doesn't say much about Joshua's family life other than that he was "the son of Nun" (Numbers 13:8, 16). He is first mentioned in Exodus 17:9, when Moses commands Joshua to choose and lead men into battle against the Amalekites, people who lived to the south of Canaan. Later, Joshua served as Moses' aide. He even accompanied Moses partway up Mount Sinai, where the older man received the Ten Commandments (see Exodus 24:12–13).

Joshua showed himself as a strong leader. That's because he had great faith in God when Moses sent him, along with eleven other spies, to scout out the promised land. When the men returned to Moses forty days later, all of them said that the land was everything God had promised it would be: "It does flow with milk and honey," they said (Numbers 13:27). However, ten of the scouts worried about fierce warriors and giants in the land, saying the Israelites would be crazy to try to take it.

Two spies Moses sent to scout out the promised land bring back a huge cluster of grapes they found growing there.

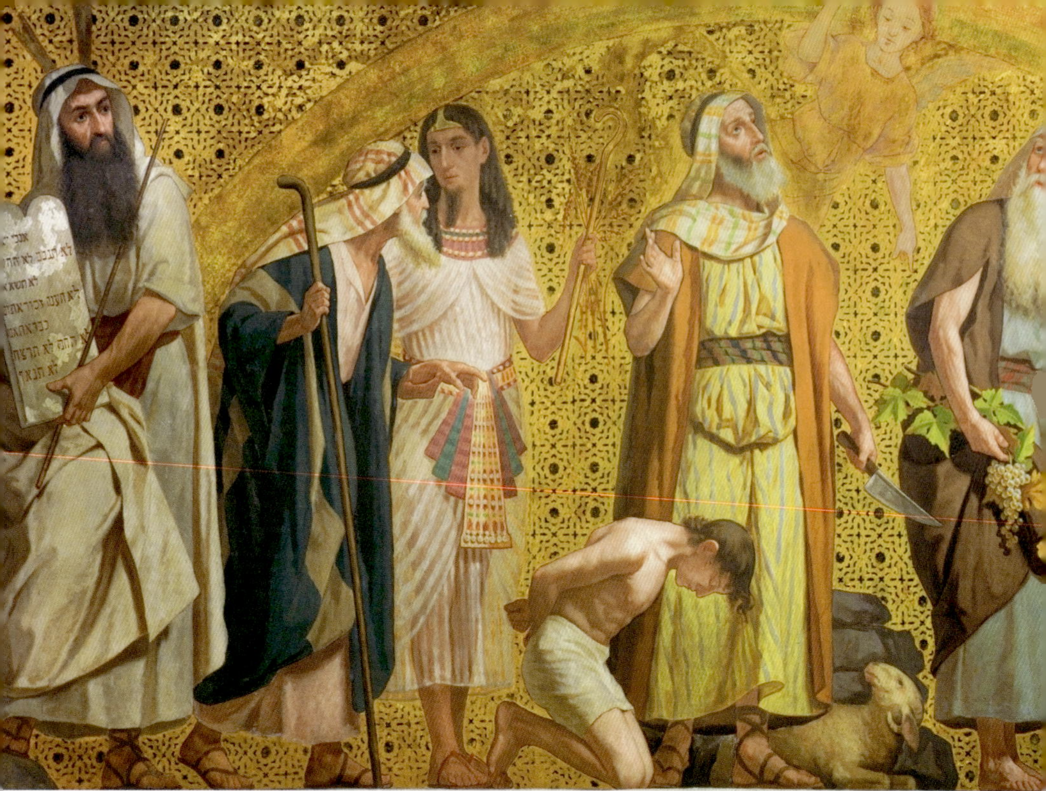

Nobody today knows exactly what the people of the Bible looked like—but this hundred-year-old painting from an Italian church shows how one artist imagined Moses (far left) and Joshua (far right). In between, from left to right, are other Bible characters we've already discussed—Jacob, Joseph, and Abraham and Isaac.

But the other two scouts—Joshua and a man named Caleb—spoke out in faith. They believed that, with God's help, the Israelites could take the land: "Do not go against the Lord. And do not be afraid of the people of the land. For they will be our food. They have no way to keep safe, and the Lord is with us. Do not be afraid of them" (Numbers 14:9).

After that day, God allowed only two of those twelve scouts to actually enter the promised land. Those two (spoiler alert!) were Caleb and Israel's new leader, Joshua.

READY TO LEAD

God could see Joshua's actions, hear his words, and look into his heart. The Lord knew that Joshua was a courageous man with the ability to lead the Israelites with wisdom. Moses had prayed that God would select a good leader to take over (Numbers 27:16–17). And God answered that prayer by commanding Moses to bring Joshua in front of all the people. He would be introduced as God's choice to lead the Israelites after Moses died. Moses did as God told him to do, laying his hands on Joshua as a sign. Now it was clear to the people who would lead them after Moses.

After Moses died, God began speaking directly to Joshua. God said, "My servant Moses is dead. So you and all these people get up and cross the Jordan River to the land I am giving to the people of Israel" (Joshua 1:2).

God was happy to give the Israelites what He had promised them decades before, and He knew He had chosen the right man for the job of leading the people into Canaan. Joshua had already proved that he was brave and faithful, but God said His Word would keep Joshua strong:

> *"This book of the Law must not leave your mouth. Think about it day and night, so you may be careful to do all that is written in it. Then all will go well with you. You will receive many good things. Have I not told you? Be strong and have strength of heart! Do not be afraid or lose faith. For the Lord your God is with you anywhere you go."*
> JOSHUA 1:8–9

Wow! After hearing these words from God's own mouth, Joshua must have been ready to roll. He immediately called the Israelite leaders together and told them, "Go among the tents and tell the people, 'Gather together the things you will need. For within three days you will cross this Jordan to go in to take the land the Lord your God is giving you for your own' " (Joshua 1:11).

TAKING THE PROMISED LAND

God performed a miracle to get the people across the Jordan River (read all about it in Joshua 3:14–17). As Joshua led the Israelites into the promised land, they soon came to the enemy city of Jericho. It had big, thick walls for protection, and its gates were shut tight because the people of Jericho were afraid of the Israelites.

God promised to give the city to the Israelites if Joshua would just follow a strange plan. He should command his soldiers to march around the city once a day for six days. On the seventh day, Joshua was to have the men march around the city seven times with the priests blowing their horns. When the priests gave one long blast on their horns, all the people of Israel would shout as loud as they could. When they did that, the city walls would fall down!

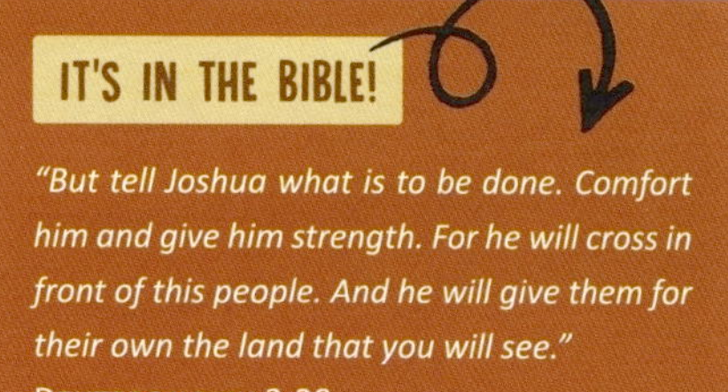

IT'S IN THE BIBLE!

"But tell Joshua what is to be done. Comfort him and give him strength. For he will cross in front of this people. And he will give them for their own the land that you will see."
DEUTERONOMY 3:28

That doesn't sound like much of a battle plan, does it? But Joshua was a man who trusted and obeyed God above everything, so he had his people do just what God had said. When they did, Jericho's walls came tumbling down and the Israelites captured the city.

But that was just the beginning. When the people living in the cities in Canaan heard that the Israelites had conquered Jericho, they became terrified that the same thing would happen to them. And it did. With God's help, Joshua led the Israelites from city to city, capturing almost all of the promised land. Along the way, the Israelites defeated a total of thirty-one kings in Canaan!

IN JOSHUA'S OWN WORDS

"If you think it is wrong to serve the Lord, choose today whom you will serve. Choose the gods your fathers worshiped on the other side of the river, or choose the gods of the Amorites in whose land you are living. But as for me and my family, we will serve the Lord."
JOSHUA 24:15

It's hard to imagine thick city walls collapsing at the sound of an army's shouts—but that's why we call Joshua's victory over Jericho a miracle.

JOSHUA'S LAST WORDS

Joshua lived his entire life serving and believing God. Not long before he died, he called the people of Israel to a place called Shechem for a farewell address. Joshua reminded the people of the amazing things God had done for them and encouraged them to choose to serve God alone.

The people, feeling encouraged and inspired by Joshua's strong faith, replied:

> *"May it never be that we turn away from the Lord and serve other gods. For the Lord our God is the One Who brought us and our fathers out of the land of Egypt, from the house where we were made to work. He did these powerful works in front of our eyes. He kept us safe everywhere we went, among all the nations we passed through. The Lord drove away from in front of us all the nations, even the Amorites who lived in the land. So we will serve the Lord. For He is our God."*
> JOSHUA 24:16–18

Not long after that, Joshua—one of the greatest heroes in the whole Bible—died at the age of 110. He was buried in a place called Timnath-serah.

WHAT WE CAN LEARN FROM JOSHUA:

Even though he lived thousands of years before Jesus came to earth, Joshua lived by the same truth we do today: "I can do all things because Christ gives me the strength" (Philippians 4:13). God had given Joshua an assignment that would have been impossible for him to accomplish on his own. But Joshua responded with faith when God said, "Be strong and have strength of heart! Do not be afraid or lose faith. For the Lord your God is with you anywhere you go" (Joshua 1:9).

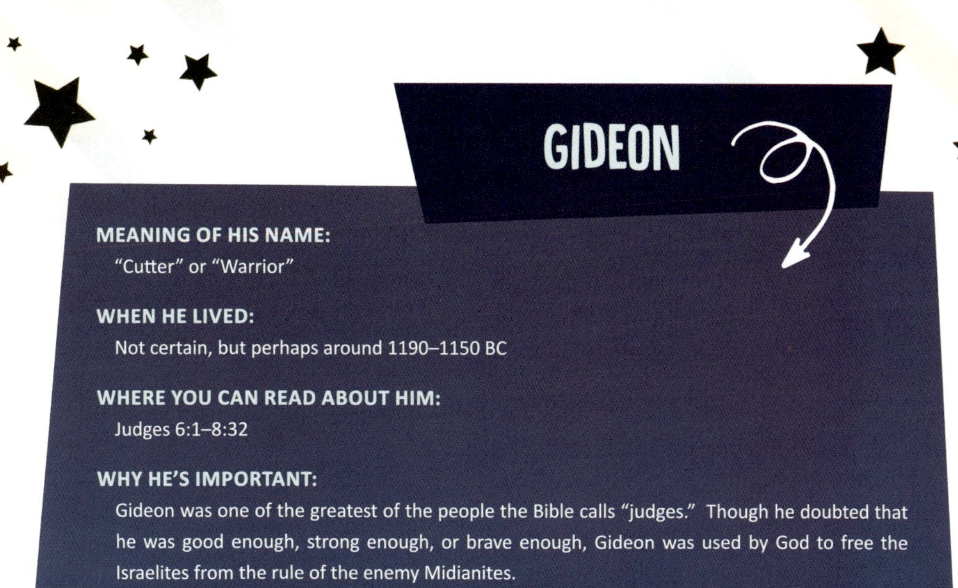

GIDEON

MEANING OF HIS NAME:
"Cutter" or "Warrior"

WHEN HE LIVED:
Not certain, but perhaps around 1190–1150 BC

WHERE YOU CAN READ ABOUT HIM:
Judges 6:1–8:32

WHY HE'S IMPORTANT:
Gideon was one of the greatest of the people the Bible calls "judges." Though he doubted that he was good enough, strong enough, or brave enough, Gideon was used by God to free the Israelites from the rule of the enemy Midianites.

The Bible tells us that there wasn't anything special about Gideon. He wasn't a great leader, and he wasn't a warrior. In fact, when God called him to lead the Israelites, Gideon argued that he was one of the youngest, smallest, and weakest people in his whole family. Still, God gave Gideon the strength and courage to serve Him and His people in a mighty way.

Gideon was the fifth of twelve biblical leaders listed in the book of Judges. When we hear the word *judge*, we usually think of a man or woman who decides legal cases in a courtroom. But the word *judge* in the Bible can also mean "deliverer"—the judges were leaders who stepped up and served bravely when the Israelites were troubled by enemies. The period of the judges lasted around 350 years, starting between 1400 and 1350 BC.

In those days, Israel didn't have a king, so the people did what they thought was right for themselves. The results were often disastrous. The Israelites would serve and follow God for a while, but then they would start worshiping idols instead. When they did that, God would allow Israel's enemies to take over. Then the people would cry out to God, and He would send a judge to deliver them—very much like Moses leading the Israelites out of their slavery in Egypt. Sadly, after God delivered the Israelites, it was always just a matter of time before they turned away from God again and began worshiping false gods.

In Gideon's day, Israel was in a terrible situation. The people had been doing things God considered very bad, so He allowed an enemy called the Midianites to invade Israel. Midian was much stronger than the Israelites, and sometimes God's people dug caves into the sides of mountains to hide from the invaders. The Midianites—as well as a group called the Amalekites—would fight against Israel, destroying crops and livestock. The Bible says that the Midianites were "like locusts, there were so many of them" (Judges 6:5).

God had a plan, though, to rid the promised land of these troublemakers. The plan started to take shape when the Israelites cried out to God for help. He first sent the people a prophet to remind them that He had provided for them in the past—before they had turned away from Him (Judges 6:6–10).

And then God brought Gideon into the picture.

GOD'S ASSIGNMENT FOR GIDEON

One day, Gideon was working on his father's farm, preparing grain so that it could be eaten. He was working in a winepress—a pit where grapes are crushed into wine—so that he wouldn't be seen by the Midianites. They would have just stolen the grain he was threshing!

Suddenly, an angel of God appeared to Gideon. "The Lord is with you, O powerful soldier," the angel said (Judges 6:12). Gideon knew he was speaking to a messenger from God, but he couldn't understand how the Lord had been "with" him or the Israelites—it seemed like nothing good had happened to them for a long, long time.

But now the Bible says it was the Lord Himself talking to Gideon: "Go in this strength of yours. And save Israel from the power of Midian. Have I not sent you?" (Judges 6:14).

Gideon must have thought God was joking with him! He wasn't strong enough to do what he was being asked to do. So Gideon wanted proof that God would really use him to save Israel. He asked

THE TWELVE JUDGES IN THE BOOK OF JUDGES

- Othniel (Judges 3:9–11)
- Ehud (Judges 3:15–30)
- Shamgar (Judges 3:31, 5:6)
- Deborah (Judges 4:4–5:31)
- Gideon (Judges 6:11–8:32)
- Tola (Judges 10:1–2)
- Jair (Judges 10:3–5)
- Jephthah (Judges 11:1–12:7)
- Ibzan (Judges 12:8–10)
- Elon (Judges 12:11–12)
- Abdon (Judges 12:13–15)
- Samson (Judges 13–16)

Deborah was Israel's only woman judge. She decided court cases under a palm tree and led the Israelite army into battle when the commander, a man named Barak, was afraid to go alone.

God for unusual and even miraculous things so he could know for sure—for example, the sign of the fleece (see Judges 6:36–40).

Finally, Gideon believed God and began preparing warriors to fight back against Midian.

TAKING THE FIGHT TO THE MIDIANITES

Gideon selected 32,000 fighting men to face the Midianites. But God told Gideon that that was too many. Otherwise, the Israelites might believe they had defeated the Midianites in their own strength, not in God's power.

By the time God was ready to send Gideon and his men to war, He had cut the number of soldiers to just three hundred. God would save the people of Israel with that tiny army! So Gideon, filled with faith and courage, took his three hundred to fight against thousands of Midianite soldiers.

With Gideon in the lead, Israel's three hundred warriors defeated the Midianites and drove them away. God had done what the Israelites probably believed wasn't possible. The Midianites were gone, and God's people were free to live their lives again.

The Israelites were so grateful to Gideon that they asked him to be their king. But Gideon refused, telling them that *God* was their king: "I will not rule over you. And my son will not rule over you. The Lord will rule over you" (Judges 8:23).

The Midianites came under Israel's control and the land of Israel had peace for forty years under Gideon. When he died, he was buried with his father, Joash.

Gideon stands over his fleece, thanking God for confirming His call to lead the people of Israel against the Midianites.

WHAT WE CAN LEARN FROM GIDEON:

Have you ever felt like you just weren't good enough, strong enough, or smart enough to accomplish something God gave you to do? If so, take encouragement from the story of Gideon. God gave him a huge job, one that Gideon didn't think he could do. But because Gideon believed God's promise, the Lord used him in an amazing way. If you trust Him, God will do the same for you!

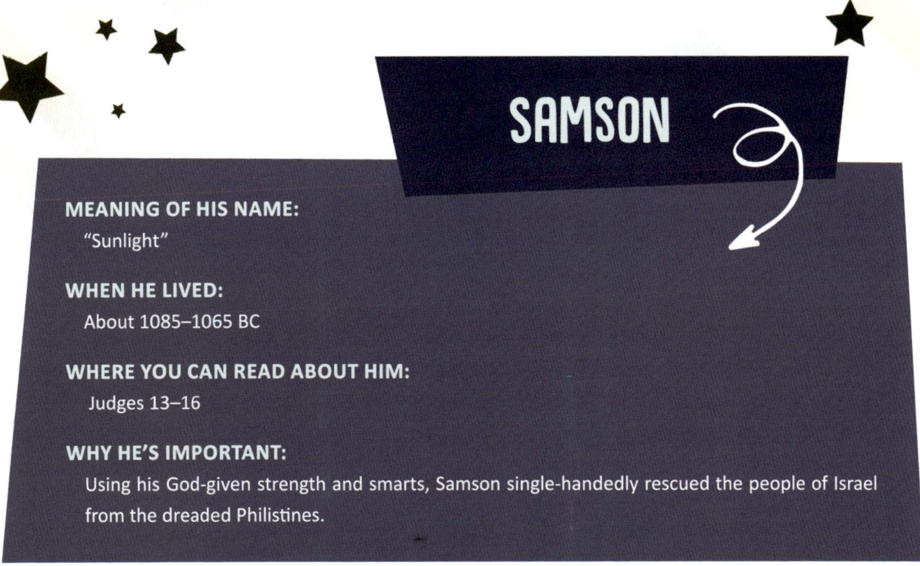

SAMSON

MEANING OF HIS NAME:
"Sunlight"

WHEN HE LIVED:
About 1085–1065 BC

WHERE YOU CAN READ ABOUT HIM:
Judges 13–16

WHY HE'S IMPORTANT:
Using his God-given strength and smarts, Samson single-handedly rescued the people of Israel from the dreaded Philistines.

Have you ever seen one of those "Strongman" competitions on TV? The goal for each competitor is to prove that he's the most powerful guy around. These competitions feature men performing amazing feats of strength.

But compared to the Bible's Samson, modern-day strongmen look like ninety-pound weaklings.

Samson was the last of twelve judges whose stories are told in the book of Judges. He was from the Israelite tribe of Dan and born at a time when the dreaded Philistines ruled over God's people. Samson's father was a man named Manoah, from a town called Zorah. The Bible doesn't tell us Samson's mother's name, but it does say that she—like Sarah, Rebekah, and Rachel—hadn't been able to have children. But that changed after an angel of God arrived to tell her that she would have a miracle son. Before he was even born, this boy—Samson—would be dedicated to serving God.

Samson grew up as a Nazirite. That means that he was set apart for God's service and had to follow some very specific rules. For example, he was not allowed to cut his hair or drink wine or other types of alcoholic drinks.

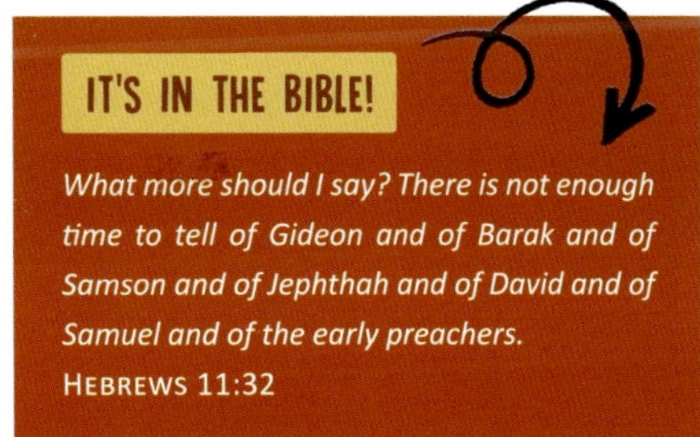

IT'S IN THE BIBLE!

What more should I say? There is not enough time to tell of Gideon and of Barak and of Samson and of Jephthah and of David and of Samuel and of the early preachers.
HEBREWS 11:32

After Samson grew up, he judged Israel for twenty years, from about 1085 to 1065 BC. His life (and death) broke forty years of Philistine rule over the Israelites. Though he could be selfish and foolish, Samson accomplished incredible things when he allowed God to work in his life.

SAMSON'S AMAZING STRENGTH

When you hear the name *Samson*, you probably think of a Bible character with superhuman strength. The book of Judges includes several accounts of Samson's amazing feats:

- He was attacked by a lion but easily killed it with his bare hands (14:5–6).
- He single-handedly killed thirty enemy Philistines (14:19).
- He killed 1,000 Philistines using the jawbone of a donkey as his weapon (15:12–15).
- He lifted and removed the big, heavy gate of a Philistine town called Gaza (16:1–3).
- He killed thousands of enemies, including their leaders, when he collapsed the Philistine temple by pushing down its pillars (16:26–30).

The Bible says Samson was able to do these mighty acts when "the Spirit of the Lord came upon him with power" (Judges 14:19). When he was faithful and obedient to God, Samson had incredible courage. All by himself, he fought the Philistines so that his people could be free.

Lions are big, ferocious cats, but one lion was no match for Samson, who killed the animal with his bare hands.

SAMSON'S WEAKNESSES

Samson was a man of incredible strength and courage, but he was far from perfect. He wasn't terribly concerned about the consequences of his actions, and he often pursued his desire for women—even women of the enemy Philistines. One woman, named Delilah, helped the Philistines in their plot to kill Samson.

Delilah nagged Samson to learn the secret of his strength. As a Nazirite, Samson knew that his uncut hair was part of what made him so strong. But he lied to Delilah three times. She wouldn't give up, though. Finally, tired of her begging, Samson told her the truth: "My hair has never been cut. For I have been a Nazirite to God from

IN SAMSON'S OWN WORDS

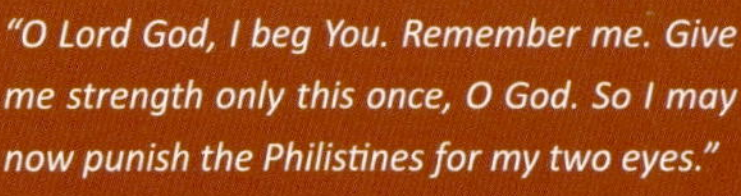

"O Lord God, I beg You. Remember me. Give me strength only this once, O God. So I may now punish the Philistines for my two eyes."
JUDGES 16:28

the time I was born. If my hair is cut, my strength will leave me. I will become weak and be like any other man" (Judges 16:17).

Samson caused the temple of Dagon to collapse, killing himself and thousands of Philistines, the enemies of Israel.

Later, as Samson slept, Delilah allowed a Philistine man to quietly shave off all of Samson's hair. When he woke up, he didn't realize that God's Spirit had left him, taking away his incredible strength. The Philistines captured Samson, gouged out his eyes, and forced him to grind grain in prison. It was a terrible situation for Samson. But the Bible points out that "the hair of his head started to grow again after it was cut off" (Judges 16:22).

Samson had been in prison for some time when the Philistine rulers held a festival in honor of their god, Dagon. Samson was brought to Dagon's temple, where the people mocked and taunted him. They didn't know that Samson had regained his strength—and it cost all of them their lives.

Standing between the two pillars holding up the temple, Samson prayed and asked God for strength. Then he placed a hand on each column and pushed with all his might. The pillars broke and the whole temple came crashing down.

Samson himself died when the temple collapsed, but he had done what God called him to do. The people of Israel were free from the rule of the Philistines!

Samson's brothers and other family members came to the ruined temple to get his body. They took Samson's remains back home to Zorah, where they buried him with his father, Manoah.

WHAT WE CAN LEARN FROM SAMSON:

Samson often chose to pursue his own desires instead of God's will for his life—but God still used him in a powerful way. All of us make mistakes and do things we know God doesn't want us to do, but He can still work through us too. We simply must hold on to our faith in Him.

RUTH AND BOAZ

MEANING OF THEIR NAMES:
"Friend" (Ruth) and "Swiftness" (Boaz)

WHEN THEY LIVED:
Not certain, but sometime during the time of the judges

WHERE YOU CAN READ ABOUT THEM:
The book of Ruth; Matthew 1:5–6; Luke 3:32

WHY THEY'RE IMPORTANT:
Boaz, an Israelite, married Ruth, a woman from Moab, and they had a son named Obed, who would become the grandfather of King David. That means Boaz and Ruth were ancestors of Jesus!

Do you like stories with happy endings? If so, you should like the Bible's book of Ruth, an Old Testament story that took place during the time of the judges.

Ruth was born and raised in a place called Moab. The Moabites didn't worship the one true God but instead followed a fake god called Chemosh. Moab was an enemy of Israel, and the two nations sometimes went to war with one another.

The story begins with an Israelite woman named Naomi and her husband, Elimelech. They lived in Bethlehem in the land of Judah with their two sons, Mahlon and Chilion. But when a terrible famine broke out, they could barely find enough food to survive. So the whole family moved to Moab, east of the Dead Sea in what is now the nation of Jordan.

Sadly, Elimelech died while the family was living in Moab.

Naomi's sons grew up and married women of Moab named Orpah and Ruth. They all stayed in Moab for ten years, when Naomi's *sons* died too. Naomi, Orpah, and Ruth were in a tough spot—they were sad because their husbands had all died, and in that culture it was hard for women to work and care for themselves.

Naomi heard that the famine in Judah had ended, so she decided to return to her hometown of Bethlehem. She hoped to either make a living or get help from her countrymen.

Orpah and Ruth started to go with Naomi, but she told the younger women that they should return to their own families in Moab. Orpah agreed and left—but Ruth refused to leave her mother-in-law alone. She clung to Naomi and promised to stay with her wherever she went, even to worship the true God of Israel. Naomi could see that she couldn't convince Ruth to stay in Moab, so the women continued their journey to Bethlehem.

Naomi and Ruth arrived in Bethlehem at the

beginning of the barley harvest. Barley is a plant like wheat, used for making bread. Ruth suggested that she should follow the harvesters in the barley fields, gathering up leftover grain that had fallen to the ground. God had told Israelite farmers to leave behind some grain for poor people to gather during the harvest (see Leviticus 23:22). So Ruth went to a nearby field to pick up food for herself and Naomi.

The owner of the field was a man named Boaz.

BOAZ MEETS RUTH

Have you heard of "making a good first impression"? That means that when someone meets you, they see things in you that make them think positive things. In the book of Ruth, Boaz makes a *great* first impression.

He was a wealthy farmer who lived and worked near the village of Bethlehem, where Jesus would be born centuries later. One day, as Boaz arrived at his fields, he saw workers gathering grain for him and called out with a hearty "May the Lord be with you." When the workers heard Boaz's greeting, they called back, "May the Lord bring good to you" (Ruth 2:4).

IN RUTH'S OWN WORDS

"Do not beg me to leave you or turn away from following you. I will go where you go. I will live where you live. Your people will be my people. And your God will be my God."
RUTH 1:16

Orpah sadly turns away from Ruth and Naomi, to go back to her family in Moab. Ruth, though, refused to leave Naomi, insisting that she would stay with her mother-in-law and worship her God.

This little scene in the Bible gives us a good clue that Boaz treated his employees well, that he genuinely cared about them. But what happens next shows us that Boaz cared about all people—and that he loved God.

When Boaz saw Ruth gathering grain in his field, he asked one of his servants who she was. The servant replied that she was a woman from Moab who had traveled with Naomi to Bethlehem. Boaz suddenly realized who Ruth was, because he had heard how kind she had been to Naomi.

Boaz quickly went to Ruth and told her to gather food only in his field. He told Ruth that he had given his servants orders not to bother her in any way. He even encouraged her to drink water from his servants' containers whenever she got thirsty. Then he quietly told his workers to leave behind some of the very best grain to make things easier for Ruth.

Ruth could hardly believe how kind Boaz was being. She bowed low before him in a sign of respect, asking why a Jewish man was treating a woman from Moab so well. Boaz looked down at Ruth and kindly said,

> *"I have heard about all you have done for your mother-in-law after the death of your husband. I have heard how you left your father and mother and the land of your birth to come to a people you did not know before. May the Lord reward you for your work. May full pay be given to you from the Lord, the God of Israel. It is under His wings that you have come to be safe."*
> RUTH 2:11–12

Ruth gathered plenty of grain for herself and Naomi, then went home and told her mother-in-law about Boaz. Naomi knew something about Boaz that Ruth didn't: he was actually a relative! Being related to Ruth's dead husband, Mahlon, meant that Boaz was a "family redeemer," someone who would help out a person like Ruth if she was in need.

Naomi wanted Ruth to have a husband to care for her, and she knew that Boaz would be perfect for her. So she told Ruth to put on her best clothes and lay down at Boaz's feet while he slept in his grain field. That would be a signal to Boaz that Ruth wanted him to marry her. He got the message!

Boaz did marry Ruth, and together they had a son named Obed. After Obed grew up, he had a son named Jesse, who became the father of David, who would become Israel's greatest king. . . and an ancestor of Jesus Christ.

Boaz and Ruth got married and began a family line that would include Jesus.

WHAT WE CAN LEARN FROM RUTH AND BOAZ:

This story is an example of how God often uses unlikely people to accomplish His purposes. Ruth was a poor widow from a country of unbelievers, while Boaz was a wealthy Israelite farmer and business-man. Yet God used their relationship to help bring Jesus into the world. That means that we *all* benefit from the story of Ruth and Boaz!

SAMUEL

MEANING OF HIS NAME:
"Heard of God"

WHEN HE LIVED:
About 1056–1004 BC

WHERE YOU CAN READ ABOUT HIM:
1 Samuel 1–3, 7–28

WHY HE'S IMPORTANT:
Samuel was the last judge of Israel and a beloved prophet who led the people to repent of their sins and turn back to God. Samuel also anointed Israel's first two kings, Saul and David.

Samuel served the nation of Israel during a time when things were about to change in a big way. Samuel was Israel's last judge because from his time on, human kings would rule over Israel.

Samuel's father was "a certain man from Ramathaim-zophim of the hill country of Ephraim. His name was Elkanah, the son of Jeroham, the son of Elihu, the son of Tohu, the son of Zuph, an Ephraimite" (1 Samuel 1:1). Did you get all that?

Samuel's mother was Hannah, one of two women that Elkanah married. His other wife, Peninnah, had children with Elkanah, but Hannah hadn't been able to have any. This made her very sad, and she cried as she prayed for a son. She even made God a promise:

> *"O Lord of All, be sure to look on the trouble of Your woman servant, and remember me. Do not forget Your woman servant, but give me a son. If You will, then I will give him to the Lord all his life."*
> 1 SAMUEL 1:11

God heard Hannah's prayer and gave her a son. She named him Samuel, and she kept her promise to God by giving him back to the Lord. When he was old enough, Hannah took Samuel to the tabernacle, the tentlike building where God met with His people. Samuel worked there with a priest named Eli, where he "grew up to serve the Lord" (1 Samuel 2:21). The Bible also says that Samuel "grew and was in favor both with the Lord and with men" (1 Samuel 2:26).

IT'S IN THE BIBLE!

Moses and Aaron were among His religious leaders. And Samuel was among those who called on His name. They called upon the Lord, and He answered them.
PSALM 99:6

GOD CALLS SAMUEL

When Samuel was a boy, God wasn't giving Israel many messages. But one day, as Samuel lay in his bed in the tabernacle, he heard a voice calling him. Samuel thought it was Eli, but the priest said he hadn't called Samuel. This happened three times. The last time, Eli realized it must be God calling to Samuel. He told the boy, "Go lie down. If He calls you, say, 'Speak, Lord, for Your servant is listening' " (1 Samuel 3:9).

Samuel went back to bed, and then for the fourth time God called out, "Samuel! Samuel!" The boy answered God, promising to listen. But what he heard was troubling.

God then told Samuel that He was going to destroy Eli's family because the priest's two sons—Hophni and Phinehas—had been sinning terribly. Like Eli, they were priests, and they should have known better. Just as bad, Eli hadn't done anything to stop them.

The following day, Eli asked Samuel what God had said in the night. Imagine how Samuel must have felt as he started telling Eli the terrible news! But Samuel served God, and that meant telling the old priest everything. Though he must have been very sad, Eli accepted what Samuel told him as God's will. A while later, Eli's sons died in a battle with the Philistines. When Eli heard about it, he fell backward off his chair, broke his neck, and died.

After Samuel spoke God's prophecy to Eli, the Bible says he grew as a man of God. And the Lord continued to speak to His people through Samuel. Israelites from every corner of the nation believed that Samuel was a true man of God.

IN SAMUEL'S OWN WORDS

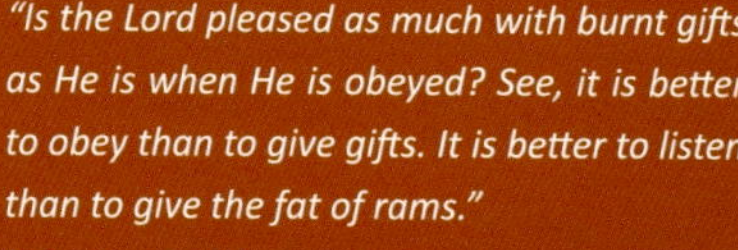

"Is the Lord pleased as much with burnt gifts as He is when He is obeyed? See, it is better to obey than to give gifts. It is better to listen than to give the fat of rams."

SAMUEL 15:22

SAMUEL'S MINISTRY

Often in Old Testament times, the Israelites refused to listen to the prophets God sent. They warned the people of God's judgment if they didn't repent of their sins and turn back to Him. But many times, the people kept doing whatever they pleased.

But with Samuel, the people often did listen. And God saved them from disaster because they did.

Earlier, you read that Eli's sons died in battle against Israel's longtime enemy, the Philistines. The Philistines had killed thousands of Israel's soldiers, and the people were frightened. Samuel knew they needed to return to the one true God, so he told them to get rid of the false gods they had been worshiping. "Turn your hearts to the Lord and worship Him alone," Samuel said. "Then He will save you from the Philistines" (1 Samuel 7:3). The people obeyed, and with God's help, Israel overcame the Philistines. As long as Samuel lived, they were never again a threat (see 1 Samuel 7:9–13).

WHEN EVERYTHING CHANGED IN ISRAEL

Samuel had two sons—Joel and Abijah—and he appointed both of them to be judges. But like the sons of Eli, Samuel's sons also sinned terribly against God. Both of them used their important position for selfish gain. When the elders of Israel learned what Joel and Abijah were doing, they complained to Samuel. He was getting too old and his sons were not trustworthy, they said. They wanted a king to rule over Israel (1 Samuel 8:1–5).

The people of Israel loved Samuel, and when he died, "all Israel gathered together and was filled with sorrow for him" (1 Samuel 25:1). He was buried in his own city of Ramah.

Samuel wasn't happy with the people's demands, so he prayed about it. God told Samuel,

> *"Listen to the voice of the people in all they say to you. For they have not turned away from you. They have turned away from Me, that I should not be king over them. They are doing to you what they have done since the day I brought them out of Egypt until now. They have turned away from Me and worshiped other gods. So listen to their voice. But tell them of the danger and show them the ways of the king who will rule over them."*
>
> 1 SAMUEL 8:7–9

Samuel warned the people that life would be much different under a human king. He would take their fields and crops, make them pay taxes, and even force their sons and daughters to work for him. But the people insisted they wanted a king, so Samuel appointed a man named Saul as Israel's first ruler. Over time, it became clear that Saul wasn't a good king, and God directed Samuel to anoint a shepherd boy named David as his replacement.

WHAT WE CAN LEARN FROM SAMUEL:

When the people of Israel demanded a king, Samuel was wise enough to immediately pray and ask God what to do. Samuel was a great example of what we should all do when we're faced with a big decision: pray!

DAVID

MEANING OF HIS NAME:
"Beloved"

WHEN HE LIVED:
About 1040–970 BC

WHERE YOU CAN READ ABOUT HIM:
1 Samuel 16–30; 2 Samuel 1–24; 1 Kings 1:1–2:10; 1 Chronicles 11–29; Psalm 23, 51

WHY HE'S IMPORTANT:
David was the second, and the greatest, king of the nation of Israel. But even though he was a great king, he wasn't a perfect man. David loved God, but he made some very bad mistakes.

One of the best-known Bible stories—one you've probably heard several times in Sunday school or church—is the battle between David and Goliath. A teenage shepherd boy faces a giant warrior and defeats him with nothing more than a sling and a single small stone.

We'll look at that story in more detail later. But there's a lot more to David than that one battle. He is a *very* important person in the Bible. Years after slaying Goliath, David became Israel's second and greatest king, taking the throne after the death of Saul. David brought the tribes of Israel together into one nation and established the city of Jerusalem as its capital. He also set the stage for the building of God's temple in Jerusalem—though it was his son Solomon who would accomplish that task decades later. And if that weren't enough, David also wrote around half of the psalms in the Bible.

David was the youngest of eight sons of a man named Jesse, who was the grandson of Ruth and Boaz. He was from Bethlehem, which is sometimes

Bethlehem, the City of David, as it looks today.

called "the City of David" in the Bible.

David is first mentioned in the book of Ruth, which identifies him as a descendant of Ruth and Boaz. But David's story begins in 1 Samuel 16, which tells us he was a shepherd in Bethlehem. David's story continues through 1 Chronicles 29. Some parts of his life are covered in more than one Old Testament book. But if you want the whole story of his kingship, 2 Samuel covers the forty years of David's reign.

David is identified with at least seventy-three of the psalms. When you read his psalms, you see David's heart for God—how he depended on God in good times and bad. The Bible calls David "the sweet song writer of Israel" (2 Samuel 23:1).

Even though God Himself described David as "a man who is pleasing to [Me] in every way" (1 Samuel 13:14), David was not perfect. Even though he accomplished some great things for his God and God's people, he also made many bad decisions—some of which led to terrible consequences.

Samuel pours oil on David's head. This "anointing" showed others that the young man was God's choice to be king of Israel.

But God was always with David, and He used this talented but flawed man to advance His plan to bring Jesus into the world.

CHOSEN TO BE KING

Way back in Deuteronomy 17, God told the Israelites that He expected them to have a king. But God wanted them to have a king *He* had chosen. Many years later, in Samuel's time, the people were demanding a king "like all the nations" (1 Samuel 8:5). God gave them what they wanted but not the king He had chosen. And things didn't turn out well at all.

The first king of Israel was Saul, and it didn't take long for him to show selfishness and a lack of obedience to God. God told the prophet Samuel that He would remove Saul from the throne, replacing him with a king who was "pleasing. . . in every way" (1 Samuel 13:14). That king would be David.

God instructed Samuel to travel to Bethlehem to anoint one of the sons of Jesse as Israel's next king. Samuel was afraid of King Saul discovering his task, but he did what God told him. Once he was in Bethlehem, Samuel invited Jesse and his seven oldest sons to make a sacrifice to God. Samuel met with each of Jesse's older boys and thought that one of them must be the next king. But all seven times God told him, "He is not the one."

Samuel asked if Jesse had any other children, and he said that his youngest, David, was watching sheep in the fields. Samuel asked to see David next.

As the young man came in from the fields, God told Samuel, "Rise up and choose him. For this is the one" (1 Samuel 16:12). Samuel anointed David with oil, and "the Spirit of the Lord came upon David with strength from that day on" (verse 13).

Many experts believe David was as young as twelve when Samuel anointed him as the second king of Israel. After this event, David returned to tending his father's sheep. He could not take the throne until after Saul's death, which wouldn't happen until David was thirty years old.

In the meantime, David's skill as a musician led him into King Saul's court. Saul would sometimes get depressed, and his servants suggested they find a good harp player to soothe his spirit. One of them knew David was a good player, and he was brought to Saul. The king loved David's music, and David himself. But that all changed when David became an overnight hero to everyone in Israel.

King Saul needed young David's harp playing to soothe his depression. But the depression became hatred after David killed Goliath.

IT'S IN THE BIBLE!

Now these are the last words of David. David the son of Jesse, the man who was raised on high, the chosen one of the God of Jacob, the sweet song writer of Israel, says, "The Spirit of the Lord spoke by me. His Word was on my tongue."
2 Samuel 23:1–2

In Saul's day, Israel was constantly at war with a people called the Philistines. One of their warriors was a gigantic man named Goliath—the Bible says he stood over nine feet tall! As the two armies faced off for battle, Goliath stepped up to taunt the Israelites and insult God. Israel's soldiers were too afraid to face Goliath alone. But when young David heard what Goliath had been saying, he volunteered to battle the giant himself.

Goliath wasn't impressed with David—he shouted, "Am I a dog, that you come to me with sticks?" (1 Samuel 17:43). Goliath figured he'd make short work of David. But the shepherd boy looked Goliath straight in the eye and said, "You come to me with a sword and spears. But I come to you in the name of the Lord of All, the God of the armies of Israel, Whom you have stood against. This day the Lord will give you into my hands" (1 Samuel 17:45–46).

David took out his sling and one of five small rocks he had brought with him. Putting the stone in his sling, he whirled the cords around and around before releasing them at the perfect moment. The stone whizzed through the air and hit Goliath square in the forehead. Stunned, the giant crashed to the ground. David then rushed over to him, took Goliath's own sword, and cut off his head.

David's victory over Goliath gave the Israelite army new courage. Soldiers rushed into battle against the Philistines and defeated them.

DAVID'S RISE TO POWER

After killing Goliath, David became famous and popular in Israel. The people were even singing songs about him! King Saul, though, became extremely jealous. He even tried several times to kill David.

IN DAVID'S OWN WORDS

O Lord my God, in You I have put my trust. Save me from all those who come for me, and keep me safe. Or they will tear me like a lion, carrying me away where there is no one to help.

Psalm 7:1–2

David knew Saul was serious—he even had to dodge a couple of spears that the king threw at him. But David never tried to fight back or kill Saul in self-defense. Instead, he ran from Saul, trying to stay out of his reach until David's time to be king arrived. (Most Bible experts believe David wrote Psalms 7, 27, 31, 34, and 54 during this time in his life—read them and see what *you* think.)

David knew that God was in control and that he needed to respect Saul as "the Lord's chosen one" (1 Samuel 24:6) until God Himself took Saul out of the picture. David knew God had chosen him to be king, but he was willing to wait for the right time. And as hard as it may be to believe, David was truly sad when Saul died.

With Saul dead in battle, David was crowned king of the southern part of Israel, called Judah. He quickly captured Jerusalem from a foreign power and made it his capital. And he soon brought the northern and southern tribes together under his rule, creating the "unified kingdom."

David accomplished many great things for the nation of Israel, making it powerful and prosperous. But he also made one huge mistake that was a disaster for both his family and the nation he had worked so hard to build.

David's weapon probably looked something like this.

DAVID'S DOWNFALL

David loved God. He usually did his best to live the way God wanted him to live. But one day, David got careless.

In a tapestry—a picture woven from colored threads—King David stares at a beautiful woman who is not his wife. His desire will cause him to commit a terrible sin.

When his army was out fighting, David stayed home. He took a walk on the flat roof of his house and noticed a beautiful neighbor woman bathing. David wanted to be with her, so he called her to his palace—and soon had her husband, who was one of his best soldiers, killed. David then married the woman, named Bathsheba.

God was not pleased.

A prophet named Nathan was sent to confront David about his sin. It took a clever story to get David's attention, but when he realized how terrible his sin was, David asked God to forgive him. But there were still consequences for his sin. First of all, the baby that he and Bathsheba had together died. And the rest of David's large family would have a lot of trouble from that time on. His own son Absalom plotted to remove David from power and take over as king.

David died at the age of seventy, after forty years as king. He was buried in Jerusalem, and Solomon—a second child he had with Bathsheba—took the throne. You can read about Solomon in the next chapter.

WHAT WE CAN LEARN FROM DAVID:

David was a great king of Israel, and he loved God. But he also had moments when he didn't walk as carefully as he should have. Because of that, David committed a terrible sin against God. The same thing can happen to any of us. So we should be careful to read God's Word, pray, and ask Him for the strength to avoid temptation.

SOLOMON

MEANING OF HIS NAME:
"Peaceful"

WHEN HE LIVED:
About 1010–950 BC

WHERE YOU CAN READ ABOUT HIM:
1 Kings 1–11; 2 Chronicles 1–9
Bible books he wrote: Proverbs, Ecclesiastes, Song of Solomon

WHY HE'S IMPORTANT:
Solomon reigned forty years as Israel's third king. During that time, he built God's temple, kept Israel from war, and also made the nation a world economic power. He was considered the wisest man in the world, but he didn't seem so wise by the time he died.

King David knew his time as king—as well as his life—was coming to an end. The people of Israel would soon need a new king to lead them, and David arranged for his son Solomon to take over. In his final days David took time to encourage Solomon, telling him,

> *"I am going the way of all the earth. So be strong. Show yourself to be a man. Do what the Lord your God tells you. Walk in His ways. Keep all His Laws and His Word, by what is written in the Law of Moses. Then you will do well in all that you do and in every place you go. Then the Lord will keep His promise to me. He has said to me, 'Your sons must be careful of their way, to walk before Me in truth with all their heart and soul. If they do, you will never be without a man on the throne of Israel.' "*
> 1 KINGS 2:2–4

Solomon was the son of David and Bathsheba—the woman David had stolen from Uriah, one of his most faithful soldiers. When David died, Solomon inherited a kingdom that had grown large and powerful during his father's reign.

As you saw in the last chapter, David was not a perfect man, but he was a great king. Solomon wanted to follow in his footsteps but wasn't so sure he would be able. He was young and inexperienced as a leader. So one of the first things he did after taking the throne was pray.

Solomon went to a place called Gibeon to worship God. One night, God came to Solomon in a dream. The Lord said the new king could ask for anything he wanted, and it would be his! Think of that—Solomon could have asked for success, a long life, tons of money. But instead he requested *wisdom*. He asked God for the ability to lead the Israelites well.

> *"O Lord my God, You have made Your servant king in place of my father David. But I am only a little child. I do not know how to start or finish. Your servant is among Your people which You have chosen. They are many people. There are too many people to number. So give Your servant an understanding heart to judge Your people and know the difference between good and bad. For who is able to judge Your many people?"*
> 1 KINGS 3:7–9

God was very happy with Solomon's request. He promised the young king, "Because you have asked this, I have done what you said. See, I have given you a wise and understanding heart. No one has been like you before, and there will be no one like you in the future" (1 Kings 3:11–12). Not only that, God promised Solomon honor and wealth too. And the Lord told him that if he walked close to God and obeyed His laws, Solomon would live a long time.

SOLOMON'S WEALTH AND WISDOM

Solomon was very different from his father, David, both as a man and as a king. David was a mighty warrior who enlarged Israel's borders by conquering other people. He made Israel a world power. Solomon, though, was a peaceful man who used his wisdom to get mind-blowing riches for himself and his nation.

Solomon opened up trade routes with other countries that brought gold and other precious metals from distant lands. He built a large fleet of ships that brought even more treasures from around the world. Some people estimate that Solomon had a personal wealth of more than *two trillion dollars* in today's money. That's a two with twelve zeroes behind it!

Because Solomon was a man of peace, leaders of other nations liked and respected him. Some came to visit with him. One time, the queen of a place called Sheba traveled to Jerusalem to see if the incredible things she had heard about Solomon were true. When she discovered they were, she gave Solomon many valuable gifts, including four and a half *tons* of gold (see 1 Kings 10:1–13).

According to 1 Kings 10:22, Solomon had a fleet of trading ships that every three years brought loads of gold, silver, ivory, apes, and peacocks.

The queen of Sheba approaches Solomon's throne. According to the Bible, "nothing like it had ever been made for the king of any other nation" (2 Chronicles 9:19).

BUILDING GOD'S TEMPLE

Solomon's father, David, loved God and wanted to build Him a huge, beautiful temple. David was eager to get started, so he began drawing up plans and gathering building materials. But before he could break ground for the temple's foundation, God stopped him. The Lord told David that he had shed too much blood as a warrior. God wanted David's son Solomon, a man of peace, to build the temple (1 Chronicles 28:1–7).

When Solomon became king, he was dedicated to God and serving Him faithfully. Like his father before him, Solomon wanted to build God a beautiful temple. This wasn't going to be an easy project, and it was going to cost a huge amount of money. But Solomon dedicated the best he and his nation had to make sure the temple was completed—and that it honored God in its spectacular beauty.

Solomon gathered huge amounts of gold and silver and bought the best lumber and other materials for the temple. He assigned more than 150,000 men to cut and carry stone from the nearby mountains. He hired the best craftspeople in the world to construct the building and to create drapes, furniture, and other items inside. By the time the temple was finished, it stood almost twenty stories tall.

SOLOMON'S WISDOM IN WRITING

Solomon stayed busy making Israel the wealthiest nation in the world and also keeping his kingdom at peace. But he still found time to write down a lot of his wisdom for later people to study. Solomon "spoke 3,000 wise sayings and wrote 1,005 songs," according to 1 Kings 4:32. And he's believed to have written all or part of three Bible books—Proverbs, Ecclesiastes, and Song of Solomon.

The book of Proverbs contains powerful instruction about loving and serving God, how to have friends, the way we treat others, seeking wisdom over foolishness, being happy in this life, choosing humility over pride, and avoiding sin. Proverbs even has a word about how we should treat our animals (Proverbs 12:10)!

If you need wisdom for any area of your life, you're likely to find it in Proverbs. Here are just a few examples:

- The fear of the Lord is the beginning of much learning (1:7).
- Do not keep good from those who should have it, when it is in your power to do it. Do not say to your neighbor, "Go, and return tomorrow, and I will give it," when you have it with you (3:27–28).
- Lips that tell the truth will last forever, but

A modern artist imagines Solomon's temple as looking like this. Notice the smoking altar at right, and the "bronze sea," a giant pool of water at left, sitting atop twelve bronze bulls.

a lying tongue lasts only for a little while (12:19).

- A wise man fears God and turns away from what is sinful, but a fool is full of pride and is not careful (14:16).
- Do not say, "I will punish wrong-doing." Wait on the Lord, and He will take care of it (20:22).

The first time you read the book of Ecclesiastes, you might wonder why it's even in the Bible. Most of the book seems to say that life on earth has no real meaning. Reading Ecclesiastes might make you sad, until the very end. That's where Solomon writes that life *does* have meaning: "The last word, after all has been heard, is: Honor God and obey His Laws. This is all that every person must do" (Ecclesiastes 12:13).

That's great wisdom, isn't it? Sadly, Solomon didn't live up to that guidance at the end of his life.

A WISE KING WHO MADE SOME VERY BAD DECISIONS

Solomon had built Israel into the richest, most powerful nation in the world. That's why the early years of his reign are sometimes called "the Golden Age of Israel." The king was successful whenever he used the wisdom God had given him.

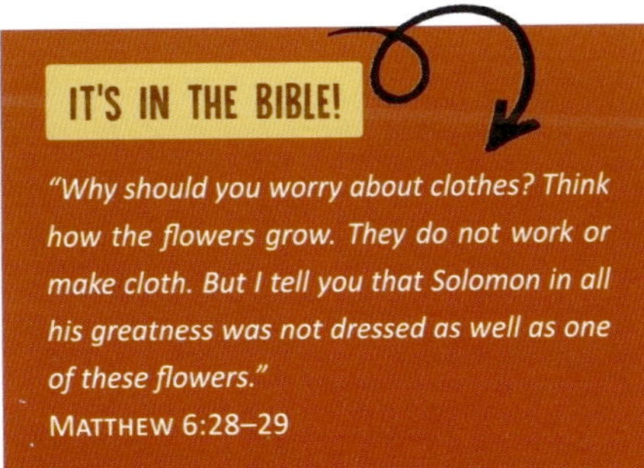

IT'S IN THE BIBLE!

"Why should you worry about clothes? Think how the flowers grow. They do not work or make cloth. But I tell you that Solomon in all his greatness was not dressed as well as one of these flowers."
MATTHEW 6:28–29

Solomon seemed destined for even greater things, but he didn't end his reign the way he started. Solomon broke several of God's laws, and God became angry with him. The king had married *seven hundred* women—and he had three hundred other women who acted as wives, even though they weren't married to him (1 Kings 11:3). Solomon wanted to build stronger relationships with the kings of other nations, and to do that, he unwisely married their daughters. These women didn't believe in the true God of Israel but instead worshiped the false gods of their own nations. Before long, Solomon's foreign wives persuaded him to build shrines—special places of worship—for their fake gods.

With Solomon leading the way, idolatry spread across the nation of Israel. The Golden Age was over. One day, God appeared to Solomon with bad news:

> *"Because you have done this and have not kept My agreement and My Laws which I told you, for sure I will tear the nation from you and will give it to your servant. But I will not do it while you are alive, because of your father David. I will tear it out of the hand of your son. But I will not tear away all the nation. I will give one family group to your son because of My servant David, and because of Jerusalem which I have chosen."*
> 1 KINGS 11:11–13

King Solomon—influenced by his many, many wives—falls into idol worship.

Sadly, Solomon had ignored the wisdom God gave him, allowing his own desires to interfere with his important job as king over Israel. Solomon disobeyed God in many ways, and as a result, he didn't live the long life God had promised if he remained faithful. The Bible doesn't say how old he was when he died, but he ruled for forty years—so he could have been in his fifties.

Not only that, the united kingdom of Israel didn't live long either. After Solomon's death, Israel split into two kingdoms—Israel to the north and Judah to the south.

WHAT WE CAN LEARN FROM SOLOMON:

God gave Solomon the gift of wisdom, which he used to accomplish great things for the nation of Israel. But he didn't always use that wisdom, making many bad decisions that led to terrible consequences for Israel. Today, we find wisdom in God's written Word, the Bible. But, as the apostle James wrote, we must obey it. "If you hear only and do not act, you are only fooling yourself. Anyone who hears the Word of God and does not obey is like a man looking at his face in a mirror. After he sees himself and goes away, he forgets what he looks like. But the one who keeps looking into God's perfect Law and does not forget it will do what it says and be happy as he does it. God's Word makes men free" (James 1:22–25).

ELIJAH

MEANING OF HIS NAME:
"Yahweh is God" or "The Lord is my God"

WHEN HE LIVED:
Born about 900 BC

WHERE YOU CAN READ ABOUT HIM:
1 Kings 17–19; 2 Kings 1–2

WHY HE'S IMPORTANT:
Elijah was one of the greatest prophets in the history of Israel. He called the people of the northern kingdom of Israel away from the worship of the false god Baal and back to the one true God.

He never wrote a book of the Bible. He appears in just a few chapters of the Old Testament. But Elijah was one of the most important and respected prophets in Israel's history.

The Bible doesn't say anything about Elijah's birth or childhood, nor does it tell us how or when God called him to serve as a prophet. He is called "the Tishbite" (1 Kings 17:1), which indicates he was from a village called Tishbe. Elijah lived during the ninth century BC, after Israel had been split into two kingdoms—a northern kingdom still called Israel and a southern kingdom called Judah.

Elijah showed up to preach in the northern kingdom, which had fallen far away from the one true God. Instead, they worshiped a false god called Baal. Elijah preached and performed miracles in the name of the Lord.

IN ELIJAH'S OWN WORDS

"How long will you be divided between two ways of thinking? If the Lord is God, follow Him. But if Baal is God, then follow him."
1 Kings 18:21

ELIJAH'S SUDDEN ARRIVAL

Elijah appears suddenly in the Bible, in 1 Kings 17. At the time, Israel was ruled by an evil king named Ahab. The Bible says that he "did what was sinful in the eyes of the Lord more than all [the kings] who were before him" (1 Kings 16:30). Elijah went boldly to Ahab and told him, "As the

Elijah tells King Ahab that God will hold back the rain from Israel—punishment for the king's bad behavior.

Lord the God of Israel lives, before Whom I stand, for sure there will be no rain or water on the grass in the early morning these years, except by my word" (1 Kings 17:1).

God knew that Ahab wouldn't take that news well, so He told Elijah to hide out for a while in a desert place near the Jordan River. God sent food to Elijah by miraculously ordering ravens to carry bread and meat to him. Later, God told Elijah to visit a town called Zarephath and go to the home of a widow who lived with her son. God promised Elijah that the woman would feed him until the drought was over—and Elijah performed a miracle that kept her food supply from running out!

Sometime later, God told Elijah to go see King Ahab. Again. The prophet told the king why Israel had gone through years of drought and famine: "I have not brought trouble to Israel. But you and your father's house have. Because you have turned away from the laws of the Lord, and have followed the false gods of Baal" (1 Kings 18:18). Elijah then made a challenge to the king: Ahab should call 450 priests of the false god Baal and 400 priests of the false goddess Asherah to Mount Carmel. There, Elijah would show all the people that there is only one true God. So Elijah, the prophets of Baal, and many people who lived in Israel gathered at Mount Carmel (1 Kings 18:17–40). The prophets of Baal called on their false god all day, but nothing happened. (Are you surprised?) But then it was Elijah's turn. He built a stone altar, dug a ditch around it, and put a sacrifice on top of wood. Knowing for sure that God would act, he also ordered water to be poured over his sacrifice. . . three times! When Elijah called on God, He sent fire from heaven to burn up the sacrifice, the wood, and even the stones Elijah used to build the altar. Not only that, all of the water was gone!

God was clearly more powerful than the false gods Baal and Asherah. And the people who witnessed this event fell on their faces and cried out, "The Lord, He is God. The Lord, He is God" (1 Kings 18:39). Elijah ordered the people to round up all the false prophets, who were then killed. Not long after that, rain started to fall in Israel for the first time in three years.

MIRACLES DURING ELIJAH'S MINISTRY

- Pronouncing drought on Israel (1 Kings 17:1)
- Being fed by ravens (1 Kings 17:2–6)
- Increasing a widow's flour and oil in Zarephath (1 Kings 17:7–15)
- Raising the widow's son from the dead (1 Kings 17:17–24)
- Calling fire from heaven to burn up an offering—and show that Baal was a false god (1 Kings 18:17–40)
- Restarting the rain in Israel (1 Kings 18:41–45)
- Being fed by an angel, twice! (1 Kings 19:5–8)
- Hearing a gentle whisper from God at Mount Sinai (1 Kings 19:11–18)
- Predicting—correctly—that dogs would eat Jezebel, Ahab's wife (1 Kings 21:23; 2 Kings 9:30–37)
- Calling fire from heaven on groups of soldiers, twice! (2 Kings 1:10–14)
- Parting the Jordan River (2 Kings 2:8)
- Being carried by a whirlwind into heaven (2 Kings 2:8–11)

Elijah never died—God took him straight to heaven in a chariot of fire.

ELIJAH ON THE RUN

Elijah had played a big part in God's victory over the false prophets of Baal. But right after that, he had to run for his life.

King Ahab told his really evil wife, Jezebel, what had happened at Mount Carmel, and she became so angry that she vowed to have Elijah killed. When Elijah heard about that, he fled into the wilderness. Amazingly, after seeing the miraculous power of God, Elijah felt so sorry for himself that he prayed for God to take his life! Later, he took a forty-day trip to Mount Horeb, also known as Mount Sinai, where God gave Moses the Ten Commandments. Elijah hid in a cave and complained to God, "I have been very careful to serve the Lord, the God of All. For the people of Israel have turned away from Your agreement.

IT'S IN THE BIBLE!

Elijah was a man as we are. He prayed that it might not rain. It did not rain on the earth for three and one-half years. Then he prayed again that it would rain. It rained much and the fields of the earth gave fruit.
JAMES 5:17–18

They have torn down Your altars and have killed with the sword the men who speak for You. Only I am left, and they want to kill me" (1 Kings 19:10).

God told Elijah to leave his cave and stand on the mountain. The Lord was going to pass by Elijah. The tired, frightened prophet heard a great wind, felt a powerful earthquake, and saw a blazing fire, but God was not in any of those things. Elijah then heard God's voice in a "gentle blowing" (1 Kings 19:12). God told Elijah what he needed to do next—and reminded the prophet that he was not alone. "I will leave 7,000 in Israel whose knees have not bowed down in front of Baal," God said (verse 18).

Elijah crawled into a cave like this and held himself a pity party.

One of God's instructions for Elijah was to appoint Elisha as Israel's next leading prophet. When Elisha was ready, Elijah was taken into heaven in a whirlwind.

He was one of two people in the Bible who never died—the other being a man named Enoch, back in Genesis 5. Here's another incredible thing about Elijah: he came back to earth again hundreds of years later—when he appeared along with Moses at what is called Jesus' "transfiguration" (see Matthew 17:1–4).

WHAT WE CAN LEARN FROM ELIJAH:

When Elijah was at his lowest point—so low that he wanted to die—God encouraged and strengthened him. He promises to do the same for us when we feel low: "We give thanks to the God and Father of our Lord Jesus Christ. He is our Father Who shows us loving-kindness and our God Who gives us comfort. He gives us comfort in all our troubles. Then we can comfort other people who have the same troubles" (2 Corinthians 1:3–4).

ELISHA

MEANING OF HIS NAME:
"My God is salvation"

WHEN HE LIVED:
Date isn't certain, but he lived during the second half of the ninth century BC.

WHERE YOU CAN READ ABOUT HIM:
1 Kings 19:19–21; 2 Kings 2–13

WHY HE'S IMPORTANT:
Elisha was Israel's leading prophet during the reigns of four evil kings: Jehoram, Jehu, Jehoahaz, and Joash. One of his greatest accomplishments was ridding Israel of the worship of the idol Baal.

Elisha knew that Elijah was going to leave him. But he still felt sad after God took his friend and teacher to heaven, leaving Elisha as Israel's leading prophet. Elijah had been like a loving father to Elisha, who had said, "As the Lord lives and as you yourself live, I will not leave you" (2 Kings 2:6).

IN ELISHA'S OWN WORDS

"Why have you torn your clothes? Let him come to me. Then he will know that there is a man of God in Israel."
2 Kings 5:8

After he saw Elijah going up in a fiery chariot, Elisha cried out, "My father, my father, the war-wagon of Israel and its horsemen!" (2 Kings 2:12). Then Elijah was gone. Elisha was so sad that he tore his own clothes in two pieces, a way of showing sorrow in that culture.

The Bible says very little about Elisha's background. We only know that his father was a man named Shaphat and that he was from a town called Abel Meholah, which was between the Sea of Galilee and the Dead Sea on the west side of the Jordan River. When Elijah first met Elisha, he was plowing a field with a team of oxen. That tells us that he was probably a farmer before he began serving God as a prophet.

GOD'S ASSIGNMENT FOR ELISHA

Elisha served as Israel's prophet during a time when very few of the people followed or honored God. The nation of Israel that David and Solomon once led had been split into two smaller kingdoms—a northern kingdom still called Israel and a southern kingdom called Judah. Most of the people of the northern kingdom worshiped an idol called Baal.

In some ways, prophets in Israel had a lot of authority. They advised kings and challenged the people to follow the one true God. They announced God's judgment on Israel's enemies and on evil people or kings. They performed miracles and made predictions about future events. But prophets' jobs could be very dangerous. If they said something that angered a king, they could risk losing their lives.

Elisha knew he had a difficult, risky job ahead. So he made one request before Elijah was taken up to heaven. Elisha said, "I ask you, let twice the share of your spirit be upon me" (2 Kings 2:9). Elijah told Elisha that he would have what he had

MIRACLES OF ELISHA

- Parts the Jordan River (2 Kings 2:13–14)
- Makes a Jericho spring drinkable (2:19–22)
- Sends bears to punish mocking youths (2:23–25)
- Floods ditches to confuse Moabites (3:1–27)
- Multiplies a widow's oil (4:1–7)
- Tells a childless woman she will have a son (4:8–17)
- Resurrects that woman's son after he died suddenly (4:18–37)
- Purifies a poisoned stew (4:38–41)
- Feeds a hundred men with twenty small loaves of bread (4:42–44)
- Heals Naaman's leprosy (5:1–14)
- Strikes Gehazi with leprosy (5:15–27)
- Causes a lost ax-head to float (6:1–7)
- Gives special sight to the king's messenger (6:16–17)
- Blinds the Aramean army (6:8–23)
- Elisha's bones bring a dead man back to life! (13:20–21)

Elisha hits the Jordan River with Elijah's cloak, causing the waters to part.

asked for, then Elijah went to heaven in a chariot of fire on a whirlwind.

Now Elisha was on his own as Israel's top prophet.

Elisha ended up serving God as a prophet of the Northern Kingdom of Israel for fifty to sixty years—during the reigns of kings Jehoram, Jehu, Jehoahaz, and Joash. None of these kings loved God or served Him, but they respected Elisha. During this time, God used Elisha to rid the nation of Israel of the worship of the false god Baal (see 2 Kings 10:18–11:18).

Because Elisha had the courage to ask for a double portion of Elijah's spirit, God strengthened Elisha to do many incredible things during his time as a prophet. God helped Elisha perform more miracles in the Bible than anyone but Jesus. Those miracles proved that God had sent Elisha, and they also demonstrated the Lord's amazing power over all things.

In addition to being a powerful prophet, Elisha was also an example of what godly love looks like. He helped poor people (see 2 Kings 4:1–7), and he helped people who were better off—such as when he healed a military commander named Naaman of a terrible skin disease (see 2 Kings 5:1–14).

Elisha had great faith in God. He was willing to ask God for big things—like a double portion of Elijah's spirit or to bring a widow's son back from the dead. He was courageous because he knew that God was in control of all things. That kept Elisha from being fearful of what other people could do to him.

Elisha died during the reign of Israel's evil king Joash. Even though Joash didn't serve Elisha's God, he still visited as Elisha was about to die. That shows us that Elisha was respected in Israel, even when people didn't like what he had to say. Close to death, Elisha continued serving God, giving the king a message from the Lord.

IT'S IN THE BIBLE!

"There were many people in the Jewish land who had a bad skin disease when the early preacher Elisha lived. None of them was healed. But Naaman from the country of Syria was healed."
LUKE 4:27

WHAT WE CAN LEARN FROM ELISHA:

Elisha had enough faith in God that he didn't shy away from asking big things from Him. We Christians today should follow Elisha's example and ask God for things we know only He can give us.

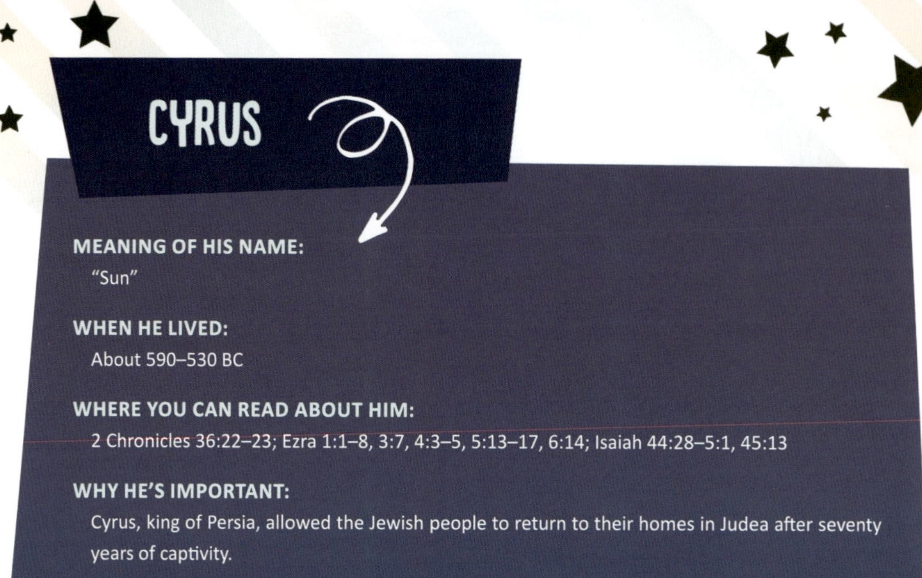

CYRUS

MEANING OF HIS NAME:
"Sun"

WHEN HE LIVED:
About 590–530 BC

WHERE YOU CAN READ ABOUT HIM:
2 Chronicles 36:22–23; Ezra 1:1–8, 3:7, 4:3–5, 5:13–17, 6:14; Isaiah 44:28–5:1, 45:13

WHY HE'S IMPORTANT:
Cyrus, king of Persia, allowed the Jewish people to return to their homes in Judea after seventy years of captivity.

The Babylonian captivity was a sad time in Israel's history. King Nebuchadnezzar of Babylon attacked Jerusalem, destroyed the temple, and took many thousands of Jewish people captive. He brought them back to Babylon to serve him.

God allowed the Babylonians to attack the southern Jewish kingdom of Judah several times over twenty years. Why? Because the people had sinned so terribly against God. Many people in Jerusalem died in the attacks, and about twenty thousand were taken away to Babylon.

But the situation wasn't hopeless. Though God had warned the Jewish people that their home would be destroyed and many of them taken captive, He also promised a restoration. God spoke to His people living in Babylon through the prophet Jeremiah (you'll read about him later in this book), saying that after seventy years in captivity, they would be allowed to return home, rebuild the temple in Jerusalem, and worship God as they did before. (You can read this great promise in Jeremiah 29:10–14.)

God always keeps His promises, and He kept

IT'S IN THE BIBLE!

The Lord, Who makes you, bought you and saves you, and the One Who put you together before you were born, says. . . "It is I Who says of Cyrus, 'He is My shepherd, and he will do all that I want him to do,' even saying of Jerusalem, 'She will be built,' and of the house of God, 'Your first stones will be laid again.' "
ISAIAH 44:24, 28

this one too! Around 539 BC, after Nebuchadnezzar died, the Babylonian Empire fell to the armies of Persia. The newly expanded Persian Empire was ruled by a man named Cyrus—also known as Cyrus the Great. Not long after the Persians defeated Babylon, Cyrus earned fame among Jewish people when he allowed the exiles who wanted to leave to return to their homes in Judah.

GETTING TO KNOW CYRUS

Cyrus was born around 590 BC and died around 530 BC. Some experts believe he died in battle, but others say he died peacefully in his palace. As king of the Persian Empire, he became known as "Cyrus the Great" because of his many military victories and because his empire spread so far and wide during his rule.

Cyrus is mentioned dozens of times in the Bible, and he was very important in the history of the Jewish people. In Old Testament times, people who studied the writings of God's prophets knew Cyrus's name—150 years before he was born! In one of the most incredible predictions in the Bible, the prophet Isaiah (who wrote his book of prophecy between around 740 and 686 BC) said this about Cyrus:

> *This is what the Lord says to Cyrus, whom He has chosen, whose right hand He has held, "I send him to put nations under his power, and to take away the power of kings. And I will open doors in front of him so that gates will not be shut. . . . For the good of Jacob My servant and Israel My chosen one, I called you by your name. I gave you a name of honor, when you had not known Me."*
> ISAIAH 45:1, 4

Amazing, huh? Not only did God tell His people that there would one day be a ruler who would show kindness and compassion to the Jewish people, He even mentioned that ruler by name! God looks out for every detail when He works out His plan for our salvation. He'll even send a king who didn't know Him.

IN CYRUS'S OWN WORDS

"Whoever there is among you of all His people, may his God be with him! Let him go up to Jerusalem which is in Judah, and build again the house of the Lord, the God of Israel. He is the God Who is in Jerusalem. Let each one who is still alive, at whatever place he may live, be helped by the men of his place with silver and gold and with good things and cattle. Let the men also give a free-will gift for the house of God in Jerusalem."
EZRA 1:3–4

When Cyrus conquered other nations, he treated their people very well. He even set up what is called the "Edict of Restoration," which allowed conquered people living in the Persian Empire to return to their homelands.

Cyrus proved that he was a friend of the Jewish people living in his empire. Even though most of the exiles originally brought to Babylon had died, Cyrus probably knew that their children and grandchildren still saw the land of Judah as their true home. It was several hundred miles away.

In his first years of his reign, Cyrus may not have known that God had promised His people that they could return home after seventy years in Babylon. But in 537 BC, God moved Cyrus' heart to allow the Jews to leave for Judah. Here's how the Bible puts it:

> *The Lord's word by the mouth of Jeremiah came true in this way also: In the first year of King Cyrus of Persia, the Lord caused the spirit of King Cyrus to send word to all his nation, and also to write it down, saying, "King Cyrus of Persia says, 'The Lord, the God of heaven, has given me all the nations of the earth. He has chosen me to build Him a house in Jerusalem, which is in Judah. Whoever is among you of all His people, may the Lord his God be with him, and let him go up.'"*
> 2 CHRONICLES 36:22–23

So a full seventy years after the first captives had been taken from Judah and marched off to Babylon—and fifty years after Jerusalem had been burned to the ground and the temple destroyed—the Jewish people were free to return to their homeland.

King Cyrus not only allowed the Jews to return home to rebuild God's temple, he also returned the temple treasures the Babylonians had taken

King Cyrus gave back to the Jews hundreds of gold and silver items that Nebuchadnezzar had taken from the temple. They included thirty gold plates, a thousand silver dishes, and numerous other items—5,400 in all.

so many years earlier. He even contributed to the work from his own treasury (see Ezra 1:4–11, 6:4–5).

After Cyrus proclaimed that the Jews could return to their homeland, three waves of former captives left Persia for Judah. The first wave, led by a man named Zerubbabel, returned in about 538 BC. This group immediately rebuilt the altar so the people could begin sacrificing to God again. They also built the foundation for a new temple.

A second party, led by a man named Ezra, returned to Judah about eighty years later. Once in Jerusalem, they worked to restore the spiritual and religious practices of the Jewish people. Finally, in about 445 BC, a man named Nehemiah led a third group to Jerusalem. These people rebuilt the city's walls.

WHAT WE CAN LEARN FROM CYRUS:

Even though Cyrus didn't worship the one true God, he helped fulfill God's promise to bring His people back to Judah after seventy years in Babylon. This shows that God can use anyone He wants to make His plans a reality.

ESTHER

MEANING OF HER NAME:
"Star"

WHEN SHE LIVED:
Not certain, but her husband, Xerxes, reigned as king of Persia from 486–465 BC.

WHERE YOU CAN READ ABOUT HER:
The book of Esther

WHY SHE'S IMPORTANT:
Esther, a beautiful Jewish woman, was chosen as queen of Persia. She risked her own life by courageously approaching her husband, King Xerxes, pleading with him to spare the lives of the Jewish people in Persia.

Who is your favorite Bible hero? Do you like Moses for standing up to Pharaoh and leading the Israelites out of their slavery in Egypt? Is Joshua at the top of your list because he led the Israelites into the promised Land? Or maybe you're impressed with Paul in the New Testament, a man who endured beatings and death threats for telling people about Jesus.

But not every hero was a guy.

There was a beautiful Jewish girl who became the queen of Persia, then risked her life to save her people from being wiped out by an evil enemy. Let's dig into the story of Esther!

When you read her story in the Old Testament (the book with her name wedged in between Nehemiah and Job), you may notice something unusual: God isn't mentioned in Esther—not even once! But if you "read between the lines," you can see He's still a very big part of this story.

Though many of God's people were living far from home, God hadn't forgotten them. He still loved them very much, and they were still His chosen people. God worked behind the scenes to make sure they survived an attempt to destroy every one of them. God put Esther in the right

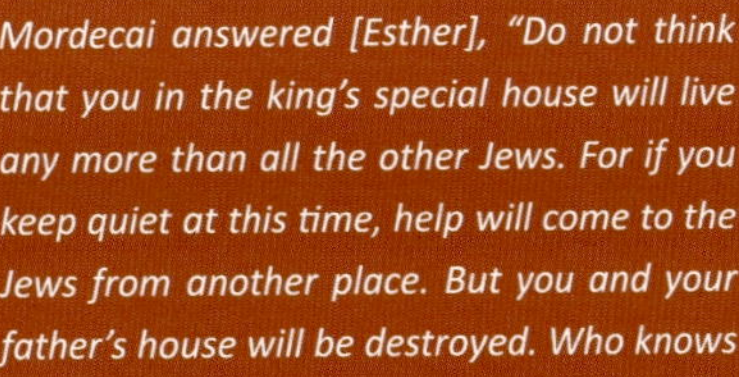

IT'S IN THE BIBLE!

Mordecai answered [Esther], "Do not think that you in the king's special house will live any more than all the other Jews. For if you keep quiet at this time, help will come to the Jews from another place. But you and your father's house will be destroyed. Who knows if you have not become queen for such a time as this?"
ESTHER 4:13–14

Queen Esther was kind of like Miss Israel, Titi Aynaw—chosen for her beauty and good personality.

place at the right time so she could speak up and save the Jews from what looked like certain death.

Esther lived in Persia (modern-day Iran) with about a million other Jewish people. The Babylonian Empire had wiped out the nation of Judah and its capital city, Jerusalem, in the sixth century BC. The invaders also took many Jewish people captive back to Babylon. In 539 BC, Persians, led by King Cyrus the Great, took over Babylon. A year later, Cyrus granted the Jews who were captive in Babylon the right to return to Judah and rebuild God's temple in Jerusalem.

Many Jews returned to Judah, but others chose to stay in Persia, where they had built homes and started families. Esther and her cousin Mordecai were among those who stayed behind. Their story is set in Susa, a capital of Persia, during the reign of King Xerxes I, also known as Ahasuerus.

Esther was also known by her Jewish name, Hadassah. Both of her parents had died, leaving her an orphan. But her cousin Mordecai stepped in to raise her as if she were his own daughter.

As a young woman, Esther became part of King Xerxes's harem—that's a group of beautiful women that kings often collect for themselves. When the king's wife, Vashti, disobeyed him in public, he removed her as queen and chose a new one. The new queen of Persia was Esther! According to the Bible, "Esther found favor in the eyes of all who saw her" (Esther 2:15).

IN ESTHER'S OWN WORDS

"Go, gather together all the Jews who are in Susa, and have them all go without food so they can pray better for me. Do not eat or drink for three days, night or day. I and my women servants will go without food in the same way. Then I will go in to the king, which is against the law. And if I die, I die."

ESTHER 4:16

FOILING HAMAN'S EVIL PLOT

A man named Haman was an advisor to King Xerxes. Haman *hated* Mordecai. When Haman had gotten an important job from the king, Mordecai refused to bow before him. As a Jew, Mordecai would only bow before God.

Haman felt insulted, and he became so angry that he hatched a plot to have Mordecai and every other Jew in Persia killed. He even built a tower to hang Mordecai from. When Mordecai learned of Haman's plans, he sent Queen Esther a message, begging her to go to the king for help. But that wasn't as easy as it sounds.

Esther loved her fellow Jews, especially Mordecai. She didn't want to see any of them die, and she knew something had to be done. But even though she was Xerxes's wife, Esther knew that approaching the king without an invitation could put her life in danger. By law, nobody could approach the king without being summoned. Both Mordecai and Esther knew that going to the king might be the last thing she ever did.

But Esther decided she had no choice. She prayed and fasted and asked Mordecai to gather all the Jews in the city of Susa, the capital of Persia, and have them pray and fast too.

Then Esther gathered up every ounce of courage within her and approached the king. Her heart was probably pounding, since what she was doing was against the law in Persia—and the penalty for breaking this law was *death*. Imagine her relief when Xerxes seemed pleased to see her. Then he held out his scepter and promised to do whatever she asked!

"If I have found favor in your eyes, O king, and if it please the king," Queen Esther said, "I ask that my life and the lives of my people be saved" (Esther 7:3). Xerxes was surprised by Esther's words, then furious when he learned of Haman's plans. The king granted Esther's request—and ordered that the evil Haman be hanged from the same tower he had built for Mordecai.

This ancient carving of a Persian king may actually be of Xerxes. Notice the special stick, or scepter, that he's holding.

Esther's willingness to risk her life to save all the Jews in Persia makes her a true hero. To this day, Jews celebrate Esther's actions in a holiday called Purim.

WHAT WE CAN LEARN FROM ESTHER:

The apostle John, one of Jesus' original twelve disciples, once wrote, "We know what love is because Christ gave His life for us. We should give our lives for our brothers" (1 John 3:16). Esther is a powerful example of that. Few of us will ever be in Esther's situation—but what are you willing to risk for someone who needs your help?

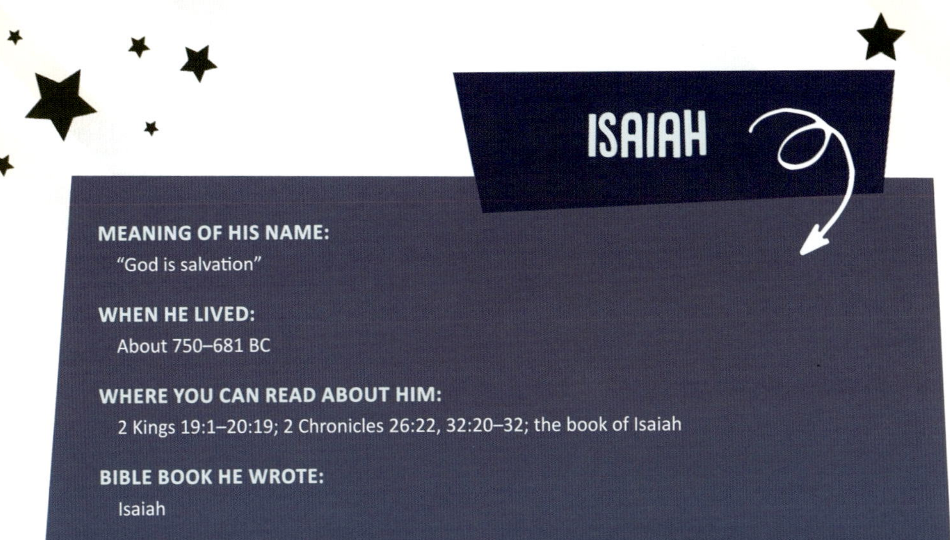

ISAIAH

MEANING OF HIS NAME:

"God is salvation"

WHEN HE LIVED:

About 750–681 BC

WHERE YOU CAN READ ABOUT HIM:

2 Kings 19:1–20:19; 2 Chronicles 26:22, 32:20–32; the book of Isaiah

BIBLE BOOK HE WROTE:

Isaiah

WHY HE'S IMPORTANT:

Isaiah not only preached to the people of Judah and Israel; he also wrote many prophecies about the birth, life, and death of the Messiah, Jesus Christ.

The Old Testament tells the stories of many people who spoke or wrote prophecies God had given them. The word *prophecy* refers to a message straight from God, and the word *prophet* describes the person God chose to speak to the people.

God called a lot of people as prophets during Old Testament times. Men such as Samuel, Elijah, Elisha, David, and many others spoke the messages God had given them. But there were other prophets God used to write down messages that became books of the Bible. The first of these books, as it appears in your Bible, is Isaiah—written by a prophet named Isaiah, who lived and preached in Judah in the eighth century BC.

The Bible doesn't tell us a lot about Isaiah's personal life. Isaiah 1:1 says that he was the son of a man named Amoz, who isn't mentioned anywhere else in the Bible. Isaiah 8:3 tells us that he was married to a lady prophet, who isn't named. But she and Isaiah had two sons—Shear-Jashub (Isaiah 7:3) and Maher-Shalal-Hash-Baz (8:3).

Isaiah spoke prophecies during the reigns of four kings: Uzziah, Jotham, Ahaz, and Hezekiah. That means he might have preached for about forty years! His messages were directed at both Judah and Israel (the southern and northern Jewish kingdoms) as well as a few other nations in that part of the world.

What he said is the most important thing about Isaiah.

ISAIAH'S MESSAGE OF PUNISHMENT. . .AND HOPE

In the sixth chapter of Isaiah's book, he tells about the day when God called him to be a prophet. Isaiah was happy to accept the job, telling God, "Here am I. Send me!" (verse 8). Then God gave Isaiah his assignment: he would give the people a message of punishment for their sins. But there would also be a message of hope when they turned back to God and changed their ways.

Isaiah is a long book. The message was very important to the Jewish people he spoke to so many centuries ago. It is also important to us today! Isaiah warned people that their sins would bring God's judgment. But he also wanted everyone to understand that God loves people. If we trust Him, worship Him the right way, and live the way He wants us to, God promises to be with us and bless us.

That's great to know, isn't it? But Isaiah's book contains some even bigger and better promises.

The most hopeful message of Isaiah was God's promise to send the Messiah to Israel. The word *messiah* means "chosen one." It has the same meaning as "Christ" in the name "Jesus Christ"—the Savior of the world! Here's an example of the

The prophet Isaiah called Jesus "Immanuel," meaning "God with us."

word: "The kings of the earth stand in a line ready to fight, and all the leaders are against the Lord and against His Chosen One" (Psalm 2:2).

Jesus is that "chosen one" that Isaiah talked about, around seven hundred years before Jesus was born. Many of Isaiah's prophecies about Jesus are very specific, which we'll see below. That was so people could see the things Jesus did and said and believe that He was the Savior God had sent to the world.

The book of Isaiah has sixty-six chapters, and almost a third of them contain prophecies about Jesus. These predictions discuss His birth, life, death, and resurrection, as well as His "second coming" at the end of time.

Let's consider some prophecies of Jesus that Isaiah wrote in his book.

JESUS' BIRTH

Every year at Christmastime, you hear the story of Jesus' birth. But did you know that Old Testament prophets like Isaiah predicted—centuries beforehand—how that birth would happen? It's true! Here are some of Isaiah's prophecies along with passages from the four Gospels (Matthew, Mark, Luke, and John) telling us how they came true:

- Jesus' mother would be a woman who had never been with a man, and Jesus would be called "Immanuel," which means "God with us" (Isaiah 7:14; Matthew 1:22–23; Luke 1:26–31).
- Jesus would be born as a baby like everyone else, and He would be called "Wonderful Counselor," "Mighty God," "Everlasting Father," and "Prince of Peace." He would also possess a kingdom that would last forever (Isaiah 9:6–7; Matthew 26:64, 28:18; John 14:27).

JESUS' WORK ON EARTH

When Jesus was about thirty years old, He started traveling around Israel, teaching, preaching, and caring for people by doing some incredible miracles. This is called Jesus' "earthly ministry." Centuries ahead of time, God showed Old Testament prophets many of the great things Jesus would do while He was on earth. Here are some things Isaiah said about Jesus' earthly ministry:

- A man (John the Baptist) would appear before Jesus' ministry started to prepare people for His arrival (Isaiah 40:3–5; Luke 3:3–6).
- Jesus would start His work in a place called Galilee (Isaiah 9:1–2; Matthew 4:13–16).
- The Holy Spirit would rest on Jesus (Isaiah 11:2; Mark 1:10).
- Jesus would come to save Jews and non-Jews alike (Isaiah 9:1–2; Luke 2:10–11).
- Jesus would perform miracles of healing (Isaiah 35:5–6; Matthew 4:23).
- Jesus would bring good news and set people free (Isaiah 61:1–2; Luke 4:18–19).

Isaiah prophesied that Jesus would heal people—and He once made a crippled man well after the man's friends lowered him down through the roof (Mark 2:1–12)!

JESUS' DEATH AND RESURRECTION

From the moment Jesus came to earth, He knew that His most important mission was to die as punishment for people's sins, and then be raised from the dead. The Old Testament prophets included a lot of details about Jesus' death on the cross and His resurrection. Here are some examples from Isaiah:

- Jesus would be ridiculed and mistreated (Isaiah 50:3–6; Matthew 26:67).
- People would reject Jesus, and He would suffer (Isaiah 53:3; Matthew 26:56).
- Jesus would be a sacrifice for sin (Isaiah 53:5–12; John 10:15, 17).
- Jesus would be wounded for our rebellion against God and die for our sin. He would be beaten so that we could be healed (Isaiah 53:2–5; Matthew 20:19).
- Jesus would die with criminals (Isaiah 53:12; Matthew 27:38; Mark 15:27–28).
- Jesus would be buried with the rich (Isaiah 53:9; Matthew 27:57–60).
- Jesus would rise from the dead (Isaiah 26:19; Matthew 28:5–6).

The Bible doesn't say when or where Isaiah died, but some people believe he was killed by the evil King Manasseh, who reigned in Judah for fifty-five years. Isaiah left behind writings that are as important today as they were when he wrote them.

Isaiah predicted the saddest thing ever—the death of Jesus as payment for people's sins. But while it was sad, it was necessary—because it allowed people to be saved.

WHAT WE CAN LEARN FROM ISAIAH:

The prophet was an important person because he was willing to go where God told him to go and say what God told him to say. When Isaiah told God, "Here am I. Send me!" he showed his Father in heaven that he was happy to serve. Are we willing to follow Isaiah's example?

JEREMIAH

MEANING OF HIS NAME:
"Raised up by God"

WHEN HE LIVED:
About 650–570 BC

WHERE YOU CAN READ ABOUT HIM:
The books of Jeremiah and Lamentations

BIBLE BOOKS HE WROTE:
Jeremiah, Lamentations

WHY HE'S IMPORTANT:
Jeremiah was a spokesman (prophet) for God during a very difficult time in the history of Judah. He warned the people of God's judgment for their sins. When the people didn't listen, Jeremiah witnessed the destruction of Jerusalem by the Babylonians.

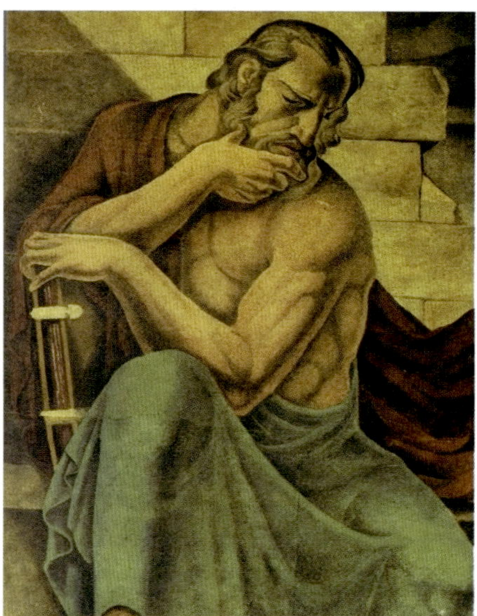

During Old Testament times, God gave His prophets some very hard assignments. But none was as difficult as the job He gave to Jeremiah. God wanted Jeremiah to preach to a very stubborn, hard-hearted people. And God told Jeremiah ahead of time that they wouldn't listen to a word he said (Jeremiah 7:27–28)!

Jeremiah was the son of a priest named Hilkiah. He was from a small village called Anathoth, about three miles northeast of Jerusalem. God called Jeremiah to be a prophet when he was just a boy (Jeremiah 1:6). In fact, the Bible says that God had set Jeremiah apart to preach before he was even born (verse 5).

God commanded Jeremiah not to get married. Why? God knew that the land of Judah would go through some terrible times in the coming years and He didn't want Jeremiah to worry about a wife and children (see Jeremiah 16:1–6).

Jeremiah preached for more than forty years. He spoke out for God during the reigns of five kings of Judah—Josiah, Jehoahaz, Jehoiakim, Jehoiachin, and Zedekiah. Jeremiah preached at the same time as other prophets whose books are in the Bible: Zephaniah, Nahum, Habakkuk, Daniel, and Ezekiel. During that time, he wrote the books of Jeremiah and Lamentations.

GOD'S MESSAGES THROUGH JEREMIAH

God sent Jeremiah to warn the people of Judah that their idolatry and disobedience would result in some very bad consequences. He warned them that the holy God—the God who had done so much for them—would allow their nation of Judah and the holy city of Jerusalem to be wiped out by a kingdom called Babylon. Many of the people who lived there would be taken into captivity.

IT'S IN THE BIBLE!

[The disciples said to Jesus,] "Some say You are John the Baptist and some say Elijah and others say Jeremiah or one of the early preachers."
MATTHEW 16:14

But Jeremiah also preached a hopeful message from God. The Lord promised Jeremiah that He would bless the nation and spare the people if they would turn back to Him and away from the terrible sins they'd been committing (see Jeremiah 7:5–7, 18:1–11).

Sadly, the kings and people of Judah hardly listened to Jeremiah. They continued in their wickedness. Early in Jeremiah's ministry, a king named Josiah worked to bring the nation and its people back to God (see 2 Chronicles 34:3). But after Josiah died, the four kings who followed him were bad. They didn't encourage the people to follow God at all.

It was bad enough that the kings and people refused to listen to Jeremiah. But they also treated him terribly because they didn't like what he was saying. Nobody enjoys hearing bad news, and they really *hate* hearing bad news because of the way they've been living!

Through Jeremiah, God said He was like a potter, making something from clay. Judah was the clay—and if the pot didn't turn out right, God could smash the clay and start over.

After King Josiah died, people treated Jeremiah worse and worse—even the people of Jeremiah's hometown of Anathoth (see Jeremiah 11:21). He received death threats, and some members of his own family plotted against him (Jeremiah 12:6). In Jerusalem, a priest named Pashhur had Jeremiah beaten and placed in stocks for a day (Jeremiah 20:1–2). Later, some evil men got permission from the evil King Zedekiah to arrest Jeremiah. They lowered him into a nearly empty well, where he sank into the mud (Jeremiah 38:1–6).

The messages Jeremiah spoke for God broke his heart. Jeremiah was treated terribly for speaking God's truth. But he had no choice but to obey God. He had to tell the people what the Lord was saying.

God had told Jeremiah, "I will make you like a strong wall of brass to these people. Even if they fight against you, they will not get power over you. For I am with you to save you and bring you out of trouble. . . . I will take you from the hand of the sinful. And I will free you from the hand of those who would hurt you" (Jeremiah 15:20–21).

Jeremiah sits in the dark, sadly remembering the destruction of Jerusalem. The picture is by the famous Dutch painter Rembrandt (1606–1669).

WHEN DISASTER CAME

Jeremiah did his very best for God. He faithfully spoke the words God had given him, and he prayed for his nation and its people. Jeremiah loved God and his people very much, and his heart was shattered when God's terrible punishment of Judah finally came.

In about 586 BC, Babylonians attacked Jerusalem and the rest of Judah. They tore down the city walls, destroyed the temple, and lit fires all around. Many people in Jerusalem died, and many more were captured and taken to Babylon. This time in Judah's history is called the "Babylonian Exile," and it lasted for seventy years.

After the Babylonian king's forces destroyed Jerusalem, Jeremiah looked around the once-great city and recorded his thoughts in what became known as the book of Lamentations. A "lament" is a sad cry. Jeremiah is known as the "weeping prophet," and this book will give you a good idea why.

Lamentations begins with these sad words: "How empty is the city that was once full of people! She was once great among the nations. But now she has become like a woman whose husband has died. She who was once a queen among the cities has become a servant made to work" (Lamentations 1:1).

IN JEREMIAH'S OWN WORDS

It is because of the Lord's loving-kindness that we are not destroyed for His loving-pity never ends. It is new every morning. He is so very faithful. "The Lord is my share." says my soul, "so I have hope in Him."

LAMENTATIONS 3:22–24

The Bible doesn't say anything about Jeremiah's death, but it tells us that he was taken to Egypt against his will. Some traditions say he was stoned to death in Egypt, sometime around 570 BC.

WHAT WE CAN LEARN FROM JEREMIAH:

Jeremiah lived in a very difficult time in Judah's history. God gave him a very difficult message to preach. But Jeremiah never shied away from telling the truth, even when the people wouldn't listen. God wants us to be like Jeremiah—to tell others the truth, even when we're not comfortable doing it.

DANIEL

MEANING OF HIS NAME:
"God is my judge"

WHEN HE LIVED:
About 620–538 BC

WHERE YOU CAN READ ABOUT HIM:
Daniel

BIBLE BOOKS HE WROTE:
Daniel

WHY HE'S IMPORTANT:
Daniel lived in a place where people didn't love or serve God, but he never compromised his faith in any way. God blessed Daniel with great influence in Babylon (which became part of Persia), and He also showed Daniel some amazing visions of the future—including details on the coming of the Messiah, Jesus Christ.

The Old Testament prophet Daniel spent most of his life living in a place and among people who didn't know or love God. But Daniel stayed faithful to God, even when he faced what looked like certain death. We'll discuss more about that later.

First, though, who was Daniel?

"No wise men, wonder-workers, or men who use secret ways can make this dream known to the king. But there is a God in heaven who makes secrets known."
DANIEL 2:27–28

He was born into the royal family of Judah, and many experts believe he was a relative of King Zedekiah. Originally called Mattaniah, Zedekiah was the last king of Judah. He was ruling during the first of King Nebuchadnezzar of Babylon's three attacks against Jerusalem.

Daniel and three of his friends—Hananiah, Mishael, and Azariah—were among the people of Judah who were captured and taken away into the Babylonian Exile. All four were very young at the time, and the Babylonians changed all of their names. Daniel was called "Belteshazzar." The other three you might recognize as Shadrach, Meshach, and Abednego.

Daniel and his friends were chosen for a

three-year training course to prepare them to serve the Babylonian king. We soon see Daniel taking a stand for what he knew was right in God's eyes: Daniel 1:8 tells us that he refused to eat the food King Nebuchadnezzar offered him. It was the best food anywhere (it was the *king's* food, after all), but Daniel and his friends said "no, thank you." That's because the food was "unclean" according to God's Law. Daniel and his friends asked for only vegetables and water, and ended up stronger and healthier than the other young men who'd eaten the king's food!

But that was just the beginning of Daniel's heroic story. He spent the rest of his days obeying God's laws, even though he was living in a very ungodly place.

LISTENING TO GOD ALONE

Daniel hadn't been in Babylon very long before he became known for his understanding of visions and dreams. The first time Daniel used his God-given gift is in Daniel 2.

King Nebuchadnezzar had had a tough night. A very strange, vivid dream was messing up his sleep. He knew the dream meant something, but he didn't know what—so he called together his "wise men" (they were actually magicians, enchanters, sorcerers, and astrologers) and ordered them to explain what he'd seen.

For a lot of kids, Daniel's rejection of the king's food would be like saying no to an all-you-can-eat pizza buffet. But Daniel and his friends knew they would dishonor God if they ate Nebuchadnezzar's treats.

King Nebuchadnezzar didn't worship the real God of the Bible, and neither did his wise men. When they told the king they couldn't help, he was furious—and issued an order that all the wise men in Babylon be put to death. Daniel and his three friends were included, even though they weren't even there when the king's wise men told him they couldn't interpret his dream!

When Daniel learned about Nebuchadnezzar's harsh order, he prayed and asked God for an answer. God honored Daniel's request, so he went to the king to interpret the dream.

Daniel told the king that the one true God had given him the ability to interpret dreams (Daniel 2:28). Then Daniel told Nebuchadnezzar what his dream meant: God would one day set up a kingdom that would last forever, and the kingdom would destroy all the man-made kingdoms that came before it (Daniel 2:44–45).

King Nebuchadnezzar was impressed by Daniel's words. He honored Daniel for his wisdom and put him in charge of all Babylon's wise men. At Daniel's request, the king also made Shadrach,

Meshach, and Abednego leaders in the nation too.

Later on, Nebuchadnezzar had another dream, this one of a big tree (see Daniel 4). There were birds in the branches and animals underneath, all eating from its fruit. But then an angel came down from heaven, ordering the tree to be stripped of its branches and cut down.

Daniel realized this dream was bad news for Nebuchadnezzar. But he gathered up his courage and told the king what it meant. The tree in the dream represented Nebuchadnezzar himself, who was proud and greedy. God was going to punish him.

Nebuchadnezzar knew Daniel spoke by God's Spirit, but the king was still proud of himself. A year later, when he looked over his capital city, he thought out loud, "Is not this the great Babylon which I have built as a beautiful place for the king? I have built it by my great strength and for the greatness of my power" (Daniel 4:30). But before he'd finished the last word, God's judgment came on Nebuchadnezzar. The king lost his mind and lived like an animal, away from any people, for seven years! When Nebuchadnezzar regained his sanity, he praised and honored Daniel's God (Daniel 4:34–37).

After some time, a man named Belshazzar became king of Babylon. During a fancy dinner he'd set up, Belshazzar ordered his servants to use the special golden cups the Babylonians had taken from God's temple in Jerusalem. God was not happy about this, and He sent a vision for the king: During the party, a hand appeared in front of the banquet-room wall. The hand spelled out a mysterious message on the wall, and Belshazzar was very afraid. Someone in the room remembered how Daniel had interpreted Nebuchadnezzar's dreams years before, so the king sent for Daniel to come. He said this vision meant that Belshazzar's reign as king was about to end.

Nebuchadnezzar's dream was of a giant statue made of different materials. Daniel told the king that he was the head of gold. Other nations, represented by silver, bronze, steel, and metal/clay, would follow him. But God was over them all.

Belshazzar promoted Daniel to the third-highest position in the kingdom—but that very night, the king was killed by soldiers of another nation. Darius the Mede became king as the Babylonian Empire ended.

A MIRACLE IN A LIONS' DEN

The new king, Darius, gave Daniel a very high position in his kingdom. But this made the king's other servants jealous, and they plotted to get Daniel in trouble. Daniel always obeyed God and had never done anything wrong, so the bad guys tried to use that against him. They talked the king into making a law that said everyone needed to pray only to *him*. If someone prayed to anyone but Darius, that person would be thrown into a den of hungry lions.

When Daniel heard about the new law, he went to his room, opened the windows, looked toward the city of Jerusalem, and knelt down and prayed to God—just like he always did, three times a day. When the king's jealous servants caught Daniel praying, they ran to Darius and tattled. Daniel had broken the king's law!

King Darius liked Daniel very much. He was sad when he realized his servants had tricked him.

The book of Daniel tells how God saved the prophet from certain death at the jaws of some hungry lions. But that isn't the only miracle of God's power in this book. Daniel 3:8–30 tells an equally amazing story of God saving Daniel's three friends—Shadrach, Meshach, and Abednego—from a blazing-hot furnace. King Nebuchadnezzar had thrown them into the flames because they refused to bow before his golden idol. It's a great story and well worth reading!

Daniel knew what the king's law said. But he wasn't about to pray to Darius. As always, Daniel prayed only to God.

Darius tried to change the new law, but the bad guys reminded him that the laws of the Medes could not be changed. So Darius had Daniel thrown into the lions' den. "May your God, Whom you are faithful to serve, save you," the king called out (Daniel 6:16). Then a large stone was placed in front of the den so Daniel couldn't escape.

That night, King Darius was so worried that he couldn't sleep a wink or eat a bite. In the morning, just as the sun was coming up, the king ran over to the lions' den to see if Daniel was still alive. "Daniel, servant of the living God," he called out, "has your God, Whom you always serve, been able to save you from the lions?" (Daniel 6:20).

Then the king heard what he had so desperately hoped to hear. Daniel answered from the den, "O king, live forever! My God sent His angel and shut the lions' mouths. They have not hurt me, because He knows that I am not guilty, and because I have done nothing wrong to you, O king" (Daniel 6:21–22).

The king was so happy that Daniel was alive, and he ordered Daniel be removed from the den immediately. Then the king threw the bad guys in with the lions! He also made a new law that said everyone in his kingdom had to respect Daniel's God—the one true God.

After God rescued Daniel from the lions, the Bible says, "Things went well for Daniel during the rule of Darius and during the rule of Cyrus the Persian" (Daniel 6:28). During that time, God gave Daniel visions of the future called *prophecies*. They include what is called the "seventy weeks prophecy," which predicted the birth and death of Jesus Christ hundreds of years later.

IT'S IN THE BIBLE!

"Son of man, if a country sins against Me by not being faithful, I will put out My hand against it. I will destroy its store of bread, and send hunger against it, and take away both man and animal from it. For even if these three men, Noah, Daniel and Job, were in this country, they would save only their own lives by being right and good," says the Lord God.
EZEKIEL 14:13–14

WHAT WE CAN LEARN FROM DANIEL:

Daniel lived in a place where people did not worship God, but he never compromised when it came to his faith—even if that meant risking his life. We all have many opportunities to compromise on what we know God wants from us. But if we follow Daniel's example, we allow God to bless us and use us for the good of His kingdom.

JONAH

MEANING OF HIS NAME:
"Dove"

WHEN HE LIVED:
About 740–681 BC

WHERE YOU CAN READ ABOUT HIM:
The book of Jonah

WHY HE'S IMPORTANT:
Jonah shows how serious God's call is. Though he tried to run from his job of preaching to Nineveh, God had no trouble finding him—and feeding him to a fish!

You probably know something about the Old Testament prophet Jonah. If nothing else, you know that his story took a very strange turn when he was swallowed by a huge fish. In this chapter, you'll learn more about Jonah—for example, *why* he was swallowed by the fish, how he got out of that situation, and what happened to him afterward.

IT'S IN THE BIBLE!

"Jonah was three days and three nights in the stomach of a big fish. The Son of Man [Jesus] will be three days and three nights in the grave also."
MATTHEW 12:40

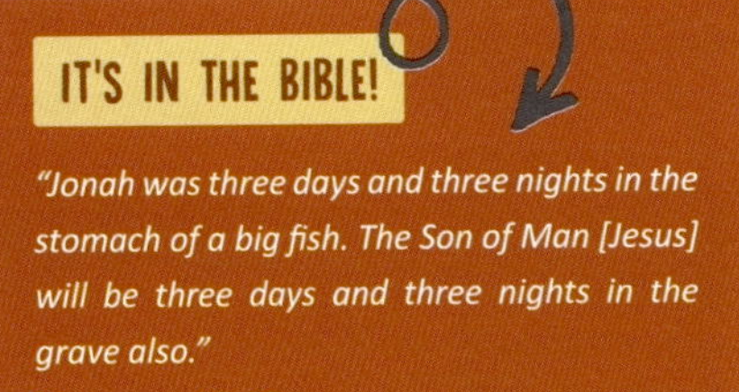

The Bible doesn't say much about Jonah's background, other than that he was the son of a man named Amittai and a prophet who lived in a place called Gath-hepher (see 2 Kings 14:25; Jonah 1:1). Jonah lived and preached in Israel about seven hundred years before Jesus was born.

The book of Jonah gets off to a very fast start. God tells him, "Get up and go to the large city of Nineveh, and preach against it. For their sin has come up before Me" (Jonah 1:2). Nineveh was the capital of the powerful Assyrian Empire. Assyria was filled with proud, harsh, idolatrous leaders who wanted to rule the world.

Jonah knew about the Assyrians, and he didn't like them one bit. He knew they were no friends of Israel, so he wished God would just destroy Assyria. Jonah didn't want God to show kindness and mercy to such a violent nation—but he knew that's exactly what God was planning.

So Jonah did something that no one can do, at least not successfully: he ran from God!

Jonah headed to a city on Israel's coast called

Joppa (today it's called Jaffa). There, he plopped down some money and boarded a ship for Tarshish, which was about 2,500 miles from Joppa. Think of that, instead of doing what God said—travel about 550 miles to Nineveh—Jonah took a much longer route. . .and a journey that turned out to be much, much more difficult.

HEADING TO A BAD PLACE

On the ship headed for Tarshish, Jonah slept. But a terrible storm arose, sending the ship's crew into a panic. The wind and waves were about to tear the boat apart. Sailors ran around the deck, throwing overboard everything that wasn't nailed down. They were hoping to lighten the ship to keep it from sinking.

The ship's captain went to Jonah and shouted, "How can you sleep? Get up and call on your god. It may be that your god will care about us, and we will not die" (Jonah 1:6). Meanwhile, the sailors were drawing names to find out who was responsible for their troubles. God actually told them when He caused Jonah's name to be drawn.

Jonah finally admitted the truth: "I am a Hebrew, and I worship the Lord God of heaven Who made the sea and the dry land," he said, admitting that he was trying to run away from the Lord (Jonah 1:9). He told them to throw him overboard to calm the sea, but the sailors didn't want to do that. But as the storm continued, they finally tossed the disobedient prophet into the sea.

The storm died down instantly. After seeing that, the men made sacrifices and promises to God.

When a person falls off a ship at sea, they often drown. But God was not finished with Jonah—He sent a huge fish that swallowed the man whole. After that, Jonah spent three days and nights in the fish's stomach! We can only imagine how dark and stinky that must have been.

In the fish's stomach, Jonah had a lot of time to think and pray. He cried out to God for help, saying, "I will give You what I have promised" (Jonah 2:9). That meant Jonah would do what he had promised years before: speak the words God gave him, to the people God sent him to.

When God saw that Jonah was ready to do his job, He caused the fish to swim toward shore and spit Jonah out onto dry land.

The Bible says it was a fish, not a whale, that swallowed Jonah. Nobody knows exactly what kind of fish, but this "Goliath grouper" might look something like Jonah's last view before he was swallowed.

ON TO NINEVEH

Now safely on dry land, Jonah listened when God again told him, "Get up and go to the large city of Nineveh, and tell the people there the news which I am going to tell you" (Jonah 3:2). This time, Jonah obeyed.

We don't know how long it took Jonah to reach Nineveh. But when he arrived, he began to warn the people that if they didn't change their ways and turn to God, their city would be destroyed in forty days. Incredibly, the people

The Bible doesn't say if anyone saw the big fish vomit Jonah onto dry land. But if anyone did, can you imagine what they were thinking?

At first, Jonah ran away when God called him to preach to the people of Nineveh. But when he finally went to Nineveh to preach, the people listened to him.

listened. They fasted and prayed, and the king called on the people to turn to God in prayer. "Everyone must pray to God with all his heart,

IN JONAH'S OWN WORDS

"I went down to the roots of the mountains. The walls of the earth were around me forever. But You have brought me up from the grave, O Lord my God. While I was losing all my strength, I remembered the Lord. And my prayer came to You, into Your holy house."
JONAH 2:6–7

so each person may turn from his sinful way and from the bad things he has done," the king said. "Who knows? God may change His mind and stop being angry so that we will not die" (Jonah 3:8–9).

When God saw how the people of Nineveh had listened to Jonah's preaching and turned to Him in prayer, He spared the city—just as He was planning when He first called Jonah to go.

You might think that Jonah would be happy that his preaching was successful. He had helped the people of Nineveh to turn away from their sinful ways. God wasn't going to destroy the city after all.

In fact, Jonah was angry. He was unhappy with God for sparing a nation that was an enemy of Israel. Jonah wanted God to destroy them.

So Jonah prayed a very strange prayer: "O Lord, is this not what I said You would do while still in my own country? That is why I ran away to Tarshish. For I knew that You are a kind and loving God Who shows pity. I knew that You are slow to anger and are filled with loving-kindness, always ready to change Your mind and not punish" (Jonah 4:2).

In the end, Jonah was so upset that he wanted to die. But God said He had compassion on the lost people who lived in the city: "Should I not have loving-pity for Nineveh, the large city where more than 120,000 people live who do not know the difference between their right and left hand, as well as many animals?" (Jonah 4:11).

WHAT WE CAN LEARN FROM JONAH:

God wants us as Christians to show mercy and forgiveness to everyone—even the people we consider our enemies. Jesus said it this way: "I tell you, love those who hate you. (Respect and give thanks for those who say bad things to you. Do good to those who hate you.) Pray for those who do bad things to you and who make it hard for you" (Matthew 5:44). When God tells you to be kind to someone you don't think deserves it, don't run away!

MARY, MOTHER OF JESUS

MEANING OF HER NAME:
"Beloved"

WHEN SHE LIVED:
About 20 BC–AD 41

WHERE YOU CAN READ ABOUT HER:
Matthew 1:16–24; Luke 1:27–56; John 19:26–27

WHY SHE'S IMPORTANT:
Mary is the most important and best-known woman in the Bible because God chose her to be the mother of Jesus, the Savior of the world.

Almost two thousand years ago, a man named Paul (you'll read more about him later) wrote, "But at the right time, God sent His Son. A woman gave birth to Him under the Law. This all happened so He could buy with His blood and make free all those who were held by the Law. Then we might become the sons of God" (Galatians 4:4–5).

This means that God waited until just the right moment to send Jesus into our world. He would live on earth as a man then die on a cross to take the punishment for our sins. And when we believe in Jesus and accept this gift, we will spend forever with Him.

But God the Father didn't only choose the right *time* to send Jesus—He chose the one special *woman* to be Jesus' mother. Mary was a young woman, probably only a teenager, who loved God and lived the way He wanted her to.

Mary came from a town called Nazareth. That was in the northern part of Israel, in an area called Galilee, about sixty-five miles north of Jerusalem. The Bible doesn't tell us anything about Mary's family, but tradition says she was the daughter of a couple named Joachim and Anne. Mary was from the family tree of King David and, going even further back, of Abraham. The Gospel of Matthew says she was engaged to a carpenter named Joseph, who also lived in Nazareth.

IT'S IN THE BIBLE!

"The Lord Himself will give you a special thing to see: A young woman, who has never had a man, will give birth to a son. She will give Him the name Immanuel."
ISAIAH 7:14

AN AMAZING JOURNEY—IN MANY WAYS

Mary's story is found mainly in the first and third Gospels. Luke tells how an angel of God, Gabriel, visited Mary in her hometown. The angel said, "You are honored very much. You are a favored woman. The Lord is with you. You are chosen from among many women" (Luke 1:28). At first, Mary didn't understand. But then Gabriel told her:

> *"Mary, do not be afraid. You have found favor with God. See! You are to become a mother and have a Son. You are to give Him the name Jesus. He will be great. He will be called the Son of the Most High. The Lord God will give Him the place where His early father David sat. He will be King over the family of Jacob forever and His nation will have no end."*
> LUKE 1:30–33

Mary didn't know what to think about what Gabriel had just said. She understood that every baby has a mom *and* a dad. She had a mom and a dad, and so did Joseph. But she and Joseph weren't yet married, and they hadn't come together in a way to make a baby. So Mary asked the angel how this would be possible.

Gabriel explained to Mary that God would do a miracle so that she could become pregnant. The angel also said that Mary's child would be holy and called the Son of God. To help Mary believe, Gabriel told her that a relative of hers would be having a baby too. And Elizabeth was an older woman who had never been able to have children—until God did a miracle in her life. Mary may have still wondered what God was doing, but she decided to trust Him. "I am willing to be used of the Lord," she told Gabriel. "Let it happen to me as you have said" (Luke 1:38).

Soon, Mary was leaving her friends and family and Joseph behind to travel to Jerusalem to see Elizabeth. In just three months, she would have a son who would be known as John the Baptist. Elizabeth was happy to see Mary, and the Holy Spirit revealed to Elizabeth exactly who her young relative's baby was. She cried out,

> *"You are honored among women! Your Child is honored! Why has this happened to me? Why has the mother of my Lord come to me? As soon as I heard your voice, the baby in my body moved for joy. You are happy because you believed. Everything will happen as the Lord told you it would happen."*
> LUKE 1:42–45

Mary stayed with Elizabeth for three months, long enough to perhaps help out with John's birth. Back in Nazareth, Mary's fiancé, Joseph, was worried—and no doubt heartbroken—to learn that Mary was expecting a baby.

Like Mary, Joseph loved God and lived the way God wanted him to. But he and Mary were not yet married, and he knew he was *not* the father of the child Mary was carrying. He decided to break off their engagement quietly so that Mary wouldn't be publicly embarrassed.

But before Joseph could do that, an angel appeared to him in a dream. The angel said, "Joseph, son of David, do not be afraid to take

The angel Gabriel makes "the annunciation" to young Mary—the announcement of the coming birth of Jesus.

Mary as your wife. She is to become a mother by the Holy Spirit. A Son will be born to her. You will give Him the name Jesus because He will save His people from the punishment of their sins" (Matthew 1:20–21).

Just like Mary had accepted Gabriel's message, Joseph did what the angel told him to do. Joseph realized that what had happened was an incredible blessing to him and Mary both. He did not break off his engagement but instead married Mary and then helped to raise Jesus as his own son.

LIFE AS JESUS' MOTHER

While she was expecting, Mary stayed with Joseph in their hometown of Nazareth. But just before Jesus was born, the Roman emperor ordered everyone to return to the town where their families originated. Caesar Augustus, who ruled from 27 BC until his death in AD 14, wanted people to register their names so the government could make sure they paid their taxes.

Joseph was a descendant of King David too, so he and Mary traveled about seventy miles from Nazareth to Bethlehem, also known as the City of David. But when they arrived, they learned that every possible place to stay was filled. So they took a spot in a stable, a place where people kept their animals.

That night, the special baby was born. Mary and Joseph wrapped little Jesus in a cloth and laid Him in a manger—a feed box for the animals. If you've heard the Christmas story before, you'll know that Mary, Joseph, and Jesus soon had some visitors—shepherds from the nearby fields, who'd been told of the baby by an army of angels.

After Jesus' birth, Mary and Joseph raised Him the way any God-loving Jewish couple would. The Gospels (Matthew, Mark, Luke, and John—the first four books of the New Testament) tell us about some things Mary did as Jesus' mother. Here are some of them, including where you can find details:

- She welcomed the wise men from the East into her home so they could worship Jesus (Matthew 2:1–12).
- She fled with Joseph and Jesus to Egypt when King Herod ordered all young boys in the Bethlehem area to be killed (Matthew 2:13–18).
- She returned with Joseph and Jesus to her hometown of Nazareth (Matthew 2:19–23).

IN MARY'S OWN WORDS

After Elizabeth spoke a blessing to Mary, the mother of Jesus responded with this song of praise, which is called "the Magnificat":

"Oh, how my soul praises the Lord.
How my spirit rejoices in God my Savior!
For he took notice of his lowly servant girl,
and from now on all generations will call me blessed.
For the Mighty One is holy,
and he has done great things for me.
He shows mercy from generation to generation
to all who fear him.
His mighty arm has done tremendous things!
He has scattered the proud and haughty ones.
He has brought down princes from their thrones
and exalted the humble.
He has filled the hungry with good things
and sent the rich away with empty hands.
He has helped his servant Israel
and remembered to be merciful.
For he made this promise to our ancestors,
to Abraham and his children forever."

LUKE 1:46–55 NLT

- She and Joseph took Jesus to Jerusalem for the Passover celebration when He was twelve (Luke 2:41–50).
- She asked Jesus to help when a wedding feast ran out of wine (John 2:1–12).
- She watched as Jesus died on the cross (John 19:25).

In the fourth Gospel, the apostle John tells us that Jesus—as He was dying on the cross—asked him to take Mary into his home (John 19:25–27). She probably lived with John until her death.

The Bible's last mention of Mary is in Acts 1:14. She was in Jerusalem, praying and worshiping with other believers after Jesus' death, resurrection, and return to heaven, waiting for Him to send His Holy Spirit.

Mary gave birth to Jesus in a stable—not exactly the place you would expect a King to be born!

WHAT WE CAN LEARN FROM MARY:

What Mary said to Gabriel was a great example of humility ("I am willing to be used of the Lord") and faith ("Let it happen to me as you have said"). This is the attitude we need in order for God to bless us.

JOHN THE BAPTIST

MEANING OF HIS NAME:
"God is gracious"

WHEN HE LIVED:
About 5 BC–AD 29

WHERE YOU CAN READ ABOUT HIM:
Matthew 3:1–17, 11:1–12, 14:1–12; Mark 1:1–14, 6:14–27; Luke 1:5–25, 3:1–18, 7:18–33; John 1:6–35, 5:33–35

WHY HE'S IMPORTANT:
God sent John the Baptist to prepare people for the arrival of Jesus. There could be no more important job!

About six months before Jesus began His ministry—preaching the good news of salvation, healing the sick, feeding the hungry—a man named John the Baptist appeared on the scene. John told people that they needed to turn away from their sins and live for God. He also said that the Savior would be coming soon.

IN JOHN THE BAPTIST'S OWN WORDS

"See! The Lamb of God Who takes away the sin of the world! I have been talking about Him. I said, 'One is coming after me Who is more important than I, because He lived before I was born.' "
John 1:29–30

Some people wondered if John himself was the Savior the Jewish people had been waiting for. But John knew—and said—that he wasn't the Messiah. He knew that his job was to prepare people to see Jesus. John's father, Zacharias, had said that about him when he was just a baby: "You will go before the Lord to make the way ready for Him. You will tell His people how to be saved from the punishment of sin by being forgiven of their sins" (Luke 1:76–77).

John was a miracle baby born to Zacharias, a Jewish priest, and his wife, Elizabeth. They were really too old to be having a child. Even though they had prayed for many years, asking God to give them a family, Elizabeth had never been able to get pregnant. But one day, when Zacharias was working in the temple in Jerusalem, the angel Gabriel appeared. Gabriel told Zacharias that he and Elizabeth would have a son. God wanted them to name the boy John. He would grow up to be a special man who would bless many people. John would preach to the Jewish people to bring them back to God, preparing them for the Messiah's arrival.

JOHN THE BAPTIST'S MESSAGE

Just as Jesus would fulfill many Old Testament promises of the coming Savior, John would fulfill God's promise of a messenger who would appear first. The Gospel of Mark puts it this way:

> *This is the Good News about Jesus the Messiah, the Son of God. It began just as the prophet Isaiah had written: "Look, I am sending my messenger ahead of you, and he will prepare your way. He is a voice shouting in the wilderness, 'Prepare the way for the LORD's coming! Clear the road for him!' "*
>
> MARK 1:1–3 NLT

What do you think a preacher should look like? John didn't look the way most people would expect. He wore clothes made out of scratchy camel hair, with a leather belt around his middle. John didn't have much to call his own, living a very simple life without any concern over "nice things"—even his own home to sleep in. He stayed in the wilderness, eating honey and locusts—bugs like grasshoppers! John's focus was telling people about the good things God could do in their lives. He just wanted to get people ready for Jesus.

Lots of people followed John the Baptist because they were interested in what he had to say. Many turned from their sins and were baptized. But John was humble, knowing that God had given him one job: get people ready for Jesus' arrival.

This locust probably doesn't look very appetizing to you, but John the Baptist had them for dinner every day!

lodern visitors are baptized in the Jordan River at a site here some believe John baptized Jesus.

John the Baptist, chained in prison, learns his fate: he will be beheaded due to a foolish promise made by Herod Antipas.

One day, some Jewish religious leaders who had heard about John came to question him about who he was. Why, they wanted to know, did he think he should be preaching to people and baptizing them? John answered, "I baptize with water. But there is One standing among you Whom you do not know. He is the One Who is coming after me. I am not good enough to get down and help Him take off His shoes" (John 1:26–27). John also explained that while he baptized people with water, Jesus would baptize with the Holy Spirit (Matthew 3:11).

The very next day, Jesus walked up to John at the Jordan River to be baptized. When Jesus waded into the water, John didn't want to baptize Him—John didn't feel like he was good enough to baptize Jesus. "I need to be baptized by You," John said. "Do You come to me?" (Matthew 3:14). But Jesus replied that it was God's will for John to baptize Him.

So John lowered Jesus into the water. When Jesus came back up, the Holy Spirit—like a dove—descended on Him. And God the Father's voice was heard saying, "This is My much-loved Son. I am very happy with Him" (Matthew 3:17).

After this, John continued to preach and confront the people of Israel about their sin.

THE DEATH OF JOHN THE BAPTIST

Jesus once told His followers, "Of those born of women, there is no one greater than John the Baptist" (Matthew 11:11). Nothing was more important to John than doing what God wanted him to do—and that was fearlessly preaching God's truth. John wasn't afraid to confront even the most powerful people in that culture.

His courage and readiness to speak hard truth eventually cost John his life.

You can read about the death of John the Baptist in Matthew 14:1–12. But here are the key points: Herod Antipas, the ruler over the Roman provinces called Galilee and Perea, had taken his brother's wife for himself. John knew that was wrong and told Herod publicly. The ruler responded by having John thrown in prison. Later, Herod had John executed.

We can focus on the sadness of John's early, violent death. Or we can be grateful for his faithful work to prepare the way for Jesus. Don't forget: John has been enjoying heaven for almost two thousand years!

IT'S IN THE BIBLE!

"See, I am going to send one with news, and he will make the way ready before Me. Then all at once the Lord you are looking for will come to His house. The one with the news of the agreement, whom you desire, is coming," says the Lord of All.
MALACHI 3:1

WHAT WE CAN LEARN FROM JOHN THE BAPTIST:

John was a great example of both courage and humility. He never stopped telling the truth, even when that meant risking his life. But he was also a humble man who never forgot the most important person in God's plan—Jesus!

NICODEMUS

MEANING OF HIS NAME:
"Victory of the people"

WHEN HE LIVED:
Over the lifetime of Jesus

WHERE YOU CAN READ ABOUT HIM:
John 3:1–21, 7:41–50, 19:39–42

WHY HE'S IMPORTANT:
Nicodemus was a Pharisee, an expert in the Jewish law, who visited Jesus one night in Jerusalem. Jesus explained to him what it means to be "born again." Nicodemus also helped with Jesus' burial after He died on a Roman cross.

During His time on earth, Jesus often taught people deep truths about God, real worship, and what a life of faith should look like. Many times, Jesus spoke to groups of people, but He occasionally took time to meet with people one on one.

One of those private conversations took place in Jerusalem at nighttime. That's when Jesus sat down with Nicodemus to share what was probably the most important part of His message.

Nicodemus was a Pharisee, a Jewish religious leader who specialized in the Old Testament law—also known as the Law of Moses. He was also a member of a group called the Sanhedrin, a council of Jewish leaders.

Many times, the Pharisees asked questions of Jesus trying to trap Him into saying something wrong. They were hoping for careless words they could use against Him. At first, it seemed, they just wanted to shut Jesus up. Later, they wanted to completely get rid of Him.

But Nicodemus was different. As he asked Jesus questions and listened to His answers, he seemed sincerely interested in knowing more—about who Jesus was and why He had come to earth.

ONE OF THE GREATEST CONVERSATIONS OF ALL TIME

Nicodemus knew about the miracles Jesus had performed, and he might even have listened as Jesus spoke to the crowds of people who followed Him. This Jewish leader realized there was something special about Jesus. As Nicodemus began his conversation, he acknowledged that Jesus had "come from God" (John 3:2). Jesus' miracles proved that God was with Him.

Jesus didn't respond to Nicodemus's kind words. He really didn't need to. Both men knew the words were truthful. Instead, Jesus changed the subject: "For sure, I tell you, unless a man is born again, he cannot see the holy nation of God" (John 3:3).

That didn't make sense to Nicodemus. "Born again"? *That isn't even possible*, he must have thought. "How can a man be born when he is old?" Nicodemus asked. "How can he get into his mother's body and be born the second time?" (John 3:4).

Jesus then explained what "born again" means. He told Nicodemus, "For sure, I tell you, unless a man is born of water and of the Spirit of God, he cannot get into the holy nation of God" (John 3:5). Being born again means the Holy Spirit gives a person a new spiritual life (verse 6). Without the Holy Spirit, Jesus said, there is no way to be born again.

IN NICODEMUS'S OWN WORDS

"Teacher, we know You have come from God to teach us. No one can do these powerful works You do unless God is with Him."
JOHN 3:2

Jesus told Nicodemus that He "must be lifted up," meaning He would die on a cross so that those who believed in Him would live forever.

Nicodemus helps remove the body of Jesus from the cross. He would provide a proper burial for God's Son.

Nicodemus knew the Old Testament scriptures, so Jesus used a story from the book of Numbers as an example. Moses once put a bronze snake up on a pole so that Israelites who had been bitten by poisonous snakes could be healed. They could get that miraculous healing if they believed God and looked at that lifted-up snake.

Then Jesus described Himself as the "Son of Man" who had come down from heaven. "As Moses lifted up the snake in the desert," He told Nicodemus, "so the Son of Man must be lifted up. Then whoever puts his trust in Him will have life that lasts forever" (John 3:14–15).

Each one of us needs to understand what Jesus told Nicodemus: Only Jesus can save us from the punishment for sin. It has nothing to do with anything good that we can ever do. It's all about what Jesus does for us. Speaking to Nicodemus, He summed up the Gospel message by making His best-known statement:

"For God so loved the world that He gave His only Son. Whoever puts his trust in God's Son will not be lost but will have life that lasts forever. For God did not send His Son into the world to say it is guilty. He sent His Son so the world might be saved from the punishment of sin by Him."
JOHN 3:16–17

As Jesus spoke, He knew that He would one day be "lifted up" so people could be saved through Him. But He wouldn't be on a bronze pole—He would be nailed to a wooden cross. Jesus would still do many great miracles and teach people how to live lives that pleased God, but His most important mission was His last. That mission was dying on the cross to provide each of us a way to be right with God. When we believe and receive Jesus, we know we will live forever with God.

NICODEMUS SERVES JESUS

After his nighttime talk with Jesus, Nicodemus disappears for a few chapters. In John 7, he reappears, telling other members of the Sanhedrin that before they made any decisions about Jesus, they should first let Him speak for Himself. But the other leaders had already made up their minds about Jesus—they wanted Him put to death, and they were willing to do whatever it took to make that happen.

In time, Jesus was arrested, tried, and crucified. And then Nicodemus comes back into the

Nicodemus was a Pharisee, a group that mainly hated Jesus. But he was wise enough to learn more, straight from Jesus Himself—and became the first person ever to hear the words of John 3:16.

picture. At great personal cost, he helped to bury Jesus.

Roman authorities had given two men permission to take Jesus' body and prepare it for burial. The men were Nicodemus and Joseph of Arimathea, another member of the group of Jewish leaders who had called for Jesus' crucifixion. Luke 23:51 tells us that he had opposed the death of Jesus because he was a secret follower of Jesus.

Jesus had died the day before the Jewish Sabbath, so Joseph and Nicodemus had little time to bury Him. The two men took the body down from the cross and wrapped it in strips of linen fabric. Nicodemus had purchased seventy-five pounds of spices to perfume the body with. Then they placed Jesus in a new tomb that belonged to Joseph. The tomb, a small cave, was in a garden not far from where Jesus had been crucified. The men placed a large stone at the entrance of the tomb, and then the Romans placed a guard so no one could steal the body.

Nicodemus is never heard from again. But his nighttime conversation with Jesus will never be forgotten.

WHAT WE CAN LEARN FROM NICODEMUS:

Back in the Old Testament, God told His people, "You will look for Me and find Me, when you look for Me with all your heart" (Jeremiah 29:13). That was true when Nicodemus took the time to seek out Jesus and learn what He was really all about. It's still true for us today.

THE APOSTLE PETER

MEANING OF HIS NAME:
"Stone" or "Rock"

WHEN HE LIVED:
Over the lifetime of Jesus, until about the AD 60s

WHERE YOU CAN READ ABOUT HIM:
The Gospels of Matthew, Mark, Luke, and John; Acts 1–5, 8–15

BIBLE BOOKS HE WROTE:
1 and 2 Peter

WHY HE'S IMPORTANT:
Peter was a leader of the disciples, the twelve men Jesus called to follow Him during His three-year ministry on earth. After the Lord returned to heaven, Peter preached with great power and thousands of people in Jerusalem became Christians.

At the start of His ministry, Jesus called twelve men to follow Him as *disciples*—people who would learn from His teaching. In time, those men became *apostles*—"sent ones" who would take the message of salvation to the world after Jesus returned to heaven. Peter was one of the very first followers Jesus called.

The Bible tells us a little about Peter's life before he met the Lord. His real name was Simon—Jesus renamed him Peter—and his father was a man named John (John 1:42). Peter was married (Matthew 8:14), and he worked with his brother Andrew as a fisherman. They lived near the Sea of Galilee in a town called Bethsaida (Matthew 4:18; John 1:44).

Peter first appears in the Bible in Matthew 4:18–19. Jesus called out to Peter and Andrew as they were fishing with their father. "Follow Me," Jesus said, "I will make you fish for men!" They immediately dropped their nets and joined Jesus.

These archaeological ruins north of the Sea of Galilee may be the apostle Peter's hometown of Bethsaida.

Peter, James, and John had been dozing when Jesus was transfigured. They awoke to find that "His face was as bright as the sun [and] His clothes looked as white as light" (Matthew 17:2).

PETER'S NEW LIFE

Peter was one of the men Jesus called to follow Him around the land of Israel. In that time, it was called Palestine and ruled by the Roman Empire. Peter walked countless miles with Jesus and the other eleven disciples. These were the men Jesus had specially selected to take His message of salvation to the world. They would be under His training for about three years, until He died on the cross, was raised from the dead, and returned to heaven.

Peter saw Jesus do amazing miracles and heard Him teach powerful lessons on how people should think, live, and worship God.

Within His twelve disciples, Jesus had an "inner circle" of three who were His closest friends—Peter and the brothers James and John. Because he was so close to Jesus, Peter got to see some things the others didn't. For example, Peter witnessed Jesus raising a little girl from the dead (Matthew 9:23–26; Mark 5:37–43; Luke 8:51–55). He was also there with James and John when Jesus was "transfigured"—meaning His normal, human body was completely changed into His shining, heavenly appearance—on a mountain (Matthew 17:1–3; Mark 9:2–3; Luke 9:29–32). Moses and Elijah, two of the most important heroes of the Old Testament, were talking with Jesus. What a sight that must have been!

Peter loved Jesus. He was excited to follow the Lord, and in his enthusiasm he sometimes said and did embarrassing things. There was a time when Jesus wanted to show His disciples how important it is to serve others, and He brought out a bowl of water to wash their feet. "I will never let You wash my feet," Peter said (John 13:8). Jesus replied, "Unless I wash you, you will not be a part of Me"—so Peter basically said, "Then wash my whole body!" Jesus told Peter that only his feet needed to be cleaned.

But one day, Peter spoke a truth that is as important today as it was when he said it. Jesus had asked Peter and the other disciples, "Who do you say that I am?" (Matthew 16:15). Peter spoke up immediately, and this time what he said was just what Jesus wanted to hear: "You are the Christ, the Son of the living God" (verse 16).

Jesus told Peter that he was blessed (or happy)

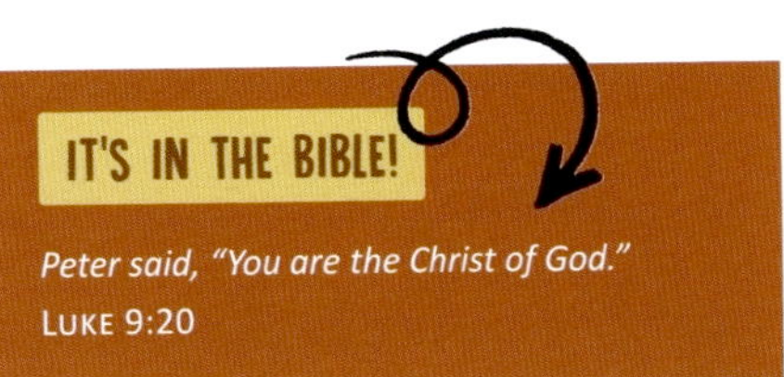

IT'S IN THE BIBLE!

Peter said, "You are the Christ of God."
LUKE 9:20

for understanding who He was. Then Jesus said,

> *"I tell you that you are Peter. On this rock I will build My church. The powers of hell will not be able to have power over My church. I will give you the keys of the holy nation of heaven. Whatever you do not allow on earth will not have been allowed in heaven. Whatever you allow on earth will have been allowed in heaven."*
> MATTHEW 16:18–19

PETER'S FALL AND RISE

Several times, Jesus had told Peter and the other disciples that one day He would suffer many things, die on a cross, and then come back to life. For some reason, Jesus' repeated messages didn't sink in.

One time when Jesus was discussing His coming suffering, Peter scolded Him for saying such a thing. But Jesus knew this was why He had come to earth, so He spoke these sharp words to Peter: "Get behind Me, Satan! You are standing in My way. You are not thinking how God thinks. You are thinking how man thinks" (Matthew 16:23).

On the night before Jesus was arrested, He gathered the disciples together to discuss what was going to happen to Him. "All of you will be ashamed of Me and leave Me tonight," He predicted. "For it is written, 'I will kill the shepherd and the sheep of the flock will be spread everywhere.' After I am raised from the dead, I will go before you to the country of Galilee" (Matthew 26:31–32).

Peter couldn't believe what Jesus was saying. "Even if all men give up and turn away because of You, I will never," he said (Matthew 26:33). But then

During Jesus' arrest, Peter defends his Lord with a sword, cutting off the ear of a man named Malchus. Jesus tells Peter to put the sword away, heals Malchus's wound, and allows Himself to be led away.

The Holy Spirit comes to live in followers of Jesus, including Peter—who will leave behind his fear and become a bold witness for Jesus.

Jesus gave Peter some specific details about how he would fail: "For sure, I tell you, before a rooster crows this night, you will say three times you do not know Me" (verse 34). Peter insisted that Jesus was wrong. "Even if I have to die with You," he said, "I will never say I do not know You" (verse 35).

Peter was probably sincere in what he said. But he didn't realize that what would happen later that night was part of God's plan. He was preparing Peter to serve Jesus even better after He returned to heaven.

Later that night, Peter was with Jesus when His enemies came to arrest Him. Peter pulled out a sword to defend Jesus, but the Lord told him to put it away: "Everyone who uses a sword will die with a sword" (Matthew 26:52). After the Roman soldiers and the Jewish religious leaders who had accused Jesus took Him away, Peter didn't know what to do.

He followed Jesus at a distance, but he was frightened. And Peter did just what he had insisted he would never do. During the trial, three different people asked Peter if he was a follower of Jesus. All three times, Peter lied, telling them that he didn't even know Jesus. The third time, Peter swore and cursed when he answered—and at that very moment, he heard a rooster crow. He was so ashamed and heartbroken that he ran away and cried (see Matthew 26:69–75).

Later that day, Jesus died on a wooden cross. But on the third day afterward, just as He had said, He was raised from the dead! Alive again, Jesus met with Peter and the other disciples at different times and places.

Once, on the shore of the Sea of Galilee, Jesus asked Peter three times, "Do you love Me?" All three times, Peter told Jesus yes. Then and there, Jesus forgave Peter and gave him a job—to feed Jesus' sheep. That meant Peter would preach and teach and serve the Christian church that would begin after Jesus returned to heaven. Peter was also told that he would one day die for Jesus.

Before that day came, Peter would show *way* more courage in preaching about Jesus than he did the night Jesus was on trial.

THE DAY EVERYTHING CHANGED FOR PETER

The day of Pentecost was a Jewish celebration that happened fifty days after Passover. On the Pentecost after Jesus' ascension to heaven, God the Father sent His Holy Spirit to live inside all Christians. (You can read about this very important day in Acts 2.) One of those Christians was Peter, who received the Spirit and got all the courage he needed to do what Jesus wanted him to. That very day, Peter stood and preached a powerful sermon to a huge crowd in Jerusalem. About three thousand people believed in Jesus!

After that, Peter preached, taught, and healed the sick—just like he had seen Jesus do. Peter couldn't *stop* talking about Jesus—even though he was threatened and arrested for doing so. He knew he was risking his life by serving Jesus, but that didn't stop him. For the rest of his life, Peter served boldly, and many people came to Jesus as a result.

Not only did he preach and perform miracles, Peter also wrote two books of the Bible. The letters that are now called 1 and 2 Peter allow us to read the thoughts of a man who spent three years of his life with Jesus!

But some people say Peter asked to be crucified head-down because he felt he wasn't worthy to die the way Jesus did.

IN PETER'S OWN WORDS

"Be sorry for your sins and turn from them and be baptized in the name of Jesus Christ, and your sins will be forgiven. You will receive the gift of the Holy Spirit. This promise is to you and your children. It is to all people everywhere. It is to as many as the Lord our God will call."
ACTS 2:38–39

Peter wrote his first letter to encourage Christians living throughout the Roman Empire. Many of them were being terribly mistreated, both by Romans and Jews. Peter wanted them to understand that it was a privilege to suffer for Jesus. His second letter warned Christians against bad teachers who showed up at their church gatherings. Peter wanted Christians to focus on good teaching so they could tell when someone was saying things that weren't true.

The Bible doesn't say when or where Peter died, but tradition says it was in the city of Rome when he was about sixty-eight years old. Tradition also says that Peter, like Jesus, was crucified.

WHAT WE CAN LEARN FROM THE APOSTLE PETER:

Though Peter loved and followed Jesus with great passion, he often said and did things that weren't part of God's plan. But after Peter received God's Holy Spirit, he preached with incredible power and led thousands of people to faith in Jesus. The same Holy Spirit that made Peter such an amazing preacher will also give *you* power to think, speak, and live the way God wants. Your part in that is to allow the Spirit to guide you.

THE APOSTLE JOHN

MEANING OF HIS NAME:
"God is gracious"

WHEN HE LIVED:
About AD 6–100

WHERE YOU CAN READ ABOUT HIM:
The Gospels of Matthew, Mark, Luke, and John; Acts 3–5, 8

BIBLE BOOKS HE WROTE:
The Gospel of John, 1 John, 2 John, 3 John, Revelation

WHY HE'S IMPORTANT:
John was one of Jesus' twelve original disciples. In fact, he was one of Jesus' closest friends. John also wrote the five New Testament books listed above.

After calling the brothers Peter and Andrew to be His disciples, Jesus turned His attention to another pair of brothers, John and James. They were fishermen too, and they were mending their father's fishing nets by the Sea of Galilee. The Bible tells us that when Jesus called them, John and his brother immediately left their father, Zebedee, and his hired workers to become disciples. They, along with Peter, would form Jesus' "inner circle" within the group of disciples. As mentioned in the previous chapter, they got to see some things none of the other disciples did—including Jesus' time of prayer in the garden of Gethsemane on the night He was arrested. Unfortunately, they were all so tired and stressed that they kept falling asleep (see Matthew 26:36–46).

Jesus once called John and his brother *Boanerges*, which means "sons of thunder" (see Mark 3:17). That's apparently because the two could become a little hotheaded at times. For example, when the people in a certain town treated Jesus and the disciples rudely, James and John asked Jesus if they could call down fire from heaven and destroy the place.

IT'S IN THE BIBLE!

They were surprised and wondered how easy it was for Peter and John to speak. They could tell they were men who had not gone to school. But they knew they had been with Jesus.
ACTS 4:13

A modern boat captain on the Sea of Galilee, casting a fishing net like Jesus' disciple John would have.

The other ten disciples once became angry at John and his brother when their mother asked Jesus to give her sons a special place in His kingdom. But Jesus told them it wasn't His place to meet such a request—only His heavenly Father's. He then used the incident to teach the disciples the importance of serving one another (see Matthew 20:20–28).

John must have calmed down over the years, because he became known as the "apostle of love." He often wrote about love in his letters. And in his Gospel, John referred to himself as "the disciple Jesus loved" several times (see John 13:23, 19:26, 20:2, 21:7). During the Last Supper, it's believed to be John who was close enough to Jesus to lean back against Him and ask who the betrayer would be (see John 21:20).

Spending three years with Jesus—hearing Him teach and watching His example—had a big effect on John. From His cross, Jesus looked down at His mother, Mary, and told John to care for her. From that day on, Mary lived in John's home, and he treated her as if she were his own mother (see John 19:25–27). After Jesus returned to heaven and sent the Holy Spirit on the day of Pentecost, John served alongside Peter as a powerful, fearless leader of the new church.

JOHN'S WRITINGS

John apparently lived a long life (some say he was the only disciple not to be killed for following Jesus), and he spent some of his later years writing. Bible experts believe he wrote his books, including the Gospel of John, around AD 80–98.

John's Gospel is different from the other three, which are called the "Synoptic Gospels." (*Synoptic* means "looking together," and those books have very similar content.) John left out some important events the other Gospel writers mentioned, including Jesus' Sermon on the Mount and His temptation by the devil just before He started His ministry. Unlike the other Gospels, John's doesn't include any accounts of Jesus casting out evil spirits or speaking parables—those stories with

Dear friends, if God loved us that much, then we should love each other. No person has ever seen God at any time. If we love each other, God lives in us. His love is made perfect in us.

1 JOHN 4:11–12

The apostle John, now an elderly man banished to an island called Patmos, receives a vision from Jesus that becomes the book of Revelation.

important spiritual lessons.

But John included a lot of material not found in the other three Gospels: Jesus' ministry in the northern region of Galilee (chapters 2–4), His raising of His good friend Lazarus from the dead (chapter 11), and what is called His "farewell discourse" (chapters 13–17).

The Bible doesn't tell us much about John's later life and death. John was probably in his seventies or eighties when Roman authorities banished him to the island of Patmos, where he was kept away from the people he loved. On Patmos, John wrote the book of Revelation, in which he said, "I, John, am your Christian brother. I have shared with you in suffering because of Jesus Christ" (Revelation 1:9).

One old church tradition says John was sentenced to death by being dunked into a pot of boiling oil—but he miraculously survived. Tradition also says that he lived to a very old age and died in the city of Ephesus around AD 100.

WHAT WE CAN LEARN FROM THE APOSTLE JOHN:

When we learn what John understood about God's love, we too can live the way God wants us to live, think the way He wants us to think, and do what He wants us to do.

THE APOSTLE PAUL

MEANING OF HIS NAME:

"Small"

WHEN HE LIVED:

Over Jesus' lifetime to the AD 60s

WHERE YOU CAN READ ABOUT HIM:

Acts 8–28

BIBLE BOOKS HE WROTE:

Romans, 1 and 2 Corinthians, Galatians, Ephesians, Philippians, Colossians, 1 and 2 Thessalonians, 1 and 2 Timothy, Titus, Philemon

WHY HE'S IMPORTANT:

God chose Paul, a Pharisee who hated Christianity, to take the message of salvation to the non-Jewish world in the first century. Paul started many churches and wrote many letters, both to these churches and to individual believers. Thirteen of those letters are now part of the New Testament.

Other than Jesus Himself, the apostle Paul is the most important person in the New Testament. He traveled thousands of miles to tell people about Jesus and to establish churches all over the Mediterranean world. He wrote letters to many churches and church leaders, and thirteen of them are in the Bible we have today. Paul was passionate about spreading the message of salvation throughout the world and teaching Christians how they should live.

But if you know anything about Paul's early life, you might wonder how God could use a man like him. Here's how that story unfolded.

MEETING JESUS

Paul's story begins in the book of Acts. He was called Saul at that time, and he was doing everything he could to stop Christians from telling others about Jesus. Many Christians were being beaten, thrown into jail, and even killed for talking about Jesus. This is called *persecution*, and Saul was a leader of the troublemakers.

He had been born and raised in a city called

Tarsus, where he grew up learning the Old Testament. As he became a man, Saul also became a Pharisee, which means he knew the Law of Moses very well. He was strict in following it and expected others to follow it too. Because he didn't believe God had a Son, Saul hated Christians. He thought he was doing God's will by persecuting them.

Jesus gets Saul's attention on the road to Damascus.

But that changed when Saul began a trip to the city of Damascus (located in present-day Syria) to arrest Christians and bring them back to Jerusalem to be jailed. But near the end of Saul's 175-mile journey, he met Jesus.

Right there on the road, a blinding light from heaven surrounded Saul. He fell to the ground and shielded his eyes. Then he heard a voice from heaven asking, "Saul, Saul, why are you working so hard against Me?" (Acts 9:4).

Shaken and confused, Saul asked, "Who are You, Lord?"

"I am Jesus, the One Whom you are working against," the voice answered. "You hurt yourself by trying to hurt Me" (Acts 9:5). Saul was probably too frightened even to move, but Jesus told him, "Get up! Go into the city and you will be told what to do" (verse 6).

The men Saul was traveling with didn't see anything—not even the light that knocked Saul to the ground—but they heard the voice speaking to Saul. When Saul got up from the ground, he couldn't see at all, so his friends led him the rest of the way to Damascus.

PAUL'S WORK ON EARTH

As Saul made his way to Damascus, God was preparing the Christians there to welcome him as a fellow believer. They would help him to become the world's most important missionary.

Christians in Damascus knew all about Saul. They knew that he had done terrible things to believers around Jerusalem, so they were very worried when they learned he was coming to their city. But God spoke to Ananias, a Christian in Damascus, telling him that he should go greet

Saul. "But Lord, many people have told me about this man," Ananias said nervously. "He came here with the right and the power from the head religious leaders to put everyone in chains who call on Your name" (Acts 9:13–14). But God answered, "Go! This man is the one I have chosen to carry My name among the people who are not Jews and to their kings and to Jews" (verse 15). So Ananias went. At Judas's home, Ananias prayed for Saul and God restored his sight.

Saul stayed for a while with the Christians of Damascus. They taught him more about Jesus, and before long, Saul began preaching and teaching in the local Jewish synagogue. People were amazed that the man who before had treated Christians so terribly was now preaching the message of salvation through Jesus (see Acts 9:22)!

Several years later, Paul went to the area that is now called Turkey. There was a big church in the city of Antioch, and Paul helped the Christians there to grow in their faith. One day, God told Paul to take a long journey and tell many more people about Jesus. God had enormous, *world-changing* plans for Paul. He was going to travel around the Mediterranean Sea preaching about Jesus and starting new churches throughout the Roman Empire.

Starting in about AD 47, Paul dedicated his life as a traveling preacher for Jesus. Over the next decade or so, he would take three different missionary journeys, travel more than ten thousand miles—mostly on foot!—and start at least fourteen churches.

Paul saw many people come to faith in Jesus. But he also suffered because people didn't always like his talk about Jesus. The Bible tells us Paul was beaten, thrown in jail, threatened, even stranded on an island called Malta after a shipwreck (see

Tourists crowd the Areopagus, also called Mars' Hill, a large rock mound where the apostle Paul discussed Jesus with the thinkers of Athens. The taller hill in the background is called the Acropolis, which is topped by a temple to the Greek goddess Athena.

In art, the apostle Paul is often shown holding a sword. There are two reasons: First, he described God's Word as "the sword of the Spirit" (Ephesians 6:17). Second, many believe he was martyred—killed for his faith in Jesus—with a sword.

Acts 27:27–28:5). But this was no surprise. God had told Ananias, "I will show [Paul] how much he will have to suffer because of Me" (Acts 9:16).

God didn't call Paul to an easy life. But because he cared deeply about people and wanted to see them saved, he never complained or thought about quitting. He kept on doing what he knew God wanted him to do.

SOME IMPORTANT MESSAGES FROM PAUL

Paul was plenty busy with traveling, preaching the message of salvation through Jesus. But he still found time to write many of the books that appear in the New Testament.

Thirteen of Paul's letters (also called "epistles") are in our Bibles today. His letters gave instructions on living for Jesus, corrected problems in the churches, and encouraged many thousands of people at the time—and many millions (probably *billions*) of Christians since then.

In the order that they appear in the Bible, those writings are Romans, 1 and 2 Corinthians, Galatians, Ephesians, Philippians, Colossians, 1 and 2 Thessalonians, 1 and 2 Timothy, Titus, and Philemon. Each of these letters can challenge you, encourage you, and answer questions you may have about your faith in Jesus. They're all worth reading!

WHY PAUL MATTERS SO MUCH

The Bible doesn't say how or when Paul died, but Christian tradition says that he was executed around AD 67 at the order of the Roman emperor Nero. Nero was treating Christians very badly, blaming them for a huge fire that broke out in Rome in AD 64.

It was around this time, when Paul was imprisoned in Rome, that he wrote the last of his biblical epistles. It was a short letter to a pastor named Timothy, who served the church in the Greek city of Ephesus. Paul thought of Timothy as a son and helped him to become a strong leader in the church. Paul's second letter to Timothy shows that he knew he would die soon. Paul wrote, "I have fought a good fight. I have finished the work I was to do. I have kept the faith" (2 Timothy 4:7).

God had sent Paul on a world-changing mission. He preached the message of salvation through Jesus to countless numbers of people, he started many churches, and he wrote life-changing letters that still instruct, challenge, and encourage Christians to this day.

We should thank God for our salvation through Jesus. But we can also be grateful for the apostle Paul. He gave his all to make sure people—including all of us—could hear the message of God's love.

WHAT WE CAN LEARN FROM THE APOSTLE PAUL:

We can learn a lot by simply reading the thirteen New Testament books Paul wrote. We can learn even more by studying the life he lived for God. Paul was focused on one thing: telling people about Jesus. No matter what people said or did to him, he kept doing what God told him to do.

LUKE

MEANING OF HIS NAME:

"Light-giving"

WHEN HE LIVED:

First century AD, probably until the 80s

WHERE YOU CAN READ ABOUT HIM:

Luke 1; Acts 1, 16–28; Colossians 4:14; Philemon v. 24; 2 Timothy 4:11

BIBLE BOOKS HE WROTE:

Luke, Acts

WHY HE'S IMPORTANT:

Luke wasn't an apostle or an eyewitness to the ministry of Jesus Christ. But using his skills as a historian, he wrote the two longest books of the New Testament. Luke's book of Acts is an amazing account of the first-century church and the leadership of men like Peter and Paul.

The Bible doesn't tell us much about the personal life of Luke, sometimes called "Luke the Evangelist." We don't know anything about his family or about how he became a Christian—though some experts believe he was saved after Jesus returned to heaven.

Most Bible scholars believe Luke was a Gentile, which means he wasn't from a Jewish family. That makes him the only non-Jewish person to write any part of the New Testament. He may have come from the cities of Troas or Antioch. The apostle Paul called Luke "the dear doctor" (Colossians 4:14), which tells us that he was a physician by profession.

Luke is an important person in the New Testament simply because he wrote so much of it! As author of the Gospel of Luke (the longest book in the New Testament) and Acts (the second-longest book), Luke wrote more of the New Testament than anyone—even more than the apostle Paul, who wrote thirteen books. Luke's two books account for one-quarter of the whole New Testament!

IN LUKE'S OWN WORDS

Dear Theophilus, I have looked with care into these things from the beginning. I have decided it would be good to write them to you one after the other the way they happened. Then you can be sure you know the truth about the things you have been taught.

Luke 1:3–4

While Luke was a doctor, he is known in Christianity as a careful historian. In his Gospel, Luke went to great trouble to record everything he had learned about Jesus (see Luke 1:1–4). He also wrote a detailed account of things that happened after Jesus returned to heaven. That would be Acts, which describes the day the Holy Spirit came to the small group of Christians gathered in Jerusalem (Acts 2). It also explains the work of important people such as Peter and John, as well as the apostle Paul and his companions, the first great missionaries of the Christian church.

Though we believe Luke wrote these two books, he never mentions himself by name in either. He is named only three times in the rest of the New Testament—each time by the apostle Paul. In Colossians 4:14, Paul calls Luke "the dear doctor." In his letter to a man named Philemon, Paul calls Luke one of his "workers with me" (Philemon v. 24). Finally, in 2 Timothy 4:11, which Paul wrote from a Roman prison cell, he said, "Luke is the only one with me here."

LUKE'S GOSPEL STORY

Luke is called "the Evangelist" because he wrote the third of the four Gospel books that start the New Testament. He states clearly that he wasn't an eyewitness to Jesus' ministry on earth but that he had "looked with care into these things from the beginning" (Luke 1:3).

A portrait of Luke from a Jerusalem church. He is often pictured with a bull, a sacrificial animal, since Luke's Gospel emphasized the sacrifice of Jesus on the cross.

Luke's books are both addressed to someone named Theophilus, a Greek name that means "friend of God." No one knows exactly who Theophilus was, but Luke wrote so that he could "be sure you know the truth about the things you have been taught" (Luke 1:4).

Of the four Gospels, Luke is the only one that is written chronologically, meaning in the order that everything happened. This Gospel, which was probably written between AD 58 and 65, includes many details the other three leave out. For example, it has the detailed story of the birth of Jesus. Many of the familiar stories you hear each Christmas come from Luke's Gospel—including the angel announcing the Messiah's birth to shepherds watching their sheep outside Bethlehem (Luke 2:8–20).

Luke is also the only Gospel writer to include

Luke's Gospel includes the story of twelve-year-old Jesus amazing some Jewish religious leaders with His understanding of the Old Testament.

anything about Jesus' childhood. Luke wrote about the boy's circumcision, His presentation at the temple in Jerusalem (where He was seen by a godly man named Simeon and a prophetess named Anna), and the way He amazed Jewish religious teachers with His understanding of Old Testament writings when He was just twelve years old. You can read those stories in Luke 2:21–52.

In his Gospel, Luke tells the story of a Savior who had come from heaven to earth to live and die for *everyone*—not just Jewish people. Luke presents Jesus as both God and man in the same person—and perfect as each. In Luke, we read about the compassionate Jesus who showed God's love to those around Him.

ACTS: LUKE'S STORY OF THE FIRST-CENTURY CHURCH

Some people have described the book of Acts as Luke's sequel (meaning "part two") to his Gospel. In Acts, Luke picks up the story where the Gospel left off. Luke again addressed the book of Acts to Theophilus. "Dear Theophilus," he wrote, "in my first writings I wrote about all the things Jesus did and taught from the beginning until the day He went to heaven. He spoke to the missionaries through the Holy Spirit. He told those whom He had chosen what they should do" (Acts 1:1–2).

Acts tells the story of the first-century church and how it grew under the courageous leadership of men like the apostle Peter, the apostle John, and the apostle Paul. That's why the book is often

A stained-glass church window in Germany shows the arrival of the Holy Spirit on the day of Pentecost. We know about this world-changing moment because of Luke's writing.

called "the Acts of the Apostles"! It starts with Jesus returning to heaven to be with His Father, then quickly describes the arrival of God's Holy Spirit, who filled the Christians in Jerusalem in a spectacular way. You can read that story in Acts 2.

The second part of the book of Acts is the story of the apostle Paul. As you know, the former Jewish leader had treated Christians terribly before he met Jesus. But then he became a Christian and traveled tirelessly preaching, teaching, and starting churches around the Roman Empire.

But Luke didn't just write those stories—he became a part of them. In Acts 16, Luke's pronouns changed from *they* to *we*, indicating that he was now a part of Paul's traveling team. "*We* took a ship from the city of Troas to the city of Samothracia. The next day *we* went to the city of Neapolis" (verse 11). After that, Luke writes three more times that he was with Paul (Acts 20:5–15, 21:1–18, 28:1–16).

After his brief appearances in the book of Acts and a few of the apostle Paul's letters, Luke disappeared from the scene. The Bible doesn't say what became of him or when and where he died. . .but ancient historical sources tell us he was killed in AD 84 for his faith. These sources say he was hanged from an olive tree.

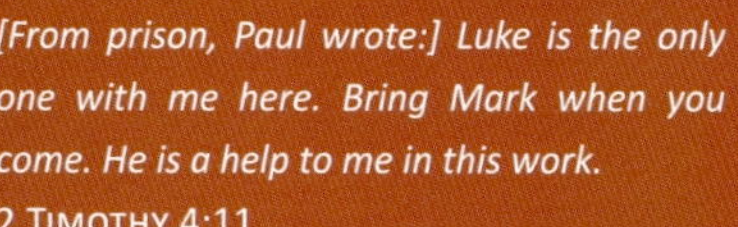

IT'S IN THE BIBLE!

[From prison, Paul wrote:] Luke is the only one with me here. Bring Mark when you come. He is a help to me in this work.
2 Timothy 4:11

WHAT WE CAN LEARN FROM LUKE:

As author of a large part of the New Testament, Luke proves that he was not only a great historian but a man with passion for Jesus and the Gospel message. He used his God-given gifts to communicate the most important message in human history—salvation through Jesus.

INRI

JESUS: THE MOST IMPORTANT MAN WHO EVER LIVED

MEANING OF HIS NAME:

The name *Jesus* means "Savior." *Christ* means "Deliverer."

WHEN HE LIVED:

About 4 BC–AD 29

WHERE YOU CAN READ ABOUT HIM:

The Gospels of Matthew, Mark, Luke, and John tell the story of Jesus' life here on earth. The rest of the New Testament tells us what His life, death, and resurrection mean to all Christians.

WHY HE'S IMPORTANT:

All through the Old Testament, God promised that He would one day send a "Messiah," a Savior who would make a way for people to be forgiven for their sins. Jesus was that Messiah. He paid the price for sin by dying on a cross. Then He was raised from the dead! Anyone who believes in Jesus can have life that lasts forever.

As you've read this book, you might have noticed that the characters were presented basically in the order they appear in the Bible. But now you're about to read of the man at the center of everything in the Bible. He's Jesus, the Savior that God sent to earth.

In other words, this book has saved the best—and most important—for last!

Jesus was the greatest man who ever lived. The first four books in the New Testament—the Gospels of Matthew, Mark, Luke, and John—tell us His story on earth. They describe His amazing, life-changing teaching and His incredible miracles. Most of all, they show how He gave up His own life so that we could be forgiven for our sins.

Jesus was a great teacher and miracle worker and an example of how we should live and treat other people. But He was a lot more than that! The Bible calls Him *Immanuel*, which means "God with us" (Matthew 1:23). That means that God Himself came to earth to live with His human creation. Jesus is God!

You probably know many details of Jesus' birth more than two thousand years ago in the little town of Bethlehem. But Jesus didn't just appear out of nowhere. Many centuries before, Old Testament prophets predicted many things about Jesus—and they all came true!

WHO WAS THIS MAN?

Jesus knew who He was—the Son of God who came to earth to save people from their sins—and He wasn't shy about saying that, even though His words made some people very angry. Here are some examples of how Jesus described Himself:

- "My Father and I are one!" (John 10:30).
- "Anyone who puts his trust in Me, puts his trust not only in Me, but in Him Who sent Me. Anyone who sees Me, sees Him Who sent Me" (John 12:44–45).
- "I am the Way and the Truth and the Life. No one can go to the Father except by Me. If you had known Me, you would know My Father also. From now on you know Him and have seen Him" (John 14:6–7).
- [After the disciple Philip said to Jesus, "Lord, show us the Father. That is all we ask," Jesus answered,] "Have I been with you all this time and you do not know Me yet? Whoever has seen Me, has seen the Father. How can you say, 'Show us the Father'?" (John 14:8–9).

But Jesus didn't just teach about Himself. He spent time sharing very important things about God the Father and how His followers should live, think, and treat other people. He taught that people needed to turn away from wrong things, confessing them to God (Matthew 4:17). He urged people to "take up [their] cross" and follow Him (Matthew 16:24–27). He wanted people to know that they needed faith in God and that they must be "like a child" to enter His kingdom (Matthew 19:13–15).

Some of Jesus' most important

Jesus has many names and titles, including "the Good Shepherd."

Jesus breaks bread with two disciples on the road to Emmaus. He called Himself "the bread of life."

teaching is found in what is called "the Sermon on the Mount," which you can read in Matthew 5–7. In this greatest sermon ever preached, Jesus taught these important truths (and many more!):

- How to be happy and blessed (Matthew 5:3–12).
- That refusing to forgive someone is as bad in God's eyes as killing that person (5:21–26).
- That looking at a woman with wrong thoughts was the same as touching her the wrong way (5:27–30).
- That we shouldn't try to get even with people when they do things to hurt or anger us (5:38–42).
- That we should love everyone, even those who don't love us in return (5:43–48).
- That we should seek what is best for God's eternal kingdom above everything else (6:19–34).
- That we should ask God, our loving heavenly Father, for the things we need, knowing that He loves us and wants to do good things for us (7:7–11).
- That we should treat others the way we want to be treated (7:12).
- That there is only one way to God—through Jesus Christ Himself (7:13–14).
- That our relationship with Jesus is based first on our faith in Him, not on the things we do (7:21–23).

IT'S IN THE BIBLE!

Jesus' Seven "I Am" claims from the book of John (NLT):

- "I am the bread of life" (John 6:35).
- "I am the light of the world" (John 8:12).
- "I am the gate for the sheep" (John 10:7).
- "I am the good shepherd" (John 10:11).
- "I am the resurrection and the life" (John 11:25).
- "I am the way, the truth, and the life" (John 14:6).
- "I am the true grapevine" (John 15:1).

JESUS' AMAZING MIRACLES

The miracles He performed were a big part of Jesus' ministry on earth. A miracle is something that happens that couldn't happen naturally—and you can read about dozens of them in the four Gospels.

The Bible says Jesus performed miracles to prove that the things He claimed about Himself were true. After Jesus had died, risen from the dead, and returned to heaven, the apostle Peter told people in Jerusalem, "Jewish men, listen to what I have to say! You knew Jesus of the town of Nazareth by the powerful works He did. God worked through Jesus while He was with you. You all know this" (Acts 2:22).

Here are just some of the miracles Jesus performed on earth:

Jesus lies asleep during a wild storm on the Sea of Galilee. When awakened by His disciples, He would simply speak to make the storm stop!

- Changing water into wine at a wedding in Cana (John 2:1–11)
- Healing a military leader's servant (Matthew 8:5–13)
- Raising a widow's son from the dead (Luke 7:11–18)
- Calming a terrible storm (Matthew 8:23–27)
- Healing a paralyzed man (Matthew 9:1–8)
- Raising a religious leader's daughter from the dead (Matthew 9:18–26)
- Feeding more than five thousand people with five loaves of bread and two fish (Matthew 14:15–21)
- Feeding more than four thousand people with seven loaves of bread and a few fish (Matthew 15:32–39)
- Giving sight to a man who had been born blind (John 9:1–38)
- Raising His friend Lazarus from the dead (John 11:1–46)

Jesus did many amazing things when He was here on earth—too many to be included in the Bible (see John 21:25). But He saved His most important miracle for last!

"I am the One Who raises the dead and gives them life. Anyone who puts his trust in Me will live again, even if he dies. Anyone who lives and has put his trust in Me will never die."
JOHN 11:25–26

JESUS' REASON FOR COMING TO EARTH

Jesus spent His last three years on earth traveling around the land of Israel doing nothing but good for people. He taught them, He encouraged them, He healed them, and He fed them. But He knew that a time was coming for something even more important. Jesus would need to complete the ultimate mission His heavenly Father had given Him.

One day, Jesus told His disciples,

> *"Listen! We are going up to Jerusalem. The Son of Man will be handed over to the religious leaders and to the teachers of the Law. They will say that He must be put to death. They will hand Him over to the people who do not know God. They will make fun of Him and will beat Him. They will nail Him to a cross. Three days later He will be raised to life."*
> MATTHEW 20:18–19

Jesus knew that God the Father had sent Him to earth to die—and it would be a terrible death on a wooden cross. But Jesus also knew this terrible event wouldn't be the end. On the third day after His death, God the Father would bring Him back to life!

That's exactly what happened. Jesus was arrested, tried, and sentenced to die. On the day of His death, Roman soldiers nailed Him to a cross where He died about six hours later. Then His followers laid Him in a tomb.

After Jesus died, His followers were heartbroken. But all four Gospels tell us that their sadness became joy when they realized that He had risen

Jesus was born to die on a cross, the perfect man taking the punishment of sin for all who would believe in Him.

from the dead—just as He had promised. You can read the story of Jesus' resurrection in Matthew 28, Mark 16, Luke 24, and John 20–21.

Alive again, Jesus appeared first to a woman named Mary Magdalene (see John 20:1–18). Over the next several days, He appeared to His apostles and to literally hundreds of His other followers.

IT'S IN THE BIBLE!

First of all, I taught you what I had received. It was this: Christ died for our sins as the Holy Writings said He would. Christ was buried. He was raised from the dead three days later as the Holy Writings said He would.
1 CORINTHIANS 15:3–4

Forty days after Mary first saw Him, Jesus returned to heaven. Now it was time for Jesus' apostles to tell others about Him. Because He had died and been raised from the dead, anyone who believed in Him could be saved.

The apostle Paul once wrote that "if Christ was not raised from the dead, your faith is worth nothing and you are still living in your sins. Then the Christians who have already died are lost in sin" (1 Corinthians 15:17–18).

Without Jesus' resurrection, death would be the most powerful thing in the universe. We would all still be separated from God for all eternity. But God raised Jesus from the dead to live forever—and we can live forever with Him!

"I'M COMING BACK!"

Jesus spent forty more days on earth—visiting His friends and giving them important instructions—before He returned to heaven. Just as Jesus ascended (went up into the sky), two angels appeared and said, "You men of the country of Galilee, why do you stand looking up into heaven? This same Jesus Who was taken from you into heaven will return in the same way you saw Him go up into heaven" (Acts 1:11).

In Jesus' "ascension," He rose up into the sky and returned to heaven. But angels soon told His disciples, "This same Jesus Who was taken from you into heaven will return in the same way you saw Him go up into heaven" (Acts 1:11).

Those words probably reminded the disciples of what Jesus had said about His "second coming," His return to earth at the end of time: "Something special will be seen in the sky telling of the Son of Man. All nations of the earth will have sorrow. They will see the Son of Man coming in the clouds of the sky with power and shining-greatness. He will send His angels with the loud sound of a horn. They will gather God's people together from the four winds. They will come from one end of the heavens to the other" (Matthew 24:30–31).

And the disciples were probably thinking of another thing Jesus had said, just before He was arrested, tried, and crucified: "There are many rooms in My Father's house. If it were not so, I would have told you. I am going away to make a place for you. After I go and make a place for you, I will come back and take you with Me. Then you may be where I am" (John 14:2–3). That's a beautiful promise to everyone who trusts Jesus for salvation.

The Bible contains many promises that Jesus will one day return to earth. And you can look forward to that day. When God makes a promise, He keeps it!

ART CREDITS

Albert H. Teich/SS—250
Anneka/SS—279
artmig/SS—184
Barbour Publishing, Inc—246
Bill Perry/SS—283
Carnby/WM—303
Darafsh/WM—251
delcarmat/SS—202, 208, 228
Dinda Yulianto/SS—199
Dream79/SS—264
Drop of Light/SS—230
euro_ace/SS—274
Everett Collection/SS—169, 170, 175
Evgenii Emelianov/SS—239
Freedom Studio/SS—256, 309, 316
Gino Santa Maria/SS—226
GoneWithTheWind/SS—288
Google Art Project/WM—201, 260
Henry and Laura Whittaker/SS—270
hramikona/SS—277
Irmhild B/SS—274, 206
jorisvo/SS—310
joshimerbin/SS—265
Kat Buslaeva/SS—266
Mary Terriberry/SS—314
Mihai_Tamasila/SS—194
Mashosh/SS—189, 198, 268
mentalmind/SS—240
Morphart Creation/SS—221
Mountains Hunter/SS—200
Nancy Bauer/SS—319
Nationalmuseum (Stockholm)/WM—225
Nejron Photo/SS—214
Nicku/SS—186, 195, 310, 217, 247, 272
Oliver Denker/SS—232
Paolo Novello/SS—282
Renata Sedmakova/SS—181, 203, 204, 218, 238, 242, 254, 271, 294, 295, 296, 297, 301, 305, 308, 315
Robert Hoetink/SS—293
Roman Sigaev/SS—304
rudall30/SS—164, 172, 178, 196, 212, 222, 252, 280, 286, 292, 298, 312
Ryan Rodrick Beiler/SS—300
Serg Zastavkin/SS—31
Shutterstock AI Generator—290
Sogno Lucido/SS—166
Volodymyr Burdiak/SS—259
Vuk Kostic/SS—168
welburnstuart/SS—257
WM—176, 185, 211, 224, 227, 231, 234, 236
Yafit/SS—262
Zvonimir Atletic/SS—258, 289
Zwiebackesser/SS—318

SS=Shutterstock
WM=Wikimedia